SHOULD THE CHURCH TEACH TITHING?
▼

SHOULD THE CHURCH TEACH TITHING?

▼

A THEOLOGIAN'S CONCLUSIONS

ABOUT A TABOO DOCTRINE

Russell Earl Kelly, Ph.D.

Writers Club Press

San Jose New York Lincoln Shanghai

Should the Church Teach Tithing?
A Theologian's Conclusions about a Taboo Doctrine

Writers Club Press
an imprint of iUniverse.com, Inc.

For information address:
iUniverse.com, Inc.
5220 S 16th, Ste. 200
Lincoln, NE 68512
www.iuniverse.com

ISBN: 0-595-15978-8

Printed in the United States of America

*This book is dedicated
with my thanks and love
to Ralph Bartlett,
my spiritual godfather,
a proven evangelist,
called and empowered
by God, and a
pre-eminent soul-winner.*

*Special thanks go to
my loving wife, Janice,
who both inspired the
research for this book
and spent many hours
proof-reading it.*

CONTENTS

Introduction xiii

Section One Definition and Pre-Law Tithing

    Chapter 1 The Origin and Definition of Tithing *3*

    Chapter 2 Genesis 14 Abraham, Melchizedek,
               and Arab Customs *12*

    Chapter 3 Genesis 28 Jacob's Bargain with God *34*

Section Two Tithing under the Mosaic Law

    Chapter 4 Numbers 18 The Statute/Ordinance of Tithing *39*

    Chapter 5 Leviticus 27: 30-34 "It Is Holy to the LORD" *47*

    Chapter 6 Tithes Replaced Land Inheritance *55*

    Chapter 7 How Many Tithes? How Much Was Required?
               10%, 20%, or 23 1/3%? *58*

    Chapter 8 Deuteronomy 12: 1-19 Deuteronomy 14:22-26
               Strange Facts about Tithing *66*

    Chapter 9 The Poor Did Not Tithe; Jesus Did Not Tithe *72*

    Chapter 10 1 Samuel 8: 14-17 1 Chronicles 23-27
               Kings, Tithes, and Taxes *79*

    Chapter 11 Amos 4: 2-6 Tithing Did Not Cover Sins *86*

    Chapter 12 2 Chronicles 31 King
               Hezekiah Restored Tithing *89*

Chapter 13 Nehemiah 10-13 Nehemiah Revived Tithing 92
Chapter 14 Malachi's Rebuke: Robbing God
            and Robbing the Poor 96
Chapter 15 Matthew 23:23 Luke 11:41-42 Jesus
            Supported Tithing under the Mosaic Law 120
Chapter 16 Luke 18: 12 A Pharisee's Boast about Tithing 130

Section Three The New Covenant and Tithing
Chapter 17 Hebrews 8; 2 Corinthians
            3 A Better New Covenant 137
Chapter 18 The Christian, the Mosaic Law,
            and the Law of Christ 147

Section Four Relevant Post-Calvary Texts
Chapter 19 Hebrews 7 Christ's High Priesthood
            Abolished Tithing 157
Chapter 20 Ephesians 2: 14-16; Colossians 2:13-17
            Ordinances of the Law Ended at Calvary 187
Chapter 21 1 Peter 2:9-10 The Priesthood of Believers
            Eliminates the Purpose of Tithing 196
Chapter 22 1 Corinthians 9:1-19 Paul Refused
            His "Right" of Support 203
Chapter 23 1 Corinthians 16 Giving to Needy Saints 224
Chapter 24 1 Timothy 5: 17-20
            Worthy of Double Honor 239
Chapter 25 Miscellaneous Objections 249

Section Five Grace Giving: The Newer and Better Replaced Tithing
Chapter 26 Chafer and Walvoord
            on New Covenant Giving 263
Chapter 27 2 Corinthians 8 and 9 Grace Principles of Giving
            Out-Perform Law Principles of Giving 267
Chapter 28 Acts 20: 16-35 A Sermon
            and Example to Preachers 277

Section Six Secular History, Ethics, and Summary

    Chapter 29 A Church History
                   of Tithing Since Calvary *295*

    Chapter 30 Ethical Considerations
                   of Tithing under Grace *316*

    Chapter 31 Summary of Reasons to Replace Tithing *326*

    Chapter 32 Spreading the Gospel
                   Remains Our Calling *334*

Bibliography *339*

About the Author *343*

INTRODUCTION

Every man according as he purposes in his heart, so let him give; not grudgingly, or of necessity; for God loves a cheerful giver (2 Cor. 9:7).

From the New Testament, it is clear that Christians should give, even sacrificially, to sustain the mysterious living organism, the church, the body of Christ, in which they are called to serve. Christian giving is an important part of the "new nature" believers have in Christ. Christians give, not because of any commandment or threatened curse for not giving, but because giving is as spontaneous as prayer, Bible study, and witnessing.

This book fully supports such giving as a freewill-offering and a faith response from the heart. However, the author is equally convinced that preaching a mandatory ten percent (tithe) of gross income, regardless of circumstances, is unscriptural and causes more harm than good to the body of Christ.

Churches within the same denomination are split over the doctrine of tithing. While many teach that tithing is a commandment and mandatory for the Christian, many others teach that principles of New Covenant giving do not include compulsory tithing. Those who teach tithing often scorn those who disagree with them as either not believing the Bible or else not being mature Christians. Positions of leadership such as pastor, deacon, and Sunday School teacher are often denied to those who do not teach tithing, even though they may be well-qualified and excel as soul-winners.

For far too long tithing has been treated as a taboo" off-limits subject among many conservative churches. Too many informed seminary professors silently stand by while persons in lower echelons write the denominational literature which promotes tithing. Their proof-text literature ignores professional biblical hermeneutical approaches. General agreement has been reached among evangelicals concerning the inspiration of the Bible, the Trinity, the deity of Christ, and the plan of salvation. Active discussion continues concerning modern prophets, the role of Israel in prophecy, and spiritual gifts. However, in many conservative, charismatic, and evangelical churches none dare question that tithing is commanded for the Christian church.

Perhaps the most ardent and vocal supporters of Christian tithing today are found in the Southern Baptist Convention. Therefore, in order to research the best available information about Christian tithing, an inquiry letter was addressed to their leadership. My letter informed them that I was preparing a Ph.D. dissertation on the subject of "tithing" and requested that they suggest the very best material available on the subject.

In May 1999, in answer to my inquiry about the best material and books on tithing, Dr. J. David Carter, Lead Stewardship Specialist for Lifeway Christian Resources of the Southern Baptist Convention, suggested that I use *Partners With God, Bible Truths About Giving*, by Bobby Eklund and Terry Austin, "as a platform for the additional research you do in designing your paper."[1] According to the copyright page, "This book is the text for Course 05-104 in the subject area Baptist Doctrine in the Church Study Course."[2]

---

1   J. David Carter, Lifeway Lead Stewardship Specialist, letter to Russell E. Kelly, 17 May 99.
2   Bobby Eklund and Terry Austin, *Partners With God, Bible Truths About Giving*, (Convention Press: The Sunday School Board of the Southern Baptist Convention, 1994), copyright page.

Partners With God has 142 pages and only devotes pages 63-79 to tithing. Eklund began his discussion of tithing by very cruelly attacking those who disagree with his position. On page 63 he introduced the section on tithing with a true story of a mother who killed her two young children and then committed suicide because she mistakenly thought she had terminal cancer. Eklund then wrote, "This tragic and extreme story illustrates an important truth: believing a lie always leads to sorrow and destruction." "The lie [of Satan] simply states that tithing is an Old Covenant practice which is no longer valid for the New Covenant Christian. This deceit has confined many Christians to financial bondage and plundered a sizeable portion of monetary resources from the church."[3]

It is past time for conservative Christians to openly discuss and research the doctrine of tithing using tried and proven biblical principles of interpretation in order to reach an agreement on this vital doctrine. What are we afraid of? Is not discovering and acting on the truth of God's Word of paramount importance for church growth? Surely the Holy Spirit does not want the church to ignore this issue!

While this book can be beneficial to all Christians, its primary focus is directed towards conservative evangelical Christians who are the strongest advocates of tithing. These also usually have a deep respect for *The New Scofield Reference Bible* and other dispensational writings. Therefore, these sources are used extensively to illustrate that these traditionally have *not* taught tithing.

Since there are many very large successful soul-winning churches on each side of the issue, evangelism, not tithing, determines financial success of a church. As previously stated, this book by no means should be interpreted to diminish the importance of Christian giving of free-will offerings to help meet sound New Covenant needs. It addresses the question,

---

3   Ibid., 63.

"Is church giving of law, necessity, exactness and compulsion, OR totally a faith response entirely from the heart?"

From Scripture it is clear that knowing the truth sets us free from error (John 8:32), and acting on that truth brings us closer to Christ (John 3:21). By avoiding this issue the church is missing out on God's blessings and sanctification (John 17:17). As in every other Bible doctrine, each Christian has an individual responsibility to know what God's Word says personally. Such is the purpose of this book and total stewardship is beyond its scope.

Every text from Genesis to Revelation that refers to tithing and its equivalent, the tenth, is included. This is followed by a look at concepts of "law" and "covenant." Next, the New Covenant principles concerning the giving of money and goods are examined. A very important survey of the early church before the Council of Nicea is included with many key quotations from renowned Christian historians on the subject of early church organization and giving.

(Quotes are from author's updated King James Version unless noted.)

The following list includes every Bible tithe text.

Genesis 14:17-20	Amos 4:2-6
Genesis 28:20-22	2 Chronicles 29:35; 31:1-12
Leviticus 27:30-34	Nehemiah 10:37-38; 12:44; 13:5, 12
Numbers 18:19-28	Malachi 3:7-10
Deuteronomy 12:1, 5-19	Matthew 23:23; Luke 11:42
Deuteronomy 14:22-29	Luke 18:9-14
Deuteronomy 26:12-13	Hebrews 7:1-19
1 Samuel 8:14-17	

Note: This book makes frequent use of the terms "Old Covenant" and "New Covenant" to distinguish those two legal documents from the divisions of the Bible normally referred to as "Old Testament" and "New Testament." It is the author's conviction that the Old Covenant properly began at Exodus 20 and the New Covenant properly began at Calvary when Jesus shed his blood. Although the four Gospels occur within the actual historical context of the Old Covenant, they are transitional and contain many New Covenant principles (excluding tithing).

▼

DEFINITION
AND
PRE-LAW TITHING

CHAPTER 1

▼

THE ORIGIN
AND
DEFINITION OF TITHING

What is a biblical tithe? A serious problem with understanding tithing appears at the very beginning of this book because of the serious disagreement about the definition of "tithe." The Hebrew and Greek words for "tithe" both simply mean "a tenth." However, beyond this simple definition, much difficulty exists in defining the contents of the tithe. If a legal court case were being held, a working definition would have to be agreed upon by all involved parties *before* the presentation of a case could proceed. However, since this is not possible, four definitions of "tithe" will be presented. Although many contend for the third definition, this book will use the fourth, precise Mosaic Law definition. Even this choice of a working definition will be of great concern to many because of long-standing traditional ideas of the *content* of the tithe.

The Pagan and General Definition

The first definition of "tithe" is a general all-inclusive definition which is not used in the main portion of this book. The *Encyclopedia Americana* defines the general tithe as "the tenth part of produce *or other income*, paid voluntarily or under the compulsion of law for the benefit of religious institutions, the support of priests and pastors, and the relief of those in need."[4] This definition does not distinguish between ecclesiastical tithes from church laws, personal tithes from trade and agricultural tithes.

The *Encyclopedia of Religion* reads, "In the ancient Near East lie the origins of a sacred offering or payment of a tenth part of stated goods or property to the deity. Often given to the king or to the royal temple, the 'tenth' was usually approximate, not exact. The practice is known from Mesopotamia, Syria-Palestine, Greece, and as far to the west as the Phoenician city of Carthage."[5]

The *Westminster Dictionary of the Bible* says, "A 10th part of one's *income* consecrated to God. The separation of a certain proportion of the products of one's *industry* or of the spoils of war as tribute to their gods was practiced by various nations of antiquity. The Lydians offered a tithe of their booty (Herod. I, 89). The Phoenicians and Carthaginians sent a tithe annually to the Tyrian Hercules. These tithes might be regular or occasional, voluntary or prescribed by law."[6]

This general tithe is of pagan origin and precedes the Mosaic Law's tithe by many centuries. In Genesis 14 Abraham was obligated to pay a tithe from the spoils of war in obedience to the Arab war custom. In New Testament times the Roman Empire received the first tithe of ten percent of grains and twenty percent of fruit trees from its conquered subjects.

---

4   *Encyclopedia Americana*, 1996 ed., s.v."tithe."

5   From *Encyclopedia of Religion, Mircea Eliad, editor*, 1987, s.v. "tithe."
       Reprinted by permission of the Gale Group.

6   John D. Davis, ed., *Westminster Dictionary of the Bible* (Philadelphia: Westminster Press, 1964), s.v. "tithe."

Although an *additional* full ten percent "spoils of war" tithe was not incorporated into the Mosaic Law, an *additional* two percent is mentioned in Numbers 31:25-47. Almost every theological commentator discusses this ancient custom in Genesis 14:21, which links it to the tithe in verse 20.

The Tithe as a General Offering

A second definition of "tithe" is most common among moderate and liberal churches which equate tithes with free-will offerings. Members are urged to begin with a small percentage of giving and gradually increase the percentage according to their ability. Among these churches there is little or no reference to an exact compulsory giving of ten percent from gross income as a legal requirement. Since many of the liberal churches assign Adam through Moses to mythology and believe the Pentateuch was written after the exile, they usually base their approach wholly on general principles rather than specific texts.

Also, many who hold this position prefer to use "tithe" to refer to "net" income with certain limitations. They are more likely to say that the poor are not required to give tithes and that tithes are only required from those who make a profit from their labor. They also are more likely to say that church support is not required from those on bare government pension or welfare. The parents' first duty is to provide essentials of food, clothing, and housing for their family.

The Tithe As Ten Percent of Gross Income

A third definition of "tithe" is taught among many more conservative and fundamental churches. For these churches "tithe" refers to ten percent of "gross" *income* and is an *expectation* from all economic classes, both rich and poor alike. In addition to paying salaries of gospel workers and providing social programs, some smaller churches also use the tithe for building funds and payment of all church debts. Their position claims that the tithe is an unchanging biblical *standard,* or *eternal principle,* which reflects the character of God, preceded the Mosaic Law and was, therefore, not abolished by the Mosaic Law. Exact tithing of ten percent of one's gross income should be observed by all Christians, and free-will offerings are to be given in addition to the mandatory tithe. Without exception, the tithe must be returned to God first, while other necessities such as shelter, child care, medicine, food, heat, and clothing must be given less priority. The church is obligated to teach tithing because it is a biblical command.

This definition is rejected and refuted in this book because it fails to consider the correct definition, the purpose, and limitations of the biblical tithe. As mentioned in the introduction, this book deliberately uses many conservative evangelical sources in an attempt to demonstrate that this definition is both legalistic and harmful to the church which should be using New Covenant principles.

The Tithe As an Old Covenant Ordinance for Israel

The fourth definition of "tithe" is the precise and narrow Scriptural definition as given in the Mosaic Law in the Old Covenant. The biblical tithe was an ordinance of the Mosaic Law for the use and benefit of national Israel under the Old Covenant. The tithe was given to the tribe of Levi, *first, in exchange for his loss of land inheritance in Israel* and, *second, because of his spiritual service* as a temporary intercessory priesthood representing God to the nation. The tithe was also given to provide food for festival occasions, and to provide welfare food for widows, fatherless, orphans and needy strangers in Israel. The basic tithe was not to be used for building houses of worship.

Since pagan dust defiled, the original tithe consisted solely of the increase of land produce from God's sanctified land of Israel and from the increase of animals herded on the land of Israel. Although the tithe could be exchanged for its monetary value, *the tithe itself never consisted of money!*

This book is a challenge to those holding the third definition to reconsider their position in light of the entire biblical teaching on giving, especially the

New Covenant after Calvary. It outlines New Covenant principles of giving which are far superior to the compulsory Old Covenant system.

Objections to This Definition

Several objections immediately emerge which challenge this definition. The first objection is that Abraham tithed *material goods* prior to the giving of the Mosaic Law. An entire chapter is given to this objection. Basically, Abraham's tithe was not commanded by God and was in obedience to Arab customs concerning the spoils of war.

A second objection to this definition is that it ignores the hermeneutic (principle of interpretation) that the tithe reflects the eternal nature of God and applies to all people of all ages. The objection is thoroughly discussed in the chapter on Leviticus 27:30-34. The phrase, "It is holy to the Lord," applies equally to every religious ordinance in the book of Leviticus. Proper interpretation must not ignore the chapter and book context of this phrase.

A third objection to this definition is the limitation of the *contents* of the tithe to land crops and animals. Certainly this is difficult to accept. However, unless the definition of "tithe" is found *within* the pages of the Bible itself, the definition cannot be called a "biblical" tithe. The church simply cannot define biblical terms with its own opinions and with extra-biblical sources. While it is true that God owns all things and that man is to be a steward of what God has placed in his hands, without a plain "because" statement, this fact does not establish tithing as an eternal biblical principle. Tithing's "chair" chapter, Numbers 18, clearly reveals the accurate "because," or reason, for the biblical tithe.

A fourth objection to this definition of biblical tithing claims that everybody must have paid a tithe, regardless of their occupation. However, again, this claim is not supported by Scripture, but is only supported by one's value systems and traditions.

The Content of the Tithe

A surprising biblical fact is that the poor did not pay tithe, but, instead, received *from* the tithe. A separate chapter on the poor discusses this truth. This fact is made especially clear in the gleaning laws and in the purpose of the tithe. Jesus did not tithe, nor did he sin by failing to tithe because he was poor and did not own land or stock animals. The poor were only expected to give free-will offerings to the best of their ability.

It is easy to demonstrate that the *content* of every recorded tithe found in the Mosaic Law is *only* from landowners and herdsmen of the land of Israel. This was a totally unexpected, yet very clear, truth about tithing that Bible study with an exhaustive concordance revealed. Also, strange as it may seem, Scriptural tithing was only intended for a society sustained almost wholly by agricultural crops and animal herds.

Biblical society included the following occupations: bakers, candle makers, carpenters, clothing makers, hired farm workers, hired herdsmen, hired household servants, jewelry craftsmen, masons, metal craftsmen, musicians, painters, perfume makers, physicians, sculptors, soldiers, tanners, teachers and tent makers. Yet NONE of these professions or products from these professions are included in any list of tithes or tithing! Why not? These sources provided much of the money for head taxes, temple taxes, tribute to foreign conquerors and, of course, free-will offerings. It is inconceivable to think that God simply *forgot* to include them in the many lists of items to be tithed.

Tithe Texts Which Reveal Its Limited Contents

Lev. 27:30, 32 And all *the tithe of the land*, whether of the seed of the land, or of the fruit of the tree, is the LORD's. It is holy to the LORD.... And concerning *the tithe of the herd*, or of the flock, even of whatsoever passes under the rod, the *tenth* shall be holy to the LORD.

Num. 18:27 And this your heave offering shall be reckoned to you, as though it were the grain of the threshing-floor, and as the fulness of the wine-press.

Num. 18:28 Thus you also shall offer a heave offering to the LORD of all your *tithes*, which you receive of the children of Israel; and you shall give thereof the LORD's heave offering to Aaron the priest.

Deut. 14:22 You shall truly *tithe all the increase of your seed*, that the field brings forth year by year.

Deut. 14:23 And you shall eat before the LORD your God, in the place which he shall choose to place his name, the *tithe* of your grain, of your wine, and of your oil, and the first offspring of your herds and of your flocks, that you may learn to fear the LORD your God always.

Deut. 26:12 When you have made an end of *tithing all the tithes of your increase* [produce: NIV, RSV] the third year, which is the year of tithing, and have given it to the Levite, the stranger, the fatherless, and the widow, that they may eat within your gates, and be filled.

2 Chron. 31:5 And as soon as the commandment was circulated, the children of Israel brought in abundance the firstfruits of grain, wine, and oil, and honey, and of all the increase of the fields; and the *tithe of all* things they brought in abundantly.

2 Chron. 31:6 And concerning the children of Israel and Judah, that lived in the cities of Judah, they also brought in the *tithe of oxen and sheep*, and the *tithe* of holy things which were consecrated to the LORD their God, and laid them by heaps.[7]

---

7   Taken from *Wycliffe Bible Commentary*, Charles F. Pfeiffer and Everett F. Harrison, editors, Moody Press, 1972. Used by permission. Concerning "2 Chron. 31:6," "The tithe of holy things may be a general term for the token percentages of certain offerings that became the property of the priests (Num. 18:6; cf. Lev. 6:16-7:36)."

Neh. 10:37 And that we should bring the firstfruits of our dough, and our offerings, and the fruit of all manner of trees, of wine and of oil, to the priests, to the chambers of the house of our God, and the tithes of our ground to the Levites, that the same Levites might have the *tithes* in all the cities of our tillage.

Neh. 13:5 And he had prepared for him a great chamber, where previously they laid the grain offerings, the frankincense, and the vessels, and *the tithes of the grain, the new wine, and the oil,* which was commanded to be given to the Levites, and the singers, and the porters, and the offerings of the priests.

Mal. 3:10 Bring *all the tithes* into the storehouse, that there may be *meat [food]* in my house.

Matt. 23:23 Woe to you, scribes and Pharisees, hypocrites! For you pay *tithe of mint and anise and cummin....*

Authorities Who Agree on This Definition of Tithe

Alfred Edersheim concurs, "And it is remarkable, that the Law seems to regard Israel as intended to be only an agricultural people—*no contribution being provided for from trade or merchandise*" (italics mine).[8]

Fausset's Bible Dictionary says, "The tithe of all produce as also of flocks and cattle belonged to Jehovah."[9]

Nelson's Illustrated Bible Dictionary says, "The law of Moses prescribed tithing in some detail. Leviticus 27:30-32 stated that the tithe of the land would include the seed of the *land* and the fruit of the *tree.* In addition the

---

8   Alfred Edersheim, *The Temple, Its Ministry and Services*, CD-ROM, (The Complete Christian Collection, Packard Technologies), chap. 19.

9   Andrew Robert Fausset, *Fausset's Bible Dictionary*, CD-ROM (Seattle: Biblesoft, 1999), s.v. "tithe."

Hebrew people were required to set apart every tenth animal of their *herds and flocks* to the Lord.... *Nowhere does the New Covenant expressly command Christians to tithe...*"(italics mine).[10]

The *New Catholic Encyclopedia* agrees, "In the Deuteronomic Code the tithe is limited to grain, wine, and oil (Deut. 12:6, 11, 17; 14:22). These texts more or less equate the tithe with other ritual offerings and sacrifices."[11]

The New Unger's Bible Dictionary says, "The tenth of all *produce, flocks, and cattle* was declared to be sacred to Jehovah by way, so to speak, of rent to Him who was, strictly speaking, the Owner of the land, and in return for the produce of the ground.... Although the law did not specify the various fruits of the field and of the trees that were to be tithed, the *Mishnah* (Maaseroth 1.1) includes *'everything eatable, everything that was stored up or that grew out of the earth...'"* (italics mine).[12]

---

10   Roland F. Youngblood, ed., *Nelson's Illustrated Bible Dictionary*, (Copyright: Nashville: Thomas Nelson 1986) CD-ROM (Seattle: Biblesoft, 1999), s.v. "tithe."

11   David I. Eggenberger, ed., *New Catholic Encyclopedia* (New York: McGraw-Hill, 1967), s.v. "tithe."

12   Taken from *New Unger's Bible Dictionary*, Merrill Unger, Moody Press, 1986, s.v. "tithe." Used by permission.

CHAPTER 2

▼

GENESIS 14
ABRAHAM, MELCHIZEDEK,
AND ARAB CUSTOMS

Melchizedek and Abraham: The Pro-Tithe Position

Genesis 14:20 is the key Bible text used to support the position that Christians should pay tithes, ten percent of gross income, to the church. Therefore, this chapter deserves, and receives, extended detailed attention in this book.

Genesis 14 is the first mention of tithing in Scripture. It involves Abraham paying tithes to the mysterious Melchizedek. Since this incident in Abraham's life precedes the Mosaic Law and the Old Covenant by over four centuries, those who teach tithing invariably use verses 18-20 as proof texts. Their position teaches that tithing, like marriage and the rest of the "moral" law are eternal principles which were not invalidated when the Mosaic Law was replaced by the New Covenant at Calvary. To many,

Melchizedek kept the worship of the true God alive over the centuries from the time of Noah until Abraham arrived in Canaan.

Eklund writes, "The idea of bringing a tithe to God can be found in the very first book of the Bible (see Gen. 14:20; 28:22). It was practiced by Abraham four hundred years before Moses. Bringing a tenth to their god was a common exercise in many ancient societies. Man has always used the number ten as a basis for enumerating. The actual number ten represents completeness. Therefore the tithe symbolized giving our all to God."[13]

In reply, however, such brief non-detailed assertions and conclusions are hardly the type of documentation required in most serious denominational doctrinal studies. There is no explanation offered concerning the purpose of the narrative in Genesis 14, who Melchizedek really was, what the title of "Most High" meant at that time in Israel's history, why Melchizedek allowed the king of Sodom to act as his ambassador, the nature of the spoil-tithe, what the significance of Abraham's announcement of "Yahweh" meant, whether or not Abraham tithed any of his personal property, why Abraham returned the remaining ninety percent to the king of Sodom, or why so much of the chapter involved the king of Sodom. While proponents give this chapter the extremely important function of the cornerstone "first use" of tithing, it is treated as if the inquisitive student is to simply accept the doctrinal position without question.

Narrative of Genesis 14
In order to properly understand why tithing was mentioned in this chapter, God clothed the incident in an extended detailed narrative because he did not want it to be taken out of its historical context. We must remember that the climax of a narrative is at the *end* of the story, not in the middle.

---

13   Eklund, 64.

Before reading the narrative, it is wise to consider its hermeneutic. "Narrative in its broadest sense is an account of specific space-time events and participants whose stories are recorded with a beginning, a middle, and an end.... Readers too often project some moral or spiritual truth over a biblical character or event, paying more attention to the moral lesson they see in the narrative than to the story itself. *The underlying objection to interpreting the Bible in a moralistic, exemplary fashion for every narrative passage is that it destroys the unity of the message of the Bible"* (italics mine).[14]

Between 2065 B.C. and 1918 B.C. four city-state kings from a large area between the Tigris and Euphrates Rivers invaded east of the Jordan River towards the southern end of the Dead Sea. Their leader was Chedorlaomer of Elam (v. 1). After traveling between 700-900 miles westward around the fertile crescent (of Mesopotamia), they defeated five small city-kings who ruled within a few miles of each other at the southern end of the Dead Sea (vv. 2-3).

After paying tribute for twelve years, these five rebelled in the thirteenth year (v. 4). The next year, the four kings of the east returned. Proceeding south from Damascus, they defeated numerous city-kings east, south, and southwest of the Dead Sea until they arrived at En-gedi. This placed them about twenty miles south of Salem.

Instead of advancing towards Hebron, Mamre, and Salem, they turned back south and fought the five kings (vv. 5-7). Chedorlaomer was again victorious. He took Abraham's nephew, Lot, all his goods, all the goods and food of Sodom and Gomorrah and started back home (probably retracing the route east) (vv. 8-12).

At that time Abraham lived near Hebron which is located approximately midway between Salem and Sodom (vv. 13, 24). When Abraham heard that Lot had been taken captive, he took 318 trained servants and

---

14   William C. Kaiser, Moises Silva, editors, *An Introduction to Biblical Hermeneutics: The Search for Meaning* (Grand Rapids: Zondervan), 69-71.

confederated Amorites and pursued the enemy (vv. 13-14, 24). Using a night attack, he defeated the enemy forces, rescued Lot, and retrieved all of the captives and goods which had been taken from the area of Sodom and Gomorrah (vv. 15-16).

On his return journey, Abraham stopped just outside Salem (which is probably Jerusalem). There he was greeted by the new king of Sodom who was followed by Melchizedek, the king of Salem, priest of El Elyon. Melchizedek brought bread and wine to feed Abraham and his men. Then Melchizedek blessed Abraham (vv. 17-20).

Abraham next honored Melchizedek by giving him a tenth of all the spoils of war that had been stolen from Sodom and Gomorrah (v. 21; Heb. 7:4). The king of Sodom insisted that Abraham keep the rest of the spoils for himself and only return the persons who had been taken from his area of rule (v. 21). Abraham told the king of Sodom that he had promised the LORD (Yahweh, Jehovah), whom he recognized as the El Elyon (Most High God), that he would not take any of the spoil (vv. 22-23). Abraham said he did not want the king of Sodom to boast about making him rich (vv. 23-24).

The Purpose of Genesis 14 in This Book

The purpose of this chapter is to demonstrate that Melchizedek does *not* provide a legitimate pre-law foundation to be used as an example of tithing for the New Covenant Christian. Although my conclusion is also held by many liberal and conservative Christian denominations, it is noteworthy that this is also the original dispensational position of the *New Scofield Reference Bible*, Moody Bible Institute, Dallas Theological Seminary and their highly respected authors such as Lewis Sperry Chafer, Charles Ryrie, Merrill Unger, and John Walvoord. These conservative evangelical scholars contend that the historical Melchizedek was never used to validate tithing in the Mosaic Law under the Old Covenant and cannot be used to validate tithing in the New Testament after Calvary. It will be shown that there is no eternal principle found in Genesis 14 which can be brought forward beyond Calvary to the church today. Ample evidence of this position exists in the writings of the previously mentioned authors which are used as textbook authorities in many colleges and seminaries today.

In order to understand the relevance of tithing from this narrative, it is first necessary to stop using verses 18-20 out of their historical context as "proof" texts and exegete the entire chapter with sound principles of interpretation. It is odd that, while many who support tithing accept dispensational eschatology, they reject dispensational giving principles which reject tithing.

Abraham's Tithe Was from the Spoils of War, but not from Personal Property

14:16 And he brought back all the goods, and also brought again his brother Lot, and his goods, and the women also, and the people.

14:20 And he gave him *tithes* of all.

Heb. 7:4 Now consider how great this man was, to whom even the patriarch Abraham gave the *tenth* of the spoils.

Abraham's tithe was clearly from the spoils of war, booty, which had been taken from Sodom and Gomorrah. It was not fruits from the much later "holy promised land" of Israel and did not match the description of tithes as detailed under the Mosaic Law (see chapter one). Neither did his tithe support a true Levitical priesthood which had forsaken land ownership in order to serve Yahweh.

Abraham still lived under the principle that the husband was the priest of each family unit. As a family priest he most likely made direct contributions of charity to the poor as he served God throughout his nomadic travels. Proper exegesis should begin the discussion of verse 20 at least at verse 16, instead of verse 18, and should continue it beyond verse 20, to at least verse 21.

When Abraham reached the outskirts of Salem he possessed the spoils of war. This included all of the goods which the defeated enemy had taken from the region of Sodom, plus all of the hostages, including Lot. Abraham very clearly gave from this bounty his "tithe" to Melchizedek. As a victorious king with Abraham as his "general," Melchizedek had first choice of the top of the heap of spoils, the first ten percent of the spoil. However, there is no hint in Scripture that Abraham ever tithed any of his personal property to Melchizedek, either at this time, or later.

Melchizedek's Ambassador Was the King of Sodom

14:17 And the king of Sodom went out to meet him after his return from the slaughter.

It is inconceivable that a true priest-king of the true God would allow a king who promoted the base immoral lifestyle of Sodom to go forth and act as his ambassador. We cannot forget God's description in chapter 18, verse 20, "The cry of Sodom and Gomorrah is great and their sin is very grievous."

The king of Sodom is an often ignored key player in the historical account of Genesis 14. While *three* verses (18-20) mention Melchizedek, *four* verses mention the successor to Bera, his friend and ally, the king of Sodom (21-24). While the last three climatic verses of the narrative are spoken by Abraham to the king of Sodom, not one spoken word is recorded from the mouth of Abraham to Melchizedek himself. The focus and climax of the narrative is Abraham's declaration to the king of Sodom, and not on his tithe to Melchizedek!

Since the incident occurred just outside the palace of the priest-king, Melchizedek, the king of Sodom must have certainly been acting as

Melchizedek's personal representative, his ambassador. Yet there is no disapproval or improper etiquette indicated.

Melchizedek Was a Pagan Canaanite Priest-King

14:18 And Melchizedek, king of Salem, brought forth bread and wine....

Although much speculation and reading back into the text exists, the text itself gives no evidence that Melchizedek was anything other than a self-appointed and self-named pagan priest-king similar to hundreds of others found in his era around 2000 B.C.

The Wycliffe Bible Commentary says, "The name of this mysterious person means either 'king of righteousness,' or 'my king is righteousness,' or 'my king is Zedek.' Zedek is the Hebrew word for 'righteousness' and also the name of a *Canaanite deity.* Melchizedek was the priest-king of Salem, which is the shortened form of 'Urusalem,' 'city of peace,' identified with Jerusalem. 'Shalom' is the Hebrew word for 'peace' and 'Shalem' probably was the *Canaanite god* of peace. This kindly priest-king, recognizing Abram's nobility and worth, supplied refreshment and sustenance for the weary warrior and his men. These gifts were tokens of friendship and hospitality."[15]

The preceding quotation comes from a commentary re-published for Southwestern Company (Southern Baptist) by Moody Press in 1968. The chapter on Genesis is written by Kyle M. Yates, Sr., Th.D., Ph.D., Professor of Old Testament, Baylor University, Waco, Texas, which is Southern Baptist. If, as Yates claims, Melchizedek worshiped the

---

15   *Wycliffe Comm.*, s.v. "Gen. 14." Although this commentary is published by Moody Press and uses authors from many denominations, it is predominantly Baptist. The author's copy is from The Southwestern Company, Nashville, Tennessee and lists over 20 Southern Baptist and independent Baptist contributors.

Canaanite gods, Zedek and Salem, then, logically, El Elyon must have also been a Canaanite god!

A second commentary says, "There is nothing mysterious about him in spite of the interpretation placed by some on Heb. vii, 3. He was king of some Semitic clan, which still occupied Salem, before the Jebusites captured it. There was never an utter extinction of the knowledge of God in the world, and here, too, God had preserved some knowledge of Himself."[16]

A third commentary says, "The rabbin, and most of our rabbinical writers, conclude that Melchizedek was Shem the son of Noah, who was king and priest to those who descended from him, according to the patriarchal model. But this is not at all probable…. The most commonly received opinion is that Melchizedek was a *Canaanitish* prince, that reigned in Salem, and kept up the true religion there; but, if so, why his name should occur here only in all the story of Abram, and why Abram should have altars of his own and not attend the altars of his neighbor Melchizedek who was greater than he, seem unaccountable."[17]

Melchizedek Could Not Have Been Pre-Incarnate Christ

If Melchizedek had been a pre-incarnate manifestation of Jesus Christ before his virgin birth, and if Jesus Christ had previously lived on earth as a priest-king, such an event would have rivaled the importance of the Christ-event! However, the Christ-event, and not Melchizedek, is when God became man and personally lived among his created beings.

It is very important to understand the difference between the "historical" Melchizedek of Genesis 14 and the "prophetic" and "typical" Melchizedek of Psalm 110 and Hebrews 7. "Negative" features of the *historical* Melchizedek are *reversed* to become "positive" features of Jesus

---

16   F. Davidson, ed., *New Bible Commentary* (London: Inter-Varsity Press, 1953), s.v. "Gen. 14."

17   Matthew Henry, *Matthew Henry Commentary on the Whole Bible*, CD-ROM (Seattle: Biblesoft, 1999), s.v. "Gen. 14."

Christ, the *typical* Melchizedek, in Psalm 110 and Hebrews 5-7. For the full discussion of this, see the comments at Hebrews 7:1-3 in a later chapter.

In addition, if Melchizedek had been a true worshiper of Yahweh, then he, and not Abraham, would have been God's choice for starting a chosen nation. Melchizedek was already an established priest-king in a large city in Canaan! However, such logic destroys the entire Bible emphasis and need of Abraham! It was precisely because God could not find a man of faith in Canaan like that of Abraham that he sought out Abraham in Ur and Haran.

Who was Melchizedek? The answer to this question varies almost as much as the number of theologians who discuss him. The impossibility of correctly identifying the historical Melchizedek leads to his typical use by the writer of Hebrews. However, for the purpose of this discussion on tithing, there is simply not enough evidence to *unreservedly* claim that his reception of tithes *must* be interpreted as positive proof that New Covenant Christians should tithe. If God had wanted this truth revealed, then God would have certainly emphasized it in the New Covenant, especially in passages like Hebrews 7 and 1 Corinthians 9. Yet neither Moses in the law nor any New Testament writer used Melchizedek as an example of Christian tithing.

Melchizedek's Jerusalem Was a Pagan City

Although we subconsciously want to associate Melchizedek's Jerusalem with that of David's Jerusalem over one thousand years later, this is simply not the case. The Tell Mardikh tablets (c. 2300 B.C.) contain the name "Urusalimum" and hundreds of other places and personal names in the region. The name probably means "founded by the god Shalem," a god of the Amorites.

When the Jebusites arrived they did not select the best location because the higher place above Kidron was already occupied by a *Canaanite* temple which the Jebusites did not want to displace. Archaeologists claim that the Jebusite fort dated back to at least 2000 B.C. which is the time period of Abraham's tribute to Melchizedek.[18]

Since the name of "Jerusalem" was known prior to the Jebusite occupation, it probably originally referred to the high hill of Melchizedek's temple beside the Valley of Zedek. The Jebusites are mentioned as early as Numbers 13:29. They called their city "Jebus" or "Jebusi." David captured it and named it "The City of David" (Josh. 15:8; 18:16, 28; Judg. 19:10; 2 Sam. 5:8; 1 Chron. 11:4). Evidently the original name of "Jerusalem" regained prominence under David.

The point of this discussion is that the place which Melchizedek called "Salem" was his pagan *Canaanite* residence and was *not* at that time God's holy city. Even the term "Zion" was originally a Jebusite name for their fort (2 Sam. 5:7). When the Jubusites arrived at the city they chose the southeastern hill rather than the higher hill north of it because it already had the remains of a Canaanite temple, possibly that of Melchizedek.

"Most High God" Was a Common Pagan Title for Both El" and "Baal"

14:18...and he was the priest of the most high God.
14:19 And he blessed him, and said, Blessed is Abram of the most high God, possessor of heaven and earth;
14:20 and blessed is the most high God, which has delivered your enemies into your hand....

A seminary textbook on hermeneutics reminds us, "*A good interpretation should not depend so heavily on inferences that it cannot stand on its own without the help of theoretical construct....* Did our theory about the historical

---

18   *Unger's*, s.v. "Jerusalem."

situation control our reading of the text, or did the text itself suggest the theory?" (italics mine).[19] Relevant to this chapter, does the common conclusion that Melchizedek's "Most High God" *must be* Jehovah rest on solid historical proof, or does it rest on the pre-conceived ideas of what interpreters and commentators would like it to mean?

It is extremely important for a correct understanding of Genesis 14 to realize that "Most High God," or "God the Most High," (Hebrew: "El Elyon") was a *common pagan designation for Baal, and even his father, El.* Again, neither syntax nor context require this identification to point exclusively to Jehovah, as most commentators conclude. It is unfortunate that "El Elyon" has been "translated," rather than merely being "transliterated," and left as "El Elyon." This error easily confuses the reader and encourages the reader towards a conclusion which is not apparent in the phrase itself. While a casual Canaanite reader would quickly identify the phrase with "El" or "Baal," a casual contemporary westerner would conclude that the term identifies Jehovah, or Yahweh. A comparative problem has been eliminated by Bible translators who have wisely chosen to retain the name "Baal," instead of translating it as "Lord."

Fausset's Bible Dictionary comments on the name "El Elyon" by saying, "The Phoenicians so named their chief god according to Sanchoniathon in Enseb. Praep. Event., doubtless from primitive revelation."[20]

The *International Standard Bible Encyclopedia* says that, like El Elyon, "Baal" (Babylonian "Bel"), the supreme Canaanite god, was also called "Lord," "master," and "possessor of heaven and earth."[21] At least from Melchizedek's point of view, "Baal" is the most logical, though usually ignored, meaning of "El Elyon." To further confuse the names, there are also sources which claim that "Elyon" was the grandfather of "El" and that

---

19   Kaiser, 127.

20   *Fausset's*, s.v. "Melchizedek."

21   James Orr, ed., *International Standard Bible Encyclopedia (ISBE)*, CD-ROM (Seattle: Biblesoft, 1999), s.v. "God, Names of, Elohim, El," also s.v. "Baal."

an eighth century Aramaic treaty stele even describes "El" and "Elyon" as two distinct deities.

Daniel, the book of Gentile prophecy, refers to God in Aramaic almost exclusively as "the Most High God," or "Most High" (Dan. 3:26; 4:17, 24, 25, 32, 34; 5:18, 21). Lucifer schemed to sit upon the throne of "the Most High" (Isa. 14:13-14). "The Most High God" is a name that relates to ALL nations, ALL heaven, and ALL earth, not just Israel. (Compare 2 Sam. 22:14; Ps. 7:17; 18:13; 21:7; 47:2; 83:18; 87:5; 91:1-2, 9; 92:1, 8; 97:9).

"El Elyon" Betrays Melchizedek as Ignorant of Yahweh

First, *Melchizedek did not know God as "Yahweh," that is, "LORD," or "Jehovah."* It is important to recognize that Melchizedek called himself the priest of "El Elyon," "Most High God" in verses 18-20 and did NOT call himself the priest of "*Yahweh*, the Most High God," as did Abraham to the king of Sodom in verse 22.

Those special to God knew His name! "Yahweh," the "LORD," is the special name through which God first revealed himself in Genesis 2:4 to Adam and Eve. God spoke to Cain as Yahweh in 4:6, to Noah in 5:29; 6:3; 7:1; 8:20 and 9:26; to Nimrod in 10:8-9; to those at the tower of Babel in 11:5; and to Abram in 12:1. The name, "Yahweh," occurs over 160 times in Genesis alone. Worshipers of all ages, especially those in Abraham's time, were very particular about knowing the *name* of the god to whom they prayed. Because of this Scriptural fact, it is almost inconceivable that Melchizedek could have been a true priest of the true God and yet *not know* his special name! Therefore, Melchizedek's ignorance about the true name of Yahweh disqualifies him from being one who carried the name from Noah's time.

Second, *Melchizedek identified himself as a pagan Gentile by calling himself priest of "El Elyon," "Most High God."* As just mentioned, this reference, "Most High God," was almost universally used by non-Hebrew Semitic people to designate their concept of "Baal," or even his father "El," the bull-god and father of the Canaanite pantheon.

"El," the Hebrew word most often translated as "God" in our Bibles, is a generic reference word and is not necessarily a "name." "El" can just as easily mean "god" with a little "g," "the might of nature," or even "an angel" (Exod. 34:14; Deut. 32:12; Judg. 9:46; Isa. 44:10). "El" (Strong's 410) and its root words, "uwl" (Strong's 193) and "ah-yil" (Strong's 352), all basically mean "might" and "strength." As previously mentioned, any Canaanite would immediately associate "El Elyon" with either "El" or "Baal"—never to Yahweh.[22]

Until Genesis 14, God had identified himself as "Elohim" and "Yahweh." He subsequently identified himself as "Almighty" in 17:1; 35:11; 43:14; and 48:3. God referred to himself in Genesis as "the God of Abraham, Isaac, and Jacob." By revelation, the non-Hebrew prophet, Balaam, identified Israel's God as Yahweh, the Almighty, and Most High in Numbers 24:13-16. While referring to *all nations*, Moses called God "Most High" in Deuteronomy 32:8. The point is that, while he is the true Most High, God did not *prefer* to be identified by El Elyon in the Pentateuch! Although Genesis 14, Numbers 24, and Deuteronomy 32 are the only three uses of "Most High" in the Pentateuch, this name for God would not appear again for over one thousand years when David uttered it in 2 Samuel 22:14—after his capture of Jerusalem from the Jebusites in 2 Samuel 5:7.

In other words, except for Abraham's declaration that his Most High was actually "Yahweh, LORD" in Genesis 14:22 and the reference by Moses to the "nations" in Deuteronomy 32:8, this name for God, El Elyon, is of very little importance to the patriarchs like Adam, Noah, Abraham, Isaac, Jacob, and Moses. When David did begin using El Elyon

---

22   Augustus Hopkins Strong, *Biblesoft's New Exhaustive Strong's Numbers and Concordance with Expanded Greek-Hebrew Dictionary*, CD-ROM (Seattle: Biblesoft, 1999), s.v. O.T. 193, 332, 410."

again, it was usually prefixed by "LORD." Thus Melchizedek's use of Most High for his god betrayed himself as a Gentile who was ignorant of God's most special covenant name, Yahweh.

Third, *Scripture does not tell us that Abraham revealed the name of the true Most High God to Melchizedek.* The key thought and climax of the narrative is found in verses 21-24, not in verses 18-20 which receive too much attention. Why? Because God's "champion" at this point in the Old Testament is Abraham, and not Melchizedek! Although Abraham must have certainly spoken to Melchizedek, *not one spoken word from Abraham to Melchizedek is recorded in Scripture*! Odd indeed if God considered their meeting so important.

In summary, the great revelation that Abraham's Most High was actually "Yahweh" was not made until he defended his actions towards the king of Sodom in verse 22. This omission of "Yahweh" concerning Melchizedek is important. Those who rush to make Genesis 14 teach tithing miss this point that, as priest of the "Most High" (El Elyon), Melchizedek did *not* know God as "LORD" (Yahweh, Jehovah), the covenant-God of Abraham and Israel. He was not priest of the "*LORD* Most High," and it was only Abraham who identified God as "LORD" Most High. (Note: English Bibles use all capitals for 'LORD' when the Hebrew word is 'Yahweh, Jehovah.')

Abraham's Tithe to Melchizedek Was an Arab War Custom

14:20…which has delivered your enemies into your hand. And he gave him *tithes* of all.
14:21 And the king of Sodom said to Abram, Give me the persons, and take the goods to yourself.

As documented in the first chapter, tithing did not originate in the Bible. It was a well-known pagan practice from Phoenicia, Egypt, Canaan, Mesopotamia and lands around the Fertile Crescent. It was a mandatory customary tax to a pagan god or ruler. The Roman Empire continued this tradition by requiring its defeated subject nations, like Israel, to return the spoil of the first tithe of the land to them! From comparison of discussions of verse 21. Abraham's tithe to Melchizedek was in obedience to this old Arab war custom and was not a command from Yahweh. Evidently, the Arab war custom specified that ten percent of the spoils of war be given to the local priest-king.

Historically, Melchizedek was a typical Canaanite priest-king. Abraham was obligated to pay a special one-time tithe-tax of the spoils of war. While those spoils usually belonged to an enemy, in this case, they belonged to Melchizedek's ally, ambassador-friend, and possible subject, the king of Sodom (and those he represented).

Many commentaries and theologians give contradictory reasons "why" Abraham tithed. Did he tithe because he *freely wanted to give* an offering to thank God and honor Melchizedek? Or did he tithe because he was *obligated* to tithe in observance of an old Arab war custom? It is clearly contradictory to interpret the *ten percent* in verse 20 as "free-will" and interpret the *ninety percent* in verse 21 as an "Arab war custom." A resolution of this contradiction is crucial for a correct understanding of Abraham's tithe and simply must be reconciled if the truth is to emerge. For example:

"Abram makes a practical acknowledgment of the absolute and exclusive supremacy of the God whom Melchizedek worshiped" (v. 20)…
    contradicts
"the king of Sodom concedes to Abram, *according to custom, the spoils of conquest as his right*, and claims for himself only his subjects who had been rescued from the foe" (v. 21).[23] Did Abraham tithe to honor God's "supremacy," or "according to Arab custom"?

---

23   Albert Barnes, *Barnes Notes*, CD-ROM (Seattle: Biblesoft, 1999), s.v . "Gen. 14:20-21."

"It was to a priest of the most high God that Abraham gave a tenth of the spoil as a token of his gratitude, and in honor of a divine ordinance" (v. 20)...

> *contradicts*

"*according to the war customs still existing among the Arab tribes*, Abram might have retained the recovered goods, and his right was acknowledged by the King of Sodom" (v. 21).[24] Was it "in honor of a divine ordinance," or "according to war customs"?

"This priestly reception Abram reciprocated by giving him the tenth of all, i.e., of the whole of the booty taken from the enemy. Giving the tenth was a practical acknowledgment of the divine priesthood of Melchizedek; for the tenth was, according to the *general custom*, the offering presented to the Deity" (v. 20)...

> *contradicts*

"the king of Sodom asked for his people only, and would have left the rest of the booty to Abram" (v. 21).[25] Was Abraham honoring Melchizedek's "divine priesthood," or was the king of Sodom acknowledging Arab war custom by telling Abraham to keep the rest of the booty?

"As an offering *vowed and dedicated* to the most high God, and therefore put into the hands of Melchizedek his priest" (v. 20)...

> *contradicts*

"where a *right* is dubious and divided, it is wisdom to compound the matter by mutual concessions rather than to contend. The king of Sodom had an *original right* both to the persons and to the goods, and it would bear a debate whether *Abram's acquired right by rescue would supersede his title and*

---

24   Robert Jamieson, A. R. Fausset and David Brown, *Jamieson, Fausset, and Brown Commentary,* CD-ROM (Seattle: Biblesoft, 1999), s.v. "Gen 14:20-21."

25   C. F. Keil and F. Delitzsch, *Keil and Delitzsch Commentary on the Old Testament,* CD-ROM (Seattle: Biblesoft, 1999), s.v. "Gen. 14:20-21."

extinguish it; but, to prevent all quarrels, the king of Sodom makes this fair proposal (v. 21)."[26] Did Abraham give ten percent as a voluntary "dedication" to God, and also have a "right" to keep the ninety percent because of Arab war custom?

"In giving tithes Abram acknowledged Melchizedek's God as the true God and Melchizedek's priesthood as a true one" (v. 20)...
   contradicts
"*according to Arab law,* and this may have obtained in Abram's time, if anyone receives booty, he gives up only the persons but is entitled to keep the remainder for himself" (v. 21).[27]

Clearly, the ten percent of verse 20 cannot be defined as Abraham's voluntary worship of the Most High God if the ninety percent of verse 21 is controlled by a demanding Arab law! The most likely and obvious reason that Abraham tithed to Melchizedek was the mandatory Arab war custom which required a tenth of the spoils of war be given to the local ruler. Abraham did not choose to freely tithe in order to proclaim that Melchizedek was a priest of his God. Otherwise, the reasoning for verse 21 is contradictory. This fact simply cannot be ignored.

Spoils of War Rules under Moses and David: Correctly Comparing Spoil-Tithes to Spoil-Tithes

Num. 31:21 And Eleazar the priest said to the men of war which went to the battle, This is the *ordinance* of the law which the LORD commanded Moses.... [Verses 22-25 discuss purification rites of spoils and persons after battle from chapter 19].
. . . .
Num. 31:25 And the LORD spoke to Moses, saying....

---

26   *Henry,* s.v. "Gen. 14:20-21."

27   *New Bible Comm.,* s.v. "Gen. 14:20-21."

[verses 25-54 discuss division of spoils after battle]
Num. 31:27 And divide the plunder into two parts—between them that took the war upon them, who went out to battle, and between all the congregation.
Num. 31:28 And levy a tribute to the LORD of the men of war which went out to battle—one soul [living creature] of five hundred.... [1 in 500]
Num. 31:29 Take it of their half, and give it to Eleazar the priest, for a heave offering of the LORD.
Num. 31:30 And of the children of Israel's half, you shall take one portion of fifty...and give them to the Levites, which keep the charge of the tabernacle of the LORD. [1 in 50]

While we are always reminded to properly compare "apples to apples" and not "apples to oranges," most commentators ignore this simple childhood rule in discussing the tithe of Genesis 14:20. While it is clear that Abraham gave a *spoil-tithe*, there is no connection between his one-time Arab tithe from spoils of war and the much later Mosaic Law tithe from a holy land which was decreed for the support of the Levitical priesthood!

In fact, if God's spoken word to Moses in Numbers 31:25 is of "ordinance" value and adds to the ordinance in verse 21, then these verses contain an *ordinance* of the Mosaic Law which sets the spoil-tax at **only two percent (2%)** and not ten percent (10%) which the Arab tradition required in Genesis 14:20! In Numbers 31:28-29 God commanded Moses to collect one part in five hundred (l/500th), or one-fifth of one percent (.2%) as a spoil-tax from the warriors to be given to the priest. In Numbers 31:30 God commanded Moses to collect one part in fifty (1/50th), or two percent (2%) as a spoil-tax from the rest of Israel to be given to the Levites. While it is noteworthy that the priests received a "tithe," or one tenth as much as the Levites received (1/500th is 10% of 1/50th), the Arab custom of a ten percent spoil-tax-tithe from Genesis 14 is greatly reduced to only two percent in the Mosaic Law. See also 1st Samuel 30:20-35.

Genesis 14 is a discussion of how Abraham reacted to the Arab custom of paying a tenth of the spoils of war to the local priest-king. It is not a discussion of tithing under the Mosaic Law. If one were to properly compare "apples to apples," then a comparable discussion should lead to the two percent in Numbers 31 and other Old Testament texts which refer to spoils of war. Only an incorrect "apples to oranges" approach changes the subject from spoils of war to Levitical tithes.

Abraham Violated Traditional Law and Also Returned the Ninety Percent

Abraham did not choose to tithe to Melchizedek because he was priest of the true Most High God. Instead, Abraham was obligated by long-standing Arab war custom to return a tithe of the spoils of war. Since there is no correlation between this tithing and that found in the Mosaic Law, the Mosaic Law *never* quotes Genesis 14 or even alludes to it in support of tithing. This is strange, indeed, since most modern tithe-advocates ignore the law as a foundation, go first to Melchizedek, and then turn to Leviticus 27 and Malachi 3. They also prefer to preach tithing and Melchizedek from Genesis 14 instead of the more dangerous Melchizedek text of Hebrews 7.

The king of Sodom followed the old tradition when he asked for return of the persons taken from him. Evidently, Canaanite custom permitted Abraham to keep the goods and only return the persons. Therefore, as soon as Abraham offered a tenth of the spoils to Melchizedek, the king of Sodom insisted that he keep the balance of the goods, the ninety percent, for himself (vv. 20-21). Verse 21 simply must be included in any discussion of verse 20.

14:22 And Abram said to the king of Sodom, I have lifted up my hand to the LORD, the most high God....

This declaration by Abraham begins the dramatic climax of the narrative and the real key point of the entire narrative in Genesis 14. Abraham declared allegiance to *"Yahweh," his LORD*, whom he knew was the real "Most High God" (v. 22). He refused to keep the customary ninety percent of the spoils (vv. 23-24).

Why Chapter 14 Divides 12-13 and 15-17

14:23 That I will not take from a thread even to a sandal thong, and that I will not take any thing that is yours, in case you should say, I have made Abram rich,
14:24 Except only that which the young men have eaten, and the portion of the men which went with me, Aner, Eshcol, and Mamre; let them take their portion.

Chapter 14 *follows* God's promises by faith to Abraham in chapters 12 and 13 and it *precedes* God's promises by faith in chapters 15 through 17. In chapter 14 Abraham had an opportunity to become suddenly very wealthy through his own works by keeping the riches of Sodom and the five kings of the southern Dead Sea. Yet Abraham, refusing to acquire wealth in such manner, returned ALL of it, not just ten percent! This event demonstrates that Abraham's justification, sanctification, and wealth ALL depended on faith, and not matters of customs and law.

Abraham represented God's covenant of grace, not the Old Covenant of law. The Arab custom concerning the spoils of war demanded a tribute of a tithe and allowed Abraham to keep the ninety percent and become instantly much more wealthy. However, while living under the constraints of Arab law, Abraham refused to be blessed through the provisions of that law. He deliberately violated the law-blessing opportunity because he knew that God was fully capable of blessing him through the operation of grace and faith in his life. Keeping the ninety percent would have meant keeping the worldly goods belonging to the king of Sodom. God had better blessings in store for Abraham which are eternal.

Again, Genesis 14 is a narrative with the climax at the end of the story, and not in the middle. The climax involves neither Melchizedek, nor tithing. Instead, it involves Abraham's assurance that God would keep his promises made by grace through faith, and not by military conquest, or Arab law-keeping.

Summary: Abraham's Tithe is Not an Example for Christians to Follow

Some believe that this passage demonstrates that tithing is commanded to the New Testament church because it existed before the law, just as marriage was before the law. But this comparison is not valid. Marriage preceded the law, was included in it, and was also repeated after the law. However, tithing, Sabbath observance and unclean foods also preceded the law, were included in it, but were not repeated after Calvary as commandments to the Christian church.

The preceding exegetical analysis of Genesis 14 used sound hermeneutical principles and did not apply an out-of-context proof text methodology. The conclusions are quite different from what many expect.

Abraham's tithe was:

1. Not a commandment of the LORD, but an observance of a common pagan custom.
2. Not of his own personal property, but was only of the spoils of war.
3. Not a Mosaic holy land tithe; he returned 100%.
4. Not a means of wealth through Arab law-keeping.
5. Not quoted to support tithing elsewhere in Scripture.
6. Not a condition of receiving God's blessings promised through faith in surrounding chapters.

7. Not to Abraham's LORD, Yahweh, but to a pagan priest who did not know and worship God as LORD. Melchizedek probably worshiped Baal as Most High God and possessor of heaven and earth. As a Canaanite priest-king, Melchizedek worshiped idols of Baal, offered child sacrifices, and promoted incest and sex with animals as part of pagan worship ritual. In paying this mandatory tribute, it is unfortunate that Abraham's pagan tithe-tax would have been used to promote such sin. (See Leviticus 18 and Deuteronomy 18:9-14.)

Chapter 3

▼

Genesis 28
Jacob's Bargain
with God

Gen. 28:20 And Jacob vowed a vow, saying, If God will be with me, and will keep me in this way that I go, and will give me bread to eat, and raiment to put on,

Gen. 28:21 So that I come again to my father's house in peace—then shall the LORD be my God,

Gen. 28:22 And this stone, which I have set for a pillar, shall be God's house; and of all that you shall give me, I will surely give the *tenth* to you.

Jacob's pre-Law promise to tithe is not an example for the church. This event records the only other pre-Mosaic Law mention of tithing. Also, this is definitely not a spoils-of-war-tithe as in Genesis 14. However, although there may have existed a tradition to help the poor, Jacob, like Abraham, was not responding to a command from Jehovah to tithe to a particular ministry of holy service. The formal law was yet centuries future.

True to his character, Jacob made a rash vow to God. He promised to give God a tenth of all his possessions. However, Jacob's promised tithe was conditional—God must first bless him and then bring him back to Isaac's house in peace. Jacob set the conditions, not God. Jacob made a vow to tithe; God did not ask for it. Although God greatly blessed Jacob in Haran, there is no further mention of tithing in Jacob's life (or in the book of Genesis).

In all fairness to the subject, we must ask ourselves, "To whom did Jacob give these tithes?" It is not enough just to say that he "gave them to God." God does not reach down from heaven and receive them to himself! Like Abraham, Jacob was surrounded by pagan Canaanite priest-kings. If he gave a tithe to them, he would actually be promoting idolatry, child sacrifices, sex with animals, and worship-prostitution! There was no God-called Levitical priesthood to receive them. Neither was there a temple in Jerusalem as commanded later in Deuteronomy. Unless we are willing to accept the extreme liberal contention that Abraham and Jacob are merely mythological traditions written after Bethel had a temple in northern Israel, this question is valid.

As the head of household before the law, Jacob served as his own priest. He asked for "food to eat and clothes to wear." He promised to give God "a tenth" "of all that you give me." Was Jacob promising to give God a tenth of food and clothes? How would he do that? We do not know. Perhaps Abraham and Jacob built and dedicated shrines to Jehovah (Yahweh). They could then bring food to those shrines for the poor and needy. We know that Jacob did build an altar at Bethel. However, if any commandment to tithe had been involved, there would have been no room for bargaining.

Many centuries later the *Didache*, paragraph XIV, would read, "For the prophets are your high priests. If you have no prophet, give them [firstfruits] to the poor." The early churches, like Jacob, followed strong traditions which compelled them to give firstfruits and offerings directly to the poor in the absence of an organized ministry.

Both Abraham's tithe and Jacob's tithe are completely out of context with tithing in the Mosaic Law. However, it must be pointed out that, under the law, Israel would later consider even the dust of the Gentile land as defiling and requiring ceremonial cleansing. Of course, there is no prohibition against the source of the tithe from a holy land in the book of Genesis.

Again, to whom did Jacob (and Abraham) tithe when they were wandering nomads? Except for the unfounded claims that Melchizedek was a faithful true priest-king serving Yahweh, no similar claim is made for any of the other priest-kings in which territories Jacob and Abraham lived. Like the temple of the moon god in Haran, except for their own shrines, all of the other shrines and priest-kings were clearly pagan.

▼

TITHING
UNDER THE
MOSAIC LAW

CHAPTER 4

▼

NUMBERS 18
THE STATUTE/ORDINANCE
OF TITHING

When Genesis 14 is removed as a candidate to support biblical tithing, the only other biblical alternative is the Mosaic Law. Therefore, tithing must fall under one of three categories of the law. Tithing must either be part of the commandments, part of the ordinances, or part of the judgments. The "commandments" expressed the righteous will of God (Exod. 20:1-26); the "judgments"governed the social life of Israel (Exod. 21:1 to 24:11); and the "ordinances" governed the religious life of Israel (Exod. 24:12 to 31:18). These three elements formed the 'law,' as the phrase is generically used in the New Testament. It is clear that tithing fell in the category or "ordinances."

Numbers 18 is the exact legislative wording of the ordinance which included tithing. Just as any person studying the history of any subject should first trace its history to its relevant origin, even so any legitimate study of tithing should logically begin with the precise wording of the *ordinance* itself. Unfortunately, however, very few Christians can open their Bibles to the exact place of the tithing ordinance—Numbers 18! Since this chapter will be referred to often in this book, it is necessary to be grounded in its wording.

An important seminary textbook on understanding biblical principles says, "The main burden of doctrinal teaching must rest on the *chair* passages."…"These passages [seats of doctrine] which we may call *chair* passages, can well function as boundary setters for interpreters as they seek guidance about the correct interpretation of texts that are textually or topically parallel. These *chair* passages contain the largest amount of material in one place on the respective doctrines. In a sense they represent a self-policing function of Scripture, one particularly important for Protestants who have typically rejected external limitations (e.g., by the church or by tradition) on their interpretations of the Bible."[28]

As you very carefully read Numbers 18, pay special attention to the words in italics because they all play important roles in this book.

Duties of Priests and Levites

18:1 And the LORD said to Aaron, You and your sons and your father's house with you shall bear the iniquity of the sanctuary; and you and your sons with you shall bear the iniquity of your priesthood.

Only Aaronic Priests Minister before God

18:2 And your brothers also of the tribe of Levi, the tribe of your father, bring with you, that they may be joined to you, and minister to you;

---

28   Kaiser, 201-02.

but you and your sons with you shall minister before the tabernacle of witness.

Most Levites Are Only Servants to the Priests

18:3 And they shall keep your charge, and the charge of all the tabernacle; only they shall not *come near* the vessels of the sanctuary and the altar, that neither they, nor you also, die.

Levite Servants Are Restricted

18:4 And they shall be joined to you, and keep the charge of the tabernacle of the congregation, for all the service of the tabernacle; and a stranger shall not *come near* to you.
18:5 And you shall keep the charge of the sanctuary, and the charge of the altar; that there may be no wrath any more upon the children of Israel.
18:6 And I, behold, I have taken your brothers the Levites from among the children of Israel; to you they are given as a gift for the LORD, to do the service of the tabernacle of the congregation.
18:7 Therefore, you and your sons with you shall keep your priest's office for every thing of the altar, and *within the veil*; and you shall serve: I have given your priest's office to you as a gift for service; and the stranger that *comes near* shall be put to death.

The Priest's Portion of the Offerings

18:8 And the LORD spoke to Aaron, Behold, I also have given you the charge of my heave offerings of all the holy things of the children of Israel; to you have I given them by reason of the anointing, and to your sons, by an *ordinance [statute]* forever.

18:9 This shall be yours of the most holy things, reserved from the fire: every oblation of theirs, every grain offering of theirs, and every sin offering of theirs, and every trespass offering of theirs, which they shall render to me, shall be *most holy* for you and for your sons.

18:10 In the most holy place shall you eat it; every male shall eat it; it shall be holy to you.

18:11 And this is yours: the heave offering of their gift, with all the wave offerings of the children of Israel; I have given them to you, and to your sons and to your daughters with you, by a *statute [ordinance]* forever; every one that is clean in your house shall eat of it.

18:12 All the best of the oil, and all the best of the wine, and of the wheat, the firstfruits of them which they shall offer to the LORD, them have I given you.

18:13 And whatsoever is first ripe in the land, which they shall bring to the LORD, shall be yours; every one that is clean in your house shall eat of it.

18:14 Every thing *devoted in Israel* shall be yours.

18:15 Every thing that opens the matrix in all flesh, which they bring to the LORD, whether it is of men or beasts, shall be yours; nevertheless, the *firstborn* of man shall you surely redeem, and the first offspring of unclean beasts shall you redeem.

18:16 And those who are to be redeemed from a month old shall you redeem, according to your estimation, for the money of five shekels, after the shekel of the sanctuary, which is twenty gerahs.

18:17 But the first offspring of a cow, or the first offspring of a sheep, or the first offspring of a goat, you shall not redeem; they are holy; you shall sprinkle their blood upon the altar, and shall burn their fat for an offering made by fire, for a sweet savor to the LORD.

18:18 And the flesh of them shall be yours, as the wave breast and as the right shoulder are yours.

18:19 All the heave offerings of the holy things, which the children of Israel offer to the LORD, I have given you, and your sons and your daughters with you, by a *statute [ordinance]* forever; it is a covenant of salt forever before the LORD to you and to your seed with you.

Priests Cannot Own or Inherit Land

18:20 And the LORD spoke to Aaron, You shall have *no inheritance* in their land, neither shall you have any part among them; I am your part and your inheritance among the children *of Israel.*

Levites Receive Food Tithes, but No Inheritance

18:21 *And, behold, I have given the children of Levi all the tenth in Israel for an inheritance, for their service which they serve, even the service of the tabernacle of the congregation.*
18:22 Neither must the children of Israel henceforth *come near* the tabernacle of the congregation, unless they bear sin, and die.
18:23 But the Levites shall do the service of the tabernacle of the congregation, and they shall bear their iniquity; it shall be a *statute [ordinance]* forever throughout your generations, that among the children of Israel they have *no inheritance.*
18:24 But the *tithes* of the children of Israel, which they offer as a heave offering to the LORD, I have given to the Levites to inherit; therefore I have said to them, Among the children of Israel they shall have *no inheritance.*

Priests' Portion: 10% of Tithes (1% Total)

18:25 And the LORD spoke to Moses, saying,
18:26 Thus speak to the Levites, and say to them, When you take of the children of Israel the *tithes* which I have given to you from them for your inheritance; then you shall offer up a heave offering of it for the LORD, even a *tenth part of the tithe.*

18:27 And this, your heave offering, shall be reckoned to you, as though it were the grain of the threshing-floor, and as the fulness of the wine-press.

18:28 Thus you also shall offer a heave offering to the LORD of all your *tithes*, which you receive of the children of Israel; and you shall give thereof the LORD's heave offering to Aaron the priest.

18:29 Out of all your gifts you shall offer every heave offering of the LORD, of all the best thereof, even the sanctified part thereof out of it.

18:30 Therefore you shall say to them, When you have heaved the best thereof from it, then it shall be counted to the Levites as the increase of the threshingfloor, and as the increase of the wine-press.

18:31 And you shall eat it in every place, you and your households; for it is your reward for your service in the tabernacle of the congregation.

18:32 And you shall bear no sin by reason of it, when you have heaved from it the best of it; neither shall you pollute the holy things of the children of Israel, unless you die.

Summary

Tithing was an ordinance (statute) at the very heart of the Mosaic Law and Numbers 18 is the exact wording of that ordinance.

1. *Only national Israel was commanded to pay tithes.* Almost every verse in the chapter makes reference to national Israel and her children under special covenant terms. This ordinance was never expanded outside of those Old Covenant terms of national Israel to the church.

2. *Only the Aaronic priests among the Levites could "come near," or "draw near"* to offer at the altar, enter the holy places, and touch the vessels and furnishings of the sanctuary (vv. 1, 2b, 4, 7). Direct worship of God was only performed "by proxy" through the priests. There was no priesthood of believers; *the priesthood* of the head of the family had been set aside in the Old Covenant; and even most Levites could not directly worship God. The reason for emphasizing the "come near" passages becomes clear in later chapters of this book

concerning how the doctrine of the priesthood of believers affects tithing. Also, see the very important discussion at Hebrews 7:19.

3. *Levites merely performed servant duties for the priests.* Even they would die if they "came near" to God (vv. 2a, 3, 4, 6). See point 6.

4. *Neither priests nor Levites could own or inherit property* (vv. 20, 23, 24, 26). Tithes replaced all property inheritance rights. This key part of Old Covenant tithing is discussed in a separate chapter in this book.

5. Priests were also given heave offerings, firstfruits of the land, the firstborn of clean animals, vow offerings, and redemption money for the firstborn of men and unclean animals (vv. 8-19). Any extension of tithes and offerings should include these also.

6. *Only Levites received tithes, not the priests* (vv. 21-24). The tithe was paid to them for their servant duties towards the "anointed" priests. Levites did **NOT** perform the actual worship ritual. This aspect has also been largely forgotten today in attempts to re-word tithing for Christians.

7. *In Numbers 18, the priests, descendants of Aaron, those who actually performed the sacrificial ritual, did **NOT** receive tithes!* They only received 1/10th of the 1/10th that was given to the Levites for all other forms of service (vv. 25-32). Therefore, priests received only one percent (1%), or a "tithe of the tithe" (v. 26). This aspect has also been largely ignored without valid biblical principles (also Neh. 10:38).

8. *Tithes only consisted of food and were eaten* (v. 31). See the full discussion in chapter one on the definition of "tithe." This is yet another unauthorized change of God's Word in order to convert Old Covenant Law into something God never intended.

9. *These instructions are clearly in the context of the Old Covenant "statutes" or "ordinances."* The term is used four times in this chapter alone (vv. 8, 11, 19, 23). This is also the context of Malachi 3:7 and 4:4 which is often ignored.

10. This foundational chapter must be thoroughly studied by any serious Bible student interested in the subject of tithing.

11. Having studied Numbers 18, it is quite difficult to understand why Eklund would say, "In spite of all that Jesus accomplished on our behalf he did not revoke God's ownership of the tithe. The Old Covenant practice of tithing was *not* a part of the legal system."[29] In reality, tithing was **the** very *"heart"* of the legal system! Tithing replaced the former system of the family priesthood and made provision for the very existence of the Levitical priesthood in order that the religious, ceremonial, and cultic provisions of the law would be enforced.

---

29   Eklund, 67.

CHAPTER 5

▼

LEVITICUS 27:30-34
"IT IS HOLY TO THE LORD"

27:30 And all the *tithe* of the land, whether of the seed of the land, or of the fruit of the tree, is the LORD's. I*t is holy to the LORD.*
27:31 And if a man will at all redeem any of his tithes, he shall add thereto the fifth part thereof.
27:32 And concerning the *tithe* of the herd, or of the flock, even of whatsoever passes under the rod, the *tenth* shall be *holy to the LORD.*
27:33 He shall not search whether it is good or bad, neither shall he change it; and if he changes it at all, then both it and the change thereof shall be holy; it shall not be redeemed.
27:34 These are the commandments, which the LORD commanded Moses for the children of Israel in Mount Sinai.

The key phrase, "It is holy to the Lord," appears in verses 30 and 32. Those who believe that New Covenant Christians should continue to obey (greatly modified) tithing laws employ this phrase as their most powerful argument for its eternal nature.

Eklund writes, "The most basic reason for tithing is the fact that Scripture clearly teaches the tithe is the Lord's. [He quotes Leviticus 27:30 and 32.] God owns everything in the heavens and on the earth (see Ps. 24:1). Yet the tithe belongs to him in a distinctive sense. God allows man to use nine tenths, but the tithe is sacred and must not be expended. The tithe is *'holy to the Lord,'* set apart, to be used only by God."[30]

The basic principle of the alternative view is presented by William Kaiser. "Law based not on the nature of God but on his particular sayings on a special occasion is called *positive* law.... The commandment about the Sabbath is the only one in the Ten Commandments that is mixed with both moral and positive aspects. It is *moral* in that it says that God is owner of all time and therefore has a right to receive back a portion of our time in worship of himself. But it is *positive*, or *ceremonial*, in that it spells out the seventh day as that time."[31] Like the Sabbath, there is a *moral* aspect of giving because God is the owner of all creation and there is a *positive*, or *ceremonial*, aspect of giving in that the exact ten, twenty, or twenty three percent was specified in the law for Israel.

A third approach by Roman Catholic theologian Thomas Aquinas is only a variation of Kaiser's statement. Both Kaiser and Aquinas conclude that the "ten percent" of the tithing ordinance was not moral law and not part of the eternal principles of God. Aquinas argues that tithing was *partially moral* because natural reason tells man to give and *partially judicial* because the divine institution of the Church had the authority to decree the exact percentage to be given" (*Summa Theologica*, Vol. 3, The Second Part of the Second Part).

---

30   Ibid., 67.
31   Kaiser, 187-188.

The Context of Verses 30-34

For many very good biblical reasons, this author disagrees with the statement by Eklund. The phrases "It is the Lord's," and "It is holy to the Lord," cannot possibly be understood as meaning, "It is an eternal moral principle which pre-existed the formal law." These phrases are very common in the book of Leviticus and apply to many other ordinances which almost all churches correctly conclude ended at Calvary when Jesus said "It is finished." In the context of verses 30-32 the tithe is "holy to the Lord," (1) because it comes from Israel's holy promised land of Canaan, (2) because it is given to the sanctified Levites in exchange of their land inheritance, and (3) because the Levitical priests had replaced the priesthood of believers with a cultic priesthood under the temporary ordinances of the Old Covenant. Consequently, those who *received* tithes were not supposed to be land owners. Yet none of these reasons for declaring the tithe holy are appealed to today!

The *Wycliffe Bible Commentary* places tithing in the same category as the ordinance for animals when it says, "The tithes belonged to the Lord and were subject to the *same* redemption rules as the clean beasts that had been dedicated (vv. 9-10)."[32]

Ps. 24:1 The earth is the LORD's, and the fulness thereof; the world, and they that dwell therein.

Tithe advocates very often refer to Psalm 24:1 in support of tithing, as if it were integrally connected to it. David, however, does not connect tithing with Psalm 24:1. As a matter of fact, the word, "tithe," *never* appears in any writing attributed to King David! While it is true that God is the Creator who made and owns everything, it is also true that the tithes of Leviticus 27 could not be received from non-Israelites, from unclean

---

32   *Wycliffe Comm.*, s.v. "Lev. 27."

animals, nor from the defiled lands outside of Israel. To use the colloquial, "Tithing was an Old Covenant Israelite thing!" There is simply no universal eternal principle stated, or implied, in the immediate context itself.

Any serious theological claim that tithing must be obeyed because it is part of the eternal law of God, which reflects his eternal character, certainly needs to be verified by other than proof text methodology or simple "because I said so" arguments. Sincere supporters of New Covenant tithing should desire to enter into advanced theological discussions and defend their position with sound reasoning. However, rarely are any attempts made to support their claim without using proof-text methodology. Consider the following:

1. When using proper principles of interpretation to exegete this passage, the literal text itself limits the *contents* of the tithe to "all the tithe of the land" and "the tithe of the herd" (vv. 30, 32). This is thoroughly discussed in chapter one under the definition and limitation of the tithe. The Mosaic Law tithe *never* went beyond products of the land of Israel to include products or profits from any of the many other occupations in Israel.

2. Most contemporary tithers only apply it to their gross income. They re-interpret the literal definition.

3. Contemporary tithers stress the best of the firstfruits, while verses 32 and 33 specifically forbid this concerning the herds. God demanded every tenth animal, whether it was the best, or not the best.

4. The context limits the tithe to the nation Israel under the Mosaic Law in verse 34. It is noteworthy that, although there are many texts such as Psalm 24:1 which declare God's ownership over the entire earth, neither God nor the Israelites ever used this world-ownership principle as authorization to gather holy tithes from pagan lands or from non-Israelites.

5. Tithes originally could come from any of the land of Israel. However, Alfred Edersheim states that this requirement later was made much more *narrow* rather than being *expanded*. After the

return from exile, the land was subdivided into three different zones of holiness. The second and third tithe could *not* come to the temple from land beyond the Jordan. While Israelite land which had been captured by King David, parts of Egypt, and part of Babylon could be used for lesser tithes to local Levites, most other land was considered defiled and incapable of producing acceptable holy tithes for the temple in Jerusalem.[33]

The Context of the Preceding Verses 28 and 29

27:28 Nevertheless, no devoted thing, that a man shall devote to the LORD of all that he has, both of man and beast, and of the field of his possession, shall be sold or redeemed; every devoted thing [to destruction: NAS] is *most holy to the LORD.*
27:29 None devoted [to destruction: NIV], which shall be devoted of men, shall be redeemed; but shall surely be put to death.

In the immediate preceding verses to the tithing verses 30-34, it is very clear that the phrase "it is *most* holy to the Lord" does not mean "it is an eternal moral principle."

"Every devoted thing is MOST holy to the LORD," in verse 28, elevates this holiness to an even higher level than tithing which is only *holy* to the LORD! People who, like Achan, were under an official ban to be put to death for their sins are called "most holy to the Lord."[34] "Most holy to the Lord" meant that the condemned criminal was under an absolute unredeemable grant to God."[35] Albert Barnes says that some even interpret

---

33   Alfred Edersheim, *Sketches of Jewish Social Life, Updated Edition* (Peabody: Hendrickson Publishers, 1994), 3-19.

34   *Wycliffe Comm.,* s.v. "Lev. 27:28,"

35   Adam Clarke, *Adam Clarke's Commentary*, CD-ROM (Seattle: Biblesoft, 1996), s.v. "Lev. 27:30-34."

this "most holy" ban as a "curse."[36] A person could even place himself under such an oath by promising not to fail to accomplish a specific purpose; however this may only mean lifelong devotion.[37] Although Israel did not *sacrifice* humans, its government did have the death penalty. (See Josh. 6:17; 7:13-26; Deut. 25:19; 1 Sam. 15:3.)

The point is that, if tithing, which is only called "holy" to the Lord, reflects an eternal moral principle, then how does one explain the "most holy" to the Lord of the previous verses? Naturally, it is extremely rare (if not non-existent) for sermons about the "holiness" of the tithe to explain the "most holiness" of the previous verses of its chapter context. Proof-text methodology is essential in order to ignore this context.

The Context of Chapter 27

In addition to tithing, the chapter also contains other things which are "holy to the Lord." Leviticus 27:9 calls all devoted offerings "holy to the Lord"; 27:14 describes sanctified houses as "holy to the Lord"; 27:21 describes fields as "holy to the LORD, as a field devoted; the possession thereof shall be the priest's." These things were "holy" *because* they, like the tithe, belonged to the Levitical priest under the Mosaic Law! They were not holy because of any inherent eternal quality.

All of chapter 27 is an "ordinance," or "statute" of "devoted" things which derives its basis from the ordinance itself, which is Numbers 18. As long as the Levitical priesthood replaced the priesthood of believers, and as long as the it received tithes in exchange for land inheritance, all devoted things, including the tithe, belonged to them and were thus "holy to the Lord."

The *Encyclopedia Judaica* even states that this tithe was voluntary. And, while the tithe in Leviticus 27:32-33 occurs in the chapter dealing with

---

36   *Barnes*, s.v. "Lev. 27:28-29."

37   *Jamieson*, s.v. "Lev. 27:28-29."

sacred *free* gifts of various kinds, the first offspring in verses 26-27 are an exception to the rule (italics mine).[38]

The Context of the Book of Leviticus "Be Holy for I Am Holy"

The book of Leviticus is clearly the most ceremonial, religious, and *cultic* book of the Mosaic Law. By "cultic," I mean "specifically and exclusively concerned with national Israel under the Old Covenant." "Holiness" and "most holiness" are its major themes in every chapter. Concerning the unclean food ordinances, God said, "For I am the LORD your God: you shall therefore sanctify yourselves, and *you shall be holy; for I am holy*: neither shall you defile yourselves with any manner of creeping thing that creeps upon the earth" (11:4). "You shall be holy: for I the LORD your God am holy" (19:2). Concerning all of his ordinances, or statutes, God said, "Sanctify yourselves therefore, and be holy: for I am the LORD your God. And you shall keep my *statutes*, and do them: I am the LORD which sanctifies you" (20:7-8). Undergirding every ordinance of the Mosaic Law, including tithing, is the principle that "God is holy." Since God is holy, the things he describes as holy under the law are holy in the context of that law. However, it is clear that this does not mean that everything under the law is an "eternal moral principle" to be observed forever.

Again, the phrases, "It is the Lord's," and "Holy to the Lord," are common in Leviticus. "Holy" things to God in Leviticus include all of its religious festivals and holy days (11 times in chapter 23), the sanctuary (4:6), the crown of the high priest (8:9), God and his people (11:4; 19:2), the linen garments of the high priest (16:4), the peace offering (19:8), the fourth year's fruit of a new tree (19:24), God's name (20:3), the priests (21:6) and, lastly, the *tithe* (27:30, 32). "Most holy" things to God in Leviticus include the priest's portion of the grain and sin offerings (Lev.

---

38   Cecil Roth, ed., *Encyclopedia Judaica* (New York: MacMillan, 1972), s.v."tithe."

2:3; 6:17), the trespass offering (7:1), the inner room of the sanctuary (16:2) and persons under a ban to be punished by death (27:28-29)—things which are even *more* holy than the tithe!

Finally, the most common division of the law for study purposes separates it into commandments, judgments, and ordinances. The book of Leviticus is almost entirely a collection of "ordinances," or "statutes" for the religious life of Israel. Leviticus instructs the priests concerning offerings, consecration, atonement, religious festivals, food laws, redemption laws, devoted things, and, lastly, *tithing*. One "misses the point" by retaining tithing while rejecting almost all of the other ordinances as merely Old Covenant! Doing such is simply using poor hermeneutics!

Again, Numbers 18 (especially verses 20 and 21), not Leviticus 27, nor Malachi 3, is the foundational, or chair, chapter which gives the *reasons* for tithing. Biblical tithing was NOT an eternal moral principle reaching to eternity with God. True biblical tithing BEGAN as a command to national Israel in Numbers 18! The "principle" it teaches is a religious ordinance of the Mosaic Law. Again, tithing was in exchange for land inheritance and was payment of service to the Levitical priesthood. Tithing was the Old Covenant "ordinance" which commanded the Israelite to return to God a portion of that which he claimed from the special promised land of Canaan.

Not only was tithing an important "part" of the Old Covenant Law, it was the "**first**" part which allowed all of the rest to function! The ordinance of tithing *established and funded* the Levitical priesthood. This, in turn, allowed for the daily ritual and religious services of the nation. Therefore, it is impossible to separate tithing from its context in Leviticus.

CHAPTER 6

▼

TITHES
REPLACED
LAND INHERITANCE

Num. 18:20 And the LORD spoke to Aaron, You shall have *no inheritance* in their land, neither shall you have any part among them; *I am your part and your inheritance* among the children of Israel.
Num. 18:21 And, behold, I have given the children of Levi all the *tenth* in Israel *for an inheritance,* for their service which they serve, even the service of the tabernacle of the congregation.

The tithe was given to the Levites as their inheritance in place of land inheritance because they served God! Period. God's original plan was that they would have no independent source of wealth other than himself. This has certainly changed in our contemporary society where gospel workers usually own and inherit property and often have great wealth gained from the churches they serve.

Because of its many repetitions in Scripture, we must assume that God knew that some would eventually forget this real purpose of tithing. It is equally important to repeat this fact in the context of this book for the same reason. While those who support tithing often quote Genesis 14:18-20, Leviticus 27:30-34 and Malachi 3:8-10, those who reject New Covenant tithing quote Numbers 18:20-26, Deuteronomy 12:11-12; 14:27-29, Ephesians 2:13-17, Colossians 2:14 and Hebrews 7:5, 12, 18. And the key texts of the key "chair" document are Numbers 18:20-21.

"Inheritance" and "land" are two of the most important concepts of the Old Covenant. While western religious thought speaks of salvation in terms of grace and faith, the Jewish mind-set is more likely to speak of salvation in terms of inheritance and land. These are also key ideas in the doctrine of tithing because God described Israel, its land and its people, as his unique inheritance. "For you separated them from among all the people of the earth, to be your inheritance" (1 Kings 8:53).

In exchange for his service to God, the Levite was denied land inheritance in Israel. This truth was repeated six times in seven verses in Numbers 18:20-26! The "no inheritance" rule for those who received tithes is also repeated in Deuteronomy 12:12; 14:27, 29; 18:1-2; Joshua 13:14, 33; 14:3; 18:7; and Ezekiel 44:28.

Take a moment now and read all of the above verses! Evidently, God wanted it abundantly clear *"why"* Levi received tithes from Israel. Whenever the reason for Levites receiving the tithe was mentioned, God also mentioned that the Levites were *not allowed any inheritance* or land ownership. The Levite and the Aaronic priest were always to be counted among, and included among, the poor of the land. They were not to become wealthy, but were to live day-by-day in the expectation that Israel would bring in the tithe to sustain them and for them to re-distribute to the *other* poor of the land.

When Paul said in 1 Corinthians 9:14, "they which preach the gospel should live of the gospel," he clearly meant gospel principles of grace and faith. For almost 300 years, until the Council of Nicea in A.D. 325, the vast majority of church bishops, presbyters, and deacons lived ascetic lives of denial and poverty in order to better serve the poor of the church. They fully understood what Paul meant.

Deut. 14:29 And the Levite, (because he has no part nor inheritance with you), and the stranger, and the fatherless, and the widow, which are within your gates, shall come, and shall eat and be satisfied, that the LORD your God may bless you in all the work of your hand which you do.

On the other hand, God would say to the Levitical priest, "they which preach the law should live of the law." This means that they would live as the poor of the land who daily depended upon God. This means that they would disavow wealth as long as there were poor whom they could help by redistributing the tithes and offerings they received.

Several Protestant denominations follow the lead of Roman Catholics and provide free parsonages and retirement homes for their pastors. This might be a partial effort to apply this principle; however, it is not clear whether or not property ownership is also forbidden by those denominations.

A problem arises, especially among churches which strongly advocate tithing, but choose not to preach the facts from these "no inheritance" texts. Very often the same pastors who insist on preaching exact tithing personally own property and inherit land. They use part of the Mosaic ordinance selfishly to teach tithing, but then ignore the majority of that same ordinance. Even while preaching law, they violate it by being partial (Mal. 2:9). God wanted the Levites to be totally dependent on him as their sole inheritance.

CHAPTER 7

▼

HOW MANY TITHES?
HOW MUCH WAS REQUIRED?
10%, 20%, OR 23 1/3%?

Was the biblical tithe only 10%, or could it have been as much as 23 1/3%?
Was there one tithe, two tithes, or three? A discussion of these questions
was not originally part of this book until it became evident why only one
answer is acceptable to most who teach New Covenant tithing.

Most casual readers of the Old Testament will conclude that there were
three separate tithes, averaging twenty three and one third percent (23
1/3%) per year, instead of only one ten (10%) percent tithe. For two
thousand years theologians have been split over whether these were separate tithes or somehow merged into either one or two tithes. The "multiple tithe" position is held by Adam Clarke, Albert Barnes, Matthew
Henry, Jamieson, Fausset, and Brown, Bruce Metzger, Charles Ryrie, the
Jewish Talmud and most Jewish writers, like Josephus.

Charles Ryrie combines the second and third tithe into one. "Two tithes were required: an annual tithe for the maintenance of the Levites (Lev. 27:30; Num. 18:21) and a second tithe brought to Jerusalem for the Lord's feasts (Deut. 14:22). Every third year, however, the second tithe was kept at home for the poor (Deut. 14:28)...."[39] However, if this were true, what would supply the food for the annual feasts every third year?

For those, like the author, who believe that New Covenant giving under principles of grace replaces the entire tithing system, there is no reason to be dogmatic about which position is correct. However, for those who believe that tithing is also expected from the New Covenant Christian, the ONE tithe of ten percent can be the only true and acceptable explanation. This position is for very obvious reasons! While it is difficult enough to ask average church members for ten percent, it would be much more difficult to ask them for twenty or even twenty three and one third percent!

Therefore, those who defend exact tithing have often placed themselves into a no-compromise position which concludes that the Old Covenant only taught one tithe of ten percent. Notice the tone of Eklund's remarks, "The notion of three separate tithes has been circulated among commentators for a long time. Nevertheless, we must remain true to Scripture and not the traditions of biblical interpreters. Some have used the idea of three distinct tithes as a means of rendering tithing an obsolete doctrine, not valid for the New Covenant believers. This is done by rendering the Levite tithe as government taxation, the festival tithe as antiquated ritual, and the welfare tithe as giving to the poor. Since taxes and welfare funding are levied by the government, it is assumed that the tithe is no longer necessary."[40]

In reply to Eklund, first, it is unprofessional to attack those who disagree by accusing them of following the "traditions of biblical interpreters" and accusing them of not remaining "true to Scripture." Such superior attitude simply will not convince scholars to concede their own researched

---

39   *Ryrie*, s.v. "Mal. 3:8."
40   Eklund, 66.

positions. Second, many of Eklund's own denominational seminary scholars and textbooks hold the opposite position which he criticizes. Third, his
discussion hints at an ulterior motive for insisting on only one tithe.

The First Yearly (Levitical) Tithe, Numbers 18: For Levitical Inheritance and Sustenance

**Num. 18:20 You shall have *no inheritance* in their land, neither shall you
have any part among them; I am your part and your inheritance among
the children of Israel.**
**Num. 18:21 And, behold, I have given the children of Levi all the tenth
in Israel *for an inheritance, for their service....***

This tithe has already been discussed in detail in previous chapters.
Unlike the second and third tithes, it replaced land inheritance rights in
Israel and provided basic sustenance for the Levite and the Aaronic priests
of the tribe of Levi, as described in Numbers 18.

The Second Yearly (Festival) Tithe: Deuteronomy 12:1-19 and 14:22-26

**Deut. 12:6 And there [Jerusalem] you shall bring your burnt offerings,
and your sacrifices, and your *tithes*, and heave offerings of your hand,
and your vows, and your freewill offerings, and the first offspring of
your herds and of your flocks:**
**Deut. 12:7 And there you shall *eat* before the LORD your God, and you
shall *rejoice* in all that you put your hand unto, you and your households, wherein the LORD your God has blessed you. ["Rejoice" is in
verses 7, 12, and 18.]**

**Deut. 14:23 And you shall *eat before the LORD* your God, in the place
which he shall choose to place his name there [Jerusalem], *the tithe* of
your grain, of your wine, and of your oil, and the first offspring of your**

herds and of your flocks; that you may learn to fear the LORD your God always. ["Rejoice" is in verse 26.]

Unlike the first tithe, the second yearly tithe was brought to Jerusalem for the festivals which accompanied the numerous gatherings. Also, unlike the first tithe, along with the Levite, the other Israelites, their family members, and servants, all *ate* portions of this tithe. Also, unlike the first tithe, this tithe was an integral part of REJOICING and celebration in the presence of the LORD. It is distinctly different from the first tithe.

The Third Year (Poor) Tithe: Deuteronomy 14:28-29 and 26:12-13

Deut. 14:28 At the end of three years you shall bring forth all the tithe of your increase the same year, and shall lay it up within your gates.
Deut. 14:29 And the Levite, (because he has no part nor inheritance with you), *and the stranger, and the fatherless, and the widow*, which are within your gates, shall come, and shall *eat* and be satisfied; that the LORD your God may bless you in all the work of your hand which you do.

Deut 26:12 When you have made an end of *tithing* all the *tithes* of your increase the third year, which is *the year of tithing*, and have given it unto the Levite, *the stranger*, the fatherless, and the widow, that they may *eat* within your gates, and be filled,
Deut. 26:13 Then you shall say before the LORD your God, I have brought away the hallowed things out of my house, and also have given them to the Levite, and unto the *stranger*, to the fatherless, and to the widow, according to all your commandments which you have commanded me; I have not transgressed your commandments, neither have I forgotten them.

Unlike the first tithe, the third-year tithe (in the year of tithing) was specifically for *all* of the needy—*including the non-Israelite stranger*! Its recipients included the Levites, widows, orphans, fatherless, and strangers. Also, unlike the second tithe which went to Jerusalem, the third tithe was to stay in the towns. This could not possibly be the same as the first, or second, tithe.

Consequences of Two or Three Tithes

Deuteronomy 14:22-23 presents a real dilemma for those who teach New Covenant tithing. First, if these verses are only a later amended part of the original tithe ordinance found in Numbers 18, then Deuteronomy should have priority over Leviticus and Numbers. This would mean that tithers should be allowed to feast off the tithes they bring to church! Failure to do so would be failure to follow the final biblical tithing revelation. Second, if the church admits that the feast tithe was indeed a second tithe, then it must also teach a minimum of twenty percent as an expectation of the church. This is a lose-lose situation!

Matthew Henry is among those who think that twenty percent tithes should be taught for the New Covenant Christian. Actually, he adds the king's tithe and totals *three* tithes of at least thirty (30) percent! "You think *the tenths, the double tenths, which the law of God has appointed for the support of the church*, grievous enough, and grudge the payment of them; but, if you have a king, there must issue *another* tenth out of your estates, which will be levied with more rigor, for the support of the royal dignity" (italics mine).[41] Yet modern taxation is much more than thirty percent.

10%: 1st tithe king's portion, 1 Sam. 8:14-17
10%: Levitical sustenance, Num. 18
10%: Festival tithe, Deut. 12 and 14

---

41   *Henry*, s.v. "1 Sam. 8:15."

3 1/3%: (10% every third year): Welfare, Deut. 14 and 26
PLUS: offerings and many other royal taxes

There are good reasons to disagree with Eklund and accept three separate tithes. First, it is extremely difficult to interpret the Scriptures otherwise. The Levites deserved support and probably fed the poor from all three tithes since a secular government welfare system did not exist. Does not our government tax us at least ten percent in order to set up judicial posts and protect its people? Remember, these texts describe a theocratic (God-ruled) government!

Second, the feasts were also important as national family-reunions; they were many and long-lasting and no government funds were allocated for them. If the citizens of Israel had combined all of the expenses at every religious and national holiday throughout the year, they would have discovered at least another ten percent spent.

The third year tithe was supplemental for the poor. Today our government, not our churches, taxes more than the extra three and one third percent from us for Medicare, public housing, food stamps, and other social programs. We must also remember that no tithes were to be collected from the land every seventh year, every fiftieth year, and when drought and famine caused no increase.

In conclusion, twenty three and one third percent is not extravagant when compared to the amount of taxation required today which provides the same kinds of services as those of the theocratic Levitical government, as originally proposed in the Old Covenant.

John MacArthur agrees. "So when someone says the Jew gave ten percent, that isn't true. The Jew gave twenty-three percent to begin with. It was for the poor people, the widows, and people who didn't have anything to eat. *So they were funding the people who ran the government, which were the Levites; they were providing for national feasts through the festival tithe; and they gave for the welfare program. All this was funding for the national entity. All three of these were taxation, not freewill giving to God.* Tithing was always taxation so that the programs of the government could run: the priestly program, the national religious program, and the welfare program" (italics mine).[42]

The *International Standard Bible Encyclopedia* says, "There is thus an obvious apparent discrepancy between the legislation in Leviticus and Deuteronomy. It is harmonized in Jewish tradition, not only theoretically but in practice, by considering the tithes as *three different tithes*, which are named the First Tithe, the Second Tithe, and the Poor Tithe, which is also called the Third Tithe; compare Tob. 1:7-8; Ant, IV, iv, 3; viii, 8; viii, 22). According to this explanation, after the tithe (the First Tithe) was given to the Levites (of which they had to give the tithe to the priests), a Second Tithe of the remaining nine-tenths had to be set apart and consumed in Jerusalem. Those who lived far from Jerusalem could change this Second Tithe into money with the addition of a 5th part of its value. Only food, drink or ointment could be bought for the money (Ma`aser Sheni 2:1; compare Deut. 14:26). The tithe of cattle belonged to the Second Tithe, and was to be used for the feast in Jerusalem (Zebhachim 5:8). In the third year the Second Tithe was to be given entirely to the Levites and the poor. But according to Josephus (Ant, IV, viii, 22) the "Poor Tithe" was actually a third one. The priests and the Levites, *if landowners*, were also obliged to give the Poor Tithe (Pe'ah 1:6)" (italics mine).[43]

The third tithe reveals that the Levite was expected to be among the poor. Israel's treatment of strangers, the fatherless, and the widows was extremely important. After being first mentioned in Exodus 22:21, and ten times in Deuteronomy, they are linked in Psalms, Isaiah, Jeremiah, Ezekiel, Zechariah, and the very important tithing text of Malachi 3:5—a total of 21 times. God commanded Old Covenant Israel to care for the needy; it was not an option!

---

42   Taken from *God's Plan for Giving*, John MacArthur, Moody Press, 1985, page 76. Used by permission.

43   ISBE, s.v. "tithe."

Again, the third year tithe remained in the towns instead of going to the temple storehouse in Jerusalem. In addition to the Levite, it included all others who had *no inheritance*. God made it the responsibility of the religious leaders to take care of the needy. *Once again, one requirement for receiving from the tithe was lack of land inheritance in Israel.*

In giving a portion of the tithe to the poor and needy, the Israelite was demonstrating his commitment to keep ALL of the law. Today, there is no valid biblical principle which allows the church to teach only one of the three types of tithes to support its ministers and then ignore the national festival tithes and the third year tithes for the poor and needy. Like the rest of the law, tithing was a complete package with three inseparable parts which cannot be divorced from the context of the entire Mosaic Law.

CHAPTER 8

▼

DEUTERONOMY 12:1-19
DEUTERONOMY 14:22-26
STRANGE FACTS ABOUT TITHING

Tithing Did Not Begin until Israel Was in the Land

Deut. 12:1 These are the *statutes and judgments*, which you shall observe to do *in the land* [Hebrew: eretz] which the LORD God of your fathers gives you to possess it, all the days that you live upon the earth [in the land: NIV; Hebrew: adamah].

Deut. 12:5 But to the place which the LORD your God shall choose out of all your tribes to put his name there, even to his habitation shall you seek, and there you shall come;

Deut. 12:6 And there you shall bring your burnt offerings, and your sacrifices, and your *tithes*, and heave offerings of your hand, and your vows,

and your freewill offerings, and the first offspring of your herds and of your flocks.
Deut. 12:19 Take heed to yourselves that you do not forsake the Levite as long as you live upon the earth [in your land: NAS; Hebrew: adamah].

Did you realize that Israel did not pay tithes during the 40 years in the desert? The tithe of the Old Covenant Mosaic Law was integrally connected to the *land* of Canaan. Therefore, there was no tithing during the 40 years in the wilderness. This is logical because no tribe had an inheritance and the Levites were not given tithes before there was an inheritance from which to tithe. According to Deuteronomy 12:1 the statutes and judgments about giving, including tithing, did not begin *until* Israel was actually *in* the land, and would last as long as Israel *stayed* in the land.

In *Sketches of Jewish Social Life*, Old Testament and Hebrew scholar, Alfred Edersheim devoted the first two chapters to discussions of the holy land of Israel which are well worth reading. After the exile, the country was subdivided into three different zones of "holiness." Only tithes from the most holy land-zone could be brought to the temple. Tithes from lesser holy land zones within Israel could provide for local shrines and the poor. However, since even the "dust" from pagan Gentile lands defiled, it is certain that no temple tithe could come from "defiled" ground.[44]

Again, although, God does indeed own all the heavens and all the earth, this fact is *never* used as the *reason* for the tithe. God's special promised land was the land of Canaan. Israel's *holy inheritance* was only the land of Canaan. Whereas the eleven tribes divided this holy land into twelve sections, the inheritance of the Levite was *the tithe from their land in Canaan*. Again, the Old Covenant concept of tithing was part of the Old Covenant concept of a holy inheritance. It is unscriptural to separate tithing from the concept of the holy land from which it came.

---

44   Edersheim, *Sketches*, 3-19.

A Legitimate Tithe Must Come Only from the Land of Canaan

When Leviticus 27:30 says "all of the tithe of *the land* is holy" it means the "the land of Canaan," not just any land! Moses prayed in Deuteronomy 26:15, "Look down from your holy habitation, from heaven, and bless your people Israel, and *the land* which you have given us, as you swore to our fathers, a land that flows with milk and honey." The reverence for the land is the reason that the body of Christ was not allowed to stay on the cross overnight. "And if a man has committed a sin worthy of death, and he is to be put to death, and you hang him on a tree, his body shall not remain all night upon the tree, but you shall surely bury him that day; (for he that is hanged is accursed of God) that your land be not defiled, which the LORD your God gives you for an inheritance" (Deut. 21:22-23).

Tithing Would Stop if Israel Were Expelled from Its Land

12:19 Take heed to yourself that you do not forsake the Levite as long as you live upon the earth. (The NKJ, NAS, NIV, and RSV all read, "as long as you live in your land.")

As previously mentioned, according to Deuteronomy 12:19, as long as Israel lived in its land, it was to give tithes to the Levite instead of any land inheritance. However, should Israel be expelled from its land of Canaan and lose its inheritance, then the Levite would also lose his inheritance of the tithe from the inherited land. Therefore, tithing should cease.

After the exile this was illegally modified to include lands on which Israelites lived in Babylon and Egypt, but even those inferior tithes were not holy enough to be brought to Jerusalem and stayed in the local synagogues. The basic concept that pagan dust defiled never changed as far as the temple tithes were concerned.

The Second Tithe Could Only Be Eaten at the Temple in Jerusalem

14:23 And you shall eat before the LORD your God, in the place which he shall choose to place his name there, the *tithe* of your grain, of your wine, and of your oil, and the first offspring of your herds and of your flocks, so that you may learn to fear the LORD your God always.

Originally, the second yearly tithe must be brought only to the city of Jerusalem for all to consume. This was to prevent competitive points of importance and false worship. After the nation split, northern Israel set up its own worship center and false worship resulted. Amos 4:4 is an example of including tithing in false worship.

The Second Tithe Could Be Exchanged for Money and Then Be Used to Buy Strong Drink

14:24 And if the way is too long for you, so that you are not able to carry it; or, if the place is too far from you, which the LORD your God shall choose to set his name there, when the LORD your God has blessed you,
14:25 Then shall you turn it into money, and bind up the money in your hand, and shall go to *the place* which the LORD your God shall choose,
14:26 And you shall spend that money for whatsoever your soul lusts after, for oxen, or for sheep, or for wine, or for *strong drink*, or for whatsoever your soul desires; and you shall eat there before the LORD your God, and you shall *rejoice*, you, and your household.

Deuteronomy 14, verses 22-26, is one of the strangest passages in the Bible. Since carrying the tithe was a physical burden when one lived too far from Jerusalem, this also proves that tithes were not money! God actually commanded the purchase of wine or fermented drink for festival celebration. Alcoholics love to discover these texts and try to justify their habits. However, this by no means authorized drunkenness or the abuse of alcohol. These texts describe worship services, not personal drinking abuse. Distillation was not practiced as modern man knows it, and the alcohol content was far below what is consumed in our time. Local drinking water was often polluted and unsafe to drink. Also, Scripture provides many texts warning of the evils of alcohol abuse and we cannot claim lack of access to safe drinking water.

Eating and drinking the tithe (14:23) at the "place" in the presence of the Lord was not the normal practice, but was reserved for special occasions—the second festival tithe. The importance of these texts is in rejoicing and giving God praise for his blessings.

There Was No Tithe from the Farmland Every Seventh Year and Every Fiftieth Jubilee Year

Exod. 23:11 But the seventh year you shall let it rest and lie still; that the poor of your people may eat; and what they leave the beasts of the field shall eat. In like manner you shall deal with your vineyard, and with your olive yard.

Lev. 25:12 A jubilee shall that fiftieth year be to you; you shall not sow, neither reap that which grows of itself in it, nor gather the grapes in it of your vine undressed.
Lev. 25:12 For it is the jubilee; it shall be holy to you; you shall eat the increase thereof out of the field.

Read Exodus 23:9-11 and Leviticus 25:3-7, 11, 20-22. On these special "sevens" the land was neither sown nor reaped. It was open for the Levite, the poor, and the hired worker to eat freely along with the landowner. Is it not fair to ask how many churches which teach tithing also tell their members NOT to bring tithes every seventh and fiftieth years? What principle gives those who support tithing the authority to delete the aspects of tithing discussed in this chapter?

When Tithing Was First Imposed, There Was No Civil Authority, King, Nor Elected Officials to Support with Taxation

At first, the freewill offerings and tithes supplied the needs of Israel. With God's approval, things changed drastically when Israel rejected God's rule through judges and God gave them a king. From that point on, which includes most of Israel's Old Testament history, the political authorities were responsible for collecting and redistributing the tithes.

CHAPTER 9

▼

THE POOR DID NOT TITHE; JESUS DID NOT TITHE

The Poor Did Not Tithe

Deut 26:12 When you have made an end of tithing all the *tithes* of your increase the third year, which is *the year of tithing*, and have given it unto the Levite, *the stranger*, the fatherless, and the widow, that they may *eat* within your gates, and be filled,

Deut. 26:13 Then you shall say before the LORD your God, I have brought away the hallowed things out of my house, and also have given them to the Levite, and unto the *stranger*, to the fatherless, and to the widow, according to all your commandments which you have commanded me; I have not transgressed your commandments, neither have I forgotten them. [See also 14:28-29.]

Mal. 3:5 And I will come near to you to judgment [against]...those who oppress the hireling in his wages, the widow, and the fatherless, and that turn aside the stranger from his right, and do not fear me, says the LORD of hosts.

Mal. 3:10 Bring all the tithes into the storehouse, that there may be food in my house....

1 Tim. 5:8 But if any does not provide for his own, and especially for those of his own house, he has denied the faith, and is worse than an infidel.

The Bible does not command the poor to tithe! As a matter of biblical fact, just the opposite is true! The Mosaic Law commanded the people of Israel to feed and care for the poor, widows, fatherless, strangers, and Levites *from* the tithe. The poor received from the tithes, offerings, gleanings, and Israel's bounty.

The Code of Jewish Law says, "He who has barely sufficient for his own needs, is not obligated to give charity, for his own sustenance takes precedence over another's."[45] Unfortunately, it is all too common to find large churches with many poor who give above and beyond their means out of fear of the Old Covenant curse of Malachi 3:9. Expecting the poor to pay tithes from welfare and Social Security checks is a disgrace. Many poor who tithe are then forced to depend even more on welfare because the church does not give more back to the poor than it receives from them. Such treatment is oppression of the poor and a modern scandal.

In his book, *Stewards Shaped by Grace*, Rhodes Thompson writes, "Some disagree that people are ever too poor to tithe. But my experience in the Third World [India] and inner-city St. Louis exposed me to people whose poverty I had wittingly or unwittingly helped to create and

---

45   Solomon Ganzfried, *Code of Jewish Law*, Translated by Hyman E. Goldin (Spencetown, New York: Hebrew Publishing, 1961), 1-111.

whose liberation from it still receives too little of my time and resources. Luke's biting words to first century scribes and Pharisees jump across the centuries: 'Woe to you twentieth-century religious leaders! For you load people with burdens hard to bear, and you yourselves do not touch the burdens with one of your fingers (Luke 1:46).' Watching poor folks in St. Louis facing the winter choice between 'meat' and 'heat,' I could not lay on them the burden of tithing that would have forced them to forego both at the risk of health and life."[46]

The Ordinance of Gleaning

Deut. 24:19 When you cut down your harvest in your field, and have forgotten a sheaf in the field, you shall not go again to get it; it shall be for the stranger, for the fatherless, and for the widow, that the LORD your God may bless you in all the work of your hands.
Deut. 24:20 When you beat your olive tree, you shall not go over the boughs again; it shall be for the stranger, for the fatherless, and for the widow.
Deut. 24:21 When you gather the grapes of your vineyard, you shall not glean it afterward; it shall be for the stranger, for the fatherless, and for the widow.

The tithe of the land did not include all of the land. God commanded landowners not to harvest the corners and not to pick up what had fallen after being harvested. These holy gleanings were for the poor. Concerning the gleaning law, Edersheim wrote, "Bicurim, terumoth, and what was to be left in the corners of the fields for the poor were always set apart before the tithing was made."[47] Certainly the poor did not tithe from gleanings!

---

46   Rhodes Thompson, *Stewards Shaped by Grace* (St. Louis: Chalice Press, 1990), 122.
47   Edersheim, *Temple*, CD-ROM, chap. 19.

Because the Levite was intended to be a poor servant of God with no land inheritance or personal wealth, he was often placed at the *top* of the list of the needy and poor. As such he and his household received tithes (Deut. 14:29; 16:11, 14; 26:11-13). However, the list of qualified tithe-receivers also included other non-landowners such as the stranger, the fatherless, the orphan, and the widow. As mentioned earlier, the stranger, the fatherless, the orphan and the widow are part of a recurring theme found in the Pentateuch and the major prophets. As poor non-landowners they received tithes, but were not exempt from certain offerings.

The Ordinance Prescribing Smaller Sacrifices from the Poor

Lev. 14:21 And if he is poor, and cannot get so much [two lambs], then he shall take [only] one lamb for a trespass offering to be waved, to make an atonement for him, and one tenth deal of fine flour mingled with oil for a grain offering, and a log of oil.

Lev. 27:8 But if he is poorer than your estimation, then he shall present himself before the priest, and the priest shall value him; *according to his ability* that vowed shall the priest value him.

In addition to receiving from the tithes, the poor were also allowed to bring smaller required offerings and were allowed to pay less redemption money. The poor had many other special laws protecting them. They were always allowed to recover property (Lev. 25:25-28); equal justice was demanded for them (Exod. 23:6; Prov. 31:9); Israel was to open its doors for them and freely lend to them without interest (Deut. 15:7-8, 11; Lev. 25:35-36); clothing given as pledges for loans must be returned before sunset (Deut. 24:12); and wages were to be paid daily before sunset (Deut. 24:15; Matt. 29:8; Jas. 5:4). These laws applied to both Israelite and strangers (Deut. 24:14).

Israel was commanded to give special gifts to the poor during festival days (Esth. 9:22) and every seventh year all farmland lay un-tilled and was available to the poor (Lev. 25:6). The same was true of every fiftieth Jubilee Year; the great Jubilee festival was especially for the poor and needy (Lev. 25:8-16, 23-35; 27:16-25; Num. 36:4; Ezek. 46:17).

God honors the amount of sacrifice in giving more than the value of the things given (Mark 12:42-44). He makes it clear that oppressing the poor is sin (Deut. 10:19; Prov. 14:31; Jer. 22:16-17; Ezek. 16:49; Amos 2:6-7; 4:1; 5:12; 6:4; Zech. 7:9-10; Mal. 3:5-6). God will certainly punish those who oppress the poor (Isa. 3:14-15; 10:1-2; 11:4), and the righteous will be known according to their treatment of the poor (Deut. 12:13; 15:11; Ps. 140:12-13; Prov. 19:17; 31:20; Jer. 22:16).

Joseph and Mary Paid the Smaller Offering of the Poor

Luke 2:22 And when the days of her [Mary's] purification [from childbirth] according to the law of Moses were accomplished, they brought him [Jesus] to Jerusalem, to present him to the Lord
Luke 2:23 (As it is written in the law of the Lord, Every male that opens the womb shall be called holy to the Lord); [Lev. 12:6-8]
Luke 2:24 And to offer a sacrifice according to that which is said in the law of the Lord, A pair of turtledoves, or two young pigeons.

Jesus' parents did not qualify to pay tithes. They were poor carpenters which were not required to tithe land and animal increase if they did not own land. When presenting the baby Jesus at the temple, the customary offering of a first-year lamb was waived because of their poverty.

Jesus Did Not Tithe

Jesus did not pay tithe! Blasphemy? Not at all. The titles of this chapter come as a real surprise to most tithe-advocates. The simple reason for these true statements is found in the biblical definition of the tithe as explained in chapter one. The Bible clearly teaches that only Israelite landowners and Israelite herdsmen *inside* Israel were required to tithe. This very narrow, but true, definition eliminates all non-landowners, all tradesmen, and all who were too unfortunate to afford raising stock animals for a living in Israel. Neither was this narrow definition of tithing ever changed among Jews for over a thousand years; it was still the definition during the time of Jesus.

Jesus Did Not Pay Tithes with His Disciples; Matthew 12:1-2; Mark 2:23-24; Luke 6:1-2

Matt. 12:1 At that time Jesus went on the Sabbath day through the grain; and his disciples were hungry, and began to pluck the heads of grain, and to eat.
Matt. 12:2 But when the Pharisees saw it, they said to him, Behold, your disciples do that which is not lawful to do upon the Sabbath day.

Jesus did not qualify as a person required to pay tithes! Jesus had been a carpenter and many of his disciples had been fishermen. If none of his twelve disciples were farmers or herdsmen, then none were required by the law to pay tithes—only freewill offerings. In addition, the above incident of the gleaning is noteworthy. First, since this was neither a sabbatical year nor a Jubilee year, this incident must have reference to the gleaning laws. Second, gleaning laws were specifically for the poor. Third, the Pharisees did *not* rebuke Jesus and his disciples for not being too poor to glean. Fourth, the Pharisees did *not* rebuke Jesus and his disciples for not paying tithe on their harvest! The only accusation is that they performed work on the Sabbath day.

In conclusion, since the poor were not in possession of land, and, since the poor actually received tithes, God did not request, or require, the poor in the Old Testament to tithe. They neither owned farmland or raised herds, and, since God is full of grace and mercy, it is not within the scope of his divine holy character to ask a poor person to tithe and deprive himself and his family of the basic necessities of life. There is not a single Old Covenant text which commands the poor to tithe. God was satisfied to accept their freewill offerings.

Those who tell the poor to give ten percent of their gross income to the church and thus cause those same poor to be deprived of basic necessities are simply not teaching either Old or New Covenant principles of grace and freewill giving.

▼

CHAPTER 10

1 SAMUEL 8:14-17
1 CHRONICLES 23-27
KINGS, TITHES, AND TAXES

1 Sam. 8:7 And the LORD said to Samuel, Heed the voice of the people in all that they say to you, for they have not rejected you, but they have rejected me, that I should not reign over them.

1 Sam. 8:14 And he [your king] will take your fields, and your vineyards, and your olive yards, *even the best of them*, and give them to his servants.

1 Sam. 8:15 And he will take *the tenth of your seed*, and of your vineyards, and give to his officers, and to his servants.

1 Sam. 8:16 And he will take your menservants, and your maidservants, and your best young men, and your asses, and put them to his work.

1 Sam. 8:17 He will take *the tenth of your sheep*: and you shall be his servants.

During the approximately 300 year-period of the book of Judges, tithing is not mentioned in the Bible. Each man did that which was right in his own eyes (Judg. 17:6; 21:25). There was no central government, no central place to worship, and most of the Levites (who owned no land) became drifters and beggars. Worship of pagan gods was common. During the period of the judges, often several tribes were in bondage to neighboring nations at different times.

As long as the Levites only performed the routine and lowly servant tasks for their Aaronic brothers, their receipt of the tithe was probably very inconsistent, or even non-existent (Numbers 3, 4, and 8 all). Tithe collection would also be sporadic during reigns of evil kings, foreign occupation, and especially during times of pagan apostasy. Some families even used Levites as personal family priests.

When Israel asked for a king to rule over them like their neighbors, God declared that they had rejected his reign and replaced himself with an anointed king. From ancient antiquity to the Roman Empire, the political ruler collected the tax-tithe (the firstfruits, and the best of crops, herds, and persons) to finance his government, pay government expenses, build government buildings and provide a national army. King Solomon used forced labor to make many citizens work every third month on the king's farms and on the king's projects without pay.

Tithes Were Taxes! Even the Jews Admit It!

As soon as Israel became a monarchy, the best tithe became part of national taxation which was collected and redistributed by the king according to his needs. First Samuel 8:10-18 says that the king, whom God would "anoint" as his representative, would take the "best" and the "tenth" which formerly belonged to God. The "tenth' was regarded as "the king's share." Ten percent was already a centuries-old tradition among Israel's Canaanite neighbors and surrounding nations. Later, as witnessed in the reforms of King David, King Hezekiah, and Governor Nehemiah, politicians supervised collection and distribution of the tithe. We must remember that, under Ezra and Nehemiah, the best and first tithe-tax went to the conquering and ruling Persians.

King David's Use of Levites

1 Chron. 23:2 And he gathered together all the princes of Israel, *with the priests and the Levites.* [Civil and religious leaders are combined in a theocracy.]

1 Chron. 23:3 Now the Levites were numbered from the age of thirty years and upward; and their number by their polls, man by man, was thirty eight thousand [38,000].

1 Chron. 23:4 Of which, twenty four thousand [24,000] were to set forward the work of the house of the LORD; and *six thousand [6,000] were officers and judges* [civil and religious].

1 Chron. 26:29 Of the Izharites, Chenaniah and his sons were for the outward business over Israel, *for officers and judges* [civil and religious].

1 Chron. 26:30 And of the Hebronites, Hashabiah and his brothers, men of valor, a thousand seven hundred [1,700], were *officers* among them of Israel on this side Jordan westward *in all the business of the LORD, and in the service of the king* [civil and religious].

1 Chron. 26:31 Among the Hebronites was Jerijah the chief, even among the Hebronites, according to the generations of his fathers. In the fortieth year of the reign of David they were sought for, and there were found among them mighty men of valor at Jazer of Gilead.

1 Chron. 26:32 And his brothers, men of valor, were two thousand seven hundred [2,700] chief fathers, whom king David made *rulers* over the Reubenites, the Gadites, and the half tribe of Manasseh, *for every matter pertaining to God, and affairs of the king* [civil and religious].

King David used tithe-receiving Levites as the core of his government.
David clearly took over control of the Levites, and whatever tithes they
might have previously collected. However, no tithes are actually mentioned in association with David. Tithes were most likely included as part
of the royal taxes paid directly to him, as was the situation in other surrounding nations.

Since God had been replaced as ruler by the king, it became the king's
responsibility to rule over the worship facilities and priests. This principle
was later used to legitimize the "divine right of kings" to collect tithes in
order to support a state church. It is noteworthy that neither God, nor any
of his prophets, ever objected to this church-state arrangement originated
by David in Israel.

Levites Were Only Partially Religious Workers

As temple workers, David re-organized the Levites' work schedules
under his political authority. Levites served in 24 divisions, each serving at
the temple only a week at a time, or about two weeks per year (1 Chron.
24 all; Luke 1:5-6). During the construction of the temple David divided
the 38,000 Levites as follows: 24,000 construction supervisors, 6,000
treasurers and judges 4,000 gatekeepers, and 4,000 musicians (1 Chron.
23:4-5). First Chronicles describes general temple duties such as bakers,
repairmen, animal skinners, and janitors (chap. 23), musicians and singers
(chap. 25), and gatekeepers (chap. 26).

After the temple construction was completed, most likely many of the
24,000 Levites who were construction supervisors continued to serve the
king in their roles as social welfare workers in the various Levitical cities
scattered among every tribe. First Chronicles, chapter 26 is a very interesting chapter for those who want to know how their tithe was used. While
only serving about two weeks a year in religious activities at the temple,
the remainder of the time many Levites were still the core of the king's

officials. Inspired by God, King David used the Levites as the base of his political support.

Levites Were Political Leaders and Rulers

In their political role as servants to the king, the government consisted of "leaders, priests, and Levites" (23:2). There were 6,000 Levites who served as governmental judges and treasurers in the Levitical cities: 1,700 judged and collected revenue in one region of the country, 2,700 in another region, and (evidently) 1,600 in a third region (26:31-32). An army commander was a Levite, the son of a priest (27:5), and 4,600 Levites were soldiers in David's army (12:23, 26). Nehemiah used Levites as guards at the gates of the city (Neh. 13:22).

Certainly David (and Solomon) would have been corrected by God, or the prophets, if they had used tithes incorrectly. As inspired writers of Scripture, the Holy Spirit was guiding their decisions. Yet Scripture records that Levites were for the outward business over Israel, (1) *"for every matter pertaining to God," and* (2) *"affairs of the king"* (26:32). Compare also Ezra 2:40-42, 61; Neh. 7:43-45; Neh. 8:9; 10:28, 39; 12:44-45.

A Theocracy Combines Both Civil and Religious Taxation

God placed all of these verses in our Bibles to remind us that Levites were public officials of the state and tithes were included as state-taxation to support them. It is difficult for some to understand that the above "political" positions were supported by the tithe for sustenance of the Levites which allowed the king to use his first tithe-tax for other purposes. Using the excess Levites (who were already due ten percent) was a simple matter of good political money management by the king.

It is even more difficult to understand how Christian tithe-advocates can ignore the Old Covenant context of tithing as a political tax. Total taxation, including tithes, easily approximated forty (40) percent, which is comparable to that found in our modern society. In addition to wholly religious duties, the Levites (who received the tithe) performed normal governmental positions such as judges, treasurers, registrars, census takers, genealogists, building and city policemen, and social service workers!

Even the *Encyclopedia Judaica* agrees that tithes were political taxes. "As may be learned from 1 Sam. 8:15, 17 and from Ugarit the tithe could also be a royal tax which the king could exact and give to his officials. This ambiguity of the tithe, as a royal due on the one hand, and as a sacred donation on the other, is to be explained by the fact that the temples to which the tithe was assigned were royal temples (*cf.* Amos 7:13) and, as such, the property and treasures in them were put at the king's disposal...."

"As is well known, the kings controlled the treasures of palace and temple alike, which is understandable, since they were responsible for the maintenance of the sanctuary and its service.... It stands to reason that the tithe, which originally was a religious tribute, came to be channeled to the court, and was therefore supervised by royal authorities."[48]

The *Wycliffe Bible Commentary* says, "This [1 Sam. 8:14-17] is the only reference in the Old Testament to the exaction of tithes by the king. However, in the East it was not unusual for the revenue of the sovereign to be derived in part from tithes, as, for example, in Babylon and Persia."[49]

The *Keil & Delitzsch Commentary* says, "All their possessions he [the king] would also take to himself: the good (i.e., the best) fields, vineyards, and olive-gardens, he would take away, and give to his servants; he would tithe the sowings and vineyards (i.e., the produce which they yielded)...and raise the tithe of the flock...."[50]

While such action was not challenged by God's prophets as being out of line with the Old Covenant Law, no Christian church would want

---

48   *Judaica*, s.v. "tithe."

49   *Wycliffe Comm.*, s.v. "1 Sam. 8:14-17."

50   *Keil*, s.v. "1 Sam. 8:14-17."

politicians to handle its finances today. Following the example of the Old Covenant should compel them to do so. However, since tithing is not New Covenant, we have no guidelines concerning its collection and redistribution.

Chapter II

▼

Amos 4:2-6
Tithing Did Not Cover Sins

4:2 The Lord GOD has sworn by his holiness, that, lo, the days shall come upon you, that he will take you away with hooks, and your posterity with fishhooks.

4:3 And you shall go out at the breaches, every cow at that which is before her; and you shall cast them into the palace, says the LORD.

4:4 Come to Bethel, and transgress; at Gilgal multiply transgression; and bring your sacrifices every morning, and your *tithes* after three years;

4:5 And offer a sacrifice of thanksgiving with leaven, and proclaim and publish the free offerings; for this you love, O you children of Israel, says the Lord GOD.

4:6 And I also have given you cleanness of teeth in all your cities, and want of bread in all your places; yet you have not returned to me, says the LORD.

After the death of Solomon, during the reign of his son, Rehoboam, the northern tribes separated from Judah and Benjamin and called themselves the kingdom of "Israel." The southern two tribes were referred to as the kingdom of "Judah."

> **1 Kings 12:28 Whereupon the king took counsel, and made two calves of gold, and said to them, It is too much for you to go up to Jerusalem; behold your gods, O Israel, which brought you up out of the land of Egypt.**
> **1 Kings 12:29 And he set the one in Bethel, and the other he put in Dan.**

Compared to southern Judah, northern Israel was prosperous and powerful. In order to keep its wealth from tithes and offerings from flowing to Jerusalem in Judah, Israel had set up false worship at Bethel and Dan with sacred cows. They still worshiped God as Yahweh and kept the same traditions as southern Judah, but projected worship of Yahweh to the sacred golden calves.

Almost two hundred years later, about 787 B.C. the prophet Amos warned of destruction to Israel which came in 722 B.C. when Assyria took them away captive. When comparing 4:1 with 5:1, it seems that Amos had a double meaning when he described Israel's sins—the rich women and the sacred cows of false worship.

The sins of Israel in chapter 4 are thus: (1) you "oppress the poor and crush the needy" (v. 1), (2) you "say to your husbands [or lords], 'Bring us some drinks'" (v. 1), and (3) you are sinning more and more by pretending to have true worship at Bethel and Gilgal (v. 4).

Northern Israel claimed that it was continuing the true worship as given to Moses. Idolatrous Israel boasted about its tithes and offerings, and they loved to brag about their faithfulness in contributions (vv. 4-5). However, although they were in the correct "land" for tithing, they were in the wrong "place," that is, they were not at God's designated temple in Jerusalem.

Tithes were brought to Bethel and Dan for idol worship. These were the royal chapels of the northern kingdom. Since most of the Levitical priests had moved south into Judah, Israel's worship was totally false. Merely going through the motions of tithing was just another way to "sin yet more." Therefore, God scorned such actions when done in defiance to his will. They were no more justified with wrong motives than was the Pharisee in Luke 11:42.

CHAPTER 12

▼

2 CHRONICLES 31
KING HEZEKIAH
RESTORED TITHING

31:2 And *Hezekiah appointed the courses of the priests and the Levites* after their courses, every man according to his service, the priests and Levites for burnt offerings and for peace offerings, to minister, and to give thanks, and to praise in the gates of the tents of the LORD.

31:3 He appointed also *the king's portion* of his substance for the burnt offerings for the morning and evening burnt offerings, and the burnt offerings for the Sabbaths, and for the New Moons, and for the set feasts, as it is written in the law of the LORD.

31:4 Moreover he *commanded* the people that lived in Jerusalem to give *the portion of the priests and the Levites,* that they might be encouraged in the law of the LORD.

31:5 And as soon as the commandment went forth, the children of Israel brought in abundance the firstfruits of grain, wine, and oil, and honey, and of all the increase of the fields; and the *tithe* of all things they brought in abundantly.

31:6 And concerning the children of Israel and Judah that lived in the cities of Judah, they also brought in the *tithe* of oxen and sheep, and the *tithe* of holy things which were consecrated to the LORD their God, and laid them by heaps.

31:11 Then *Hezekiah commanded* to prepare chambers in the house of the LORD; and they prepared them;

31:12 And brought in the offerings and the *tithes* and the dedicated things faithfully, over which Cononiah the Levite was ruler, and Shimei his brother was the next.

From Deuteronomy 26:13 until 2 Chronicles 31:5, the word, "tithe," is not mentioned in Scripture. This period reached from the Judges, the united kingdom under Kings Saul and David until King Hezekiah's attempted reforms around 700 B.C.—approximately 800 years!

When tithing is again mentioned, it is commanded, collected and stored by the king, the political authority, who delegated political authority to the priests. Temple worship, observance of the Mosaic Law, and tithing had suffered under bad kings who often paid tribute to other nations and often worshiped false gods.

King Hezekiah practically had to start all over again in following David's tradition by appointing priests and separating them into various ministries of the sanctuary (31:2). He even gave up some of his king's portion of the best, his first tithe-tax, which had originally belonged to God (v. 3; cf. 1 Sam. 8:14-17). Hezekiah commanded restoration of tithing (vv. 5-6). After four months of abundant tithing (vv. 5-7), storehouses were built for the surplus (vv. 8-12).

In summary, tithing here is a political tax initiated, commanded, and enforced by the king (31:4). At the same time, all of this activity by the king of Judah seems to be in full accordance with the Mosaic Law (31:4). A Levite, Cononiah, not a priest, was in charge of the collections. Again, there was no opposition to the concept of political control of the tithes.

CHAPTER 13

▼

NEHEMIAH 10-13
NEHEMIAH REVIVED TITHING

10:37 And that we should bring the firstfruits of our dough, and our offerings, and the fruit of all manner of trees, of wine and of oil, to the priests, to the storerooms of the house of our God; and the *tithes* of our ground to the Levites, that the same Levites might have the *tithes* in all the cities of our tillage.

10:38 And the priest the son of Aaron shall be with the Levites, when the Levites take *tithes*; and the Levites shall bring up the *tithe of the tithes* to the house of our God, to the chambers, into the treasure house [storehouse: NAS].

12:44 And at that time some were appointed over the chambers for the treasures, for the offerings, for the firstfruits, and for the *tithes*, to gather into them out of the fields of the cities the portions of the law for the priests and Levites, for Judah rejoiced for the priests and for the Levites that waited. [Governor Nehemiah's appointments]

12:47 And all Israel in the days of Zerubbabel, and in the days of Nehemiah, gave the portions of the singers and the porters, every day his portion; and they consecrated holy things to the Levites; and the Levites consecrated them to the children of Aaron.

13:4 And before this, Eliashib the priest, having the oversight of the chamber of the house of our God, was allied to Tobiah.

13:5 And he had prepared for him a great chamber, where previously they laid the grain offerings, the frankincense, and the vessels, and the *tithes* of the grain, the new wine, and the oil, which was commanded to be given to the Levites, and the singers, and the porters; and the offerings of the priests.

13:12 Then all Judah brought the *tithe* of the grain and the new wine and the oil to the treasuries.

13:13 And I [Nehemiah] made treasurers over the treasuries, Shelemiah the priest, and Zadok the scribe, and of the Levites, Pedaiah; and next to them was Hanan the son of Zaccur, the son of Mattaniah; for they were counted faithful, and their office was to distribute to their brothers.

While Judah was out of its land in exile, temple-tithing from land inheritance from Israel naturally ceased. When allowed to return, the vast majority of Levites chose to stay in Babylon. The *Encyclopedia Judaica* says "It is quite possible that the priestly law was not implemented at all after the disruption of the monarchy."[51] Once back in the land, Governor Nehemiah again commanded tithing for support of the Levites and the Aaronic priesthood. The priests, the gatekeepers and the singers

---

51   *Judaica*, s.v. "tithe."

are mentioned several times as receivers of the tithe (10:39; 11:18-23; 12:23-28; 12:40-43; 13:5).

While many tithe-advocating churches are against paying the salaries of other church workers from the tithe, the Old Covenant examples from Nehemiah and Chronicles included Levites who functioned as gatekeepers and singers. Actually, tithing included every kind of Levitical sanctuary worker from the brick-layer and animal-skinner to the janitor, because the Levites, not the priests, received the *whole* tithe (Num. 18:20-24). The non-priestly Levites were to give only one tenth of the whole tithe to the ministering priests (Num. 18:26; Neh. 10:38).

Numerous discrepancies exist between Old Covenant tithing and what is falsely presented as New Covenant tithing. The Old Covenant system could not possibly work in our society. First, many small churches, who give all the tithe to the pastor, do not have enough other workers to receive the ninety percent (90%) of the tithe, and a full-time pastor could not survive on only one-tenth of the whole tithe. Thus, while a distorted form of tithing is taught in order to support the pastor, the pastor receives up to one hundred percent (100%) instead of only ten percent (10%) of the tithe. Again, compare Numbers 18:20-24 with 18:26 and Nehemiah 10:38.

A second discrepancy with modern tithe-teaching is, once again, the *contents* of the tithe. Nehemiah occurs at least twelve hundred (1,200) years after the contents of the tithe were first described in Numbers 18 and Leviticus 27. While hundreds of other occupations must have existed, the tithe is still only required from land owners who farmed or had herd animals. It is the tithe of the grain, the wine, and the oil. Although, this formula was magnified by the Pharisees to include minute garden spices, at no point does the true biblical tithe refer to products and money obtained through crafts and non land-use occupations.

Thirdly, the political authority is still primarily in charge of worship services, commanding tithing, and delegating spiritual leaders. He is

God's anointed ruler of the theocracy. Church-state union is the rule under the Old Covenant in which tithing applied.

CHAPTER 14

▼

MALACHI'S REBUKE: ROBBING GOD AND ROBBING THE POOR

"Will a man rob God? Yet you have robbed me. But you say, Wherein have we robbed you? In tithes and offerings" (Mal. 3:8).

Malachi 3:8 is the most often quoted "tithing" text in the Bible. Exactly what does this verse mean in its proper historical and exegetical context? What application does it have to Christians in the New Covenant relationship with God? Because of its importance, a detailed study of Malachi was warranted for this book. This brief commentary on Malachi reveals a more diversified meaning of Malachi 3:8.

We hear so many sermons about Malachi 3:8 that we tend to forget its Old Covenant context. Although John the Baptist was actually an Old Covenant prophet, Malachi was the last one recognized by Israel.

Although tradition says he was a Levite born in Zebulon, Malachi could have also been merely a "ghost writer" for Nehemiah. His book is the last one accepted by most Jews in the Old Testament canon. Malachi was written between 450-400 B.C. to those whom Persia had allowed to return from Babylonian captivity. It is important to realize that, in order to understand Malachi, one must also study Ezra, Haggai, Zechariah, and, especially Nehemiah, which are addressed to the *same* group of Israelites. All four immediately precede Malachi and provide its context. Malachi confronted the same problems as did Nehemiah concerning insincere religious leaders (Neh. 13:1-9), tithes (Neh. 13:10-13, and intermarriage with those in pagan religions (Neh. 13:23-28). Judgment is prominent in the context of the several curses of the Mosaic Covenant (Mal. 2:2-3, 12; 3:1-5; 4:1). However, the grace and love of God is also prominent and the righteous should not fear God's judgment (3:16-17; 4:2-3).

Malachi is presented as a conversation between God and the priests and people of Israel through the prophet. The priests and people asked six questions, and God replied (1:2-5; 1:6 to 2:9; 2:10-16; 2:17 to 3:6; 3:7-12; 3:13 to 4:3; 4:4-6).

God Addresses the Nation (1:1-5)
1:1 The name "Malachi" means "My Messenger."
1:2 God's love for Israel is the cornerstone of Malachi's message. The prophecy is addressed from God to his unique nation, Israel. The people had shown no piety or trust in God. When questioned about his love, God reminded Israel that he had chosen them before they existed as a nation.
1:3 As a nation, God chose to hate Esau because of his excessive wicked traits (Gen. 26:34; 27:41; Obad. 10-14). By grace he elected to favor Jacob (Israel).

1:4 God promised that the Edomites (Esau's descendants) would never remain restored; this was fulfilled when the Nabatean Arabs removed them from their land forever.

1:5 When Israel sees that God will perform what he promised concerning Jerusalem and Edom, then the LORD should be magnified beyond the borders of Israel.

God Addresses the Priests (1:6 to 2:9)

The religious leaders are especially guilty. While it is clear that chapter 1, verses 1-5 address the entire nation, and verse 6 begins addressing the Levitical priests specifically, it is not clear if, or where, Malachi's message returns to addressing all of the people. This author believes that the remainder of Malachi addresses primarily the Levitical priesthood and not the nation as a whole. Therefore, the sins of Malachi are primarily the sins of the priests.

1:6 "O **priests!**" *Priests specifically* despise God's name and show no honor.

1:7 The priests offer polluted bread on the altar.

1:8 The priests offer imperfect animals as sacrifice.

1:9 The priests are told to pray to God for mercy.

1:10-12 The priests' offerings are rejected.

1:13a The priests verbally express their contempt for God.

1:13b The priests offer to God what they took by robbery [NAS], [violence: RSV], [stolen: NKJ]. This is a key text which is difficult to understand unless the Levites and priests, under the authority and protection of Nehemiah, either took *more* than they should have taken, or else hoarded the best for themselves. Compare Nehemiah 12:44 and 13:13.

1:14 The priests are **cursed** because they give God a blemished sacrifices when they had better to give. They are deceivers, swindlers (NAS), and cheats (NIV).

2:1 "And now, O you priests, this commandment is for you." Again, God specifically addresses the priests. Chapter 2 continues the address to the priests from chapter 1.

2:2 God says he will send his **curse** upon the priests. He will **curse** their blessings. He has already **cursed** their blessings.

2:3 God promised to spread dung from their feasts onto their faces. They shall be taken away along with the dung.

2:4-5 The priests' special covenant with Levi, with its blessings and curses, is discussed. The "**covenant** with Levi" is very important for understanding the context of Malachi. Chapter 2 mentions it in verses 4, 5 and 8. The "covenant with Levi" was a special covenant within the Old Mosaic Covenant. In Numbers 3:10-13; 18:1-32, and 25:12-13 God changed the system of priesthood. No longer was the firstborn child of every tribe a priest before God—the patriarchal priesthood had ended. Under the Old Covenant only the descendants of Aaron from Levi would serve as priests. (See also Num. 18:1, 2b, 4, 7). Levi's "covenant of peace" (2:5) is a quotation from Numbers 25:11-13. When the nation Israel rebelled and made a golden calf to worship, only Levi left the others to stand with Moses (Exod. 32:26).

2:6 During their best times the Levitical priests had taught the truth, walked with God, and turned many away from sin.

2:7 "For he [the priest] is the messenger of the LORD of hosts." Here, we need to be reminded that "Malachi" means "my messenger." This verse also has important relevance to 3:1.

2:8 Priests have "**corrupted the covenant of Levi**" and caused others to stumble.

2:9 The priests are contemptible; they have used the law impartially.

The Difficult Context of 2:10-12a

At this point most believe that God begins addressing the nation again, and not only the Levitical priests. If this is true, the switch only lasts until verse 12b, where God again addresses the priests. Key questions are: "Who is meant by 'we' and 'our'?", and "Which 'covenant' is referred to in verse 10?" If Malachi is a Levitical priest himself, then "we" and "us" in verse 10 refers only to the "priests," and the "covenant" is that made with Levi, which has already been mentioned three times in verses 4-8. However if Malachi is not a priest, then "we" refers to "all Israel" and "covenant" refers to the general Old Covenant. The context does not clarify which is correct.

2:10 God is most likely continuing his rebuke of the priests. They were treating fellow Israelites treacherously and were profaning the covenant of Levi which their fathers had honored.

2:11 When the priests in Judah profane God's holiness with inferior worship, their sin affects all the citizens of Judah.

2:12 God will cut off those who offer false worship. "Master and scholar" is "priest or layman" in *The Living Bible*, but neither translation appears in the better versions.

2:13 It is the priests who literally cover the altar with tears, weeping, and wailing.

Neh. 13:28 And one of the sons of Joiada, the son of Eliashib the high priest, was son in law to Sanballat the Horonite; therefore *I chased him from* me.

2:14-16 The priests are to be punished because they also had divorced their Israelite wives to marry pagan wives (Ezra 9 and 10).

2:17 The priests ask, **"Where is the God of judgment?"** It is the priests who ask this question because its answer is directed towards them.

God Answers the Priests' Question about Judgment
3:1-6 God answers the question, **"Where is the God of judgment?"** with a fiery tone to the priests, **"I will come near to you in judgment"** (3:5).

Using the *apotelesmatic principle* of multiple fulfillments, these texts have at least three possible fulfillments. The first fulfillment is obvious to those familiar with the New Testament. Jesus himself quoted these texts in reference to John the Baptist who paved the way for his ministry and his temple cleansing activity (Mal. 4:5; Matt. 3:3; 11:10-11; Mark 1:2-3; Luke 1:76; 3:4; 7:26-28; John 1:6-7, 23; Isa. 40:3-5).

A second fulfillment is the LORD himself because the pronoun in the texts refers to God coming in wrath and fire. It is the Messiah, not John the Baptist, who appeared as a refiner's fire to cleanse and correct the Levitical priesthood at his first coming. Also, the great Messianic hope of Israel anticipates the Messiah who will establish pure temple worship at coming in glory at the end of the age.

Neh. 13:29 Remember them, O my God, because they have defiled *the priesthood, and the covenant of the priesthood,* **and of the Levites. Neh. 13:30 Thus** *I cleaned* **them from all strangers, and appointed the wards of the priests and the Levites, every one in his business.**

However, no matter how true the two previously mentioned fulfillments may be, the historical (not prophetic) context points to either a literal priest named Malachi, or else the governor himself, with Nehemiah using "my messenger" as a pen name. If indeed Malachi is a real person, he is still the spokesman for God and Nehemiah. It was Nehemiah who had the literal zeal to literally cleanse the defiled priesthood and restore the priests to their covenant (Neh. 10-13). We should not forget the historical context of the book of Malachi.

Tithing and the Widow, the Fatherless, and the Stranger
3:5 And I will come near to you to judgment; and I will be a swift witness against the sorcerers, and against the adulterers, and against false swearers, and against those who oppress the hireling in his wages, the

widow, and the fatherless, and that turn aside the stranger from his right, and do not fear me, says the LORD of hosts.

Tithing in Malachi is integrally connected to its context. Therefore, for the purpose of understanding tithing in Malachi, the entire preceding discussion is to clarify the CONTEXT of chapter 3, verse 5. From 1:6 until 3:4 the context addresses primarily the priests and not the entire nation.

Is verse 5 a shift from the priests of 1-4 back to the general audience of the nation, or is it a continuation of the rebuke to the priests which is evident in verses 1-4 in answer to their question of 2:17? The answer affects the very important interpretation of the key verses on tithing—verses 8-10. The guilty of verse 5 are those who are sorcerers, adulterers, false swearers, and those who oppress the poor—the hired worker, the widow, the fatherless, and the stranger. In the context of Malachi, is this a description of the nation as a whole, or specifically the corrupt priesthood?

While 2:10-17 could apply generally to both the nation and the priests, if Malachi (or even Nehemiah) is a priest himself, then the address to the Levites continues. Since the only covenant mentioned thus far is the "covenant of Levi," then the latter half of verse 10 also refers to the Levites. Verse 11 is not clear because what the priests do in Judah affects all Judah. However, Malachi did rebuke the priests previously for profaning the sanctuary and marrying pagans. Verse 12 is not clear either; this could be a reference to all Israelites, or to those who specifically present offerings, that is, the priests. Some say that the questionable translation of "the master and the scholar" refers to the priests and their students. Verse 13 could refer to either class, but especially the priests whose tears literally touch the altar. Verses 14-16 could be understood as references to a call back to either the national covenant or to the covenant of Levi (2:4-5, 8). Verse 17 very strongly favors an address to the priesthood since their question is answered in the following six verses of the next chapter, especially verse 6.

Mal. 1:14 But cursed is the deceiver, who has in his flock a male, and vows, and sacrifices to the LORD a corrupt thing....

Deut. 27:19 Cursed is he who perverts the judgment of the stranger, fatherless, and widow. And all the people shall say, Amen.

If Malachi occurred before Nehemiah 10-13, then verse 5 refers to the sins of the whole nation. The *International Standard Bible Encyclopedia*, supports this view. "Opinions vary as to the prophet's exact date.... Yet, it is doubtful whether Malachi preached during Nehemiah's active governorship.... On the other hand, the abuses which Malachi attacked correspond so exactly with those which Nehemiah found on his second visit to Jerusalem in 432 B.C. (Neh. 13:7 ff.) that it seems reasonably certain that he prophesied shortly *before* that date, i.e. between 445 and 432 B.C."[52]

For the following reasons, this author believes that those who deserve judgment in chapter 3, verse 5, are probably the Levitical priests, and not the nation as a whole.

1. It can just as easily be argued that Malachi occurred immediately *after* Nehemiah 10-13 and is a description of the sins of the priests in hoarding the tithe, not giving God the best, and not providing food for the needy in verse 5. Dates for Malachi range from 455 to 397 B.C.

Fausset's Bible Dictionary says, "He [Malachi] supported or followed up the governor Nehemiah in the restoration of the national polity civil and religious, as Haggai and Zechariah previously had supported Joshua the high priest and Zerubbabel the civil governor in building the temple."[53]

2. The priests were guilty of "sorcery." As the responsible religious leaders, they had set the example. The Levites had said that "the table of the Lord is contemptible" (1:7, 12; 2:8). The priests were also guilty

---

52   *ISBE*, s.v. "Malachi."

53   *Fausset's*, s.v. "Malachi."

of "adultery" because they had exchanged Hebrew wives for pagan wives and were disciplined by Nehemiah (Ezra 10; Neh. 13:28-30). They were also guilty of "false swearing" (1:13-14).

3. A very important *omission* from the list in verse 5 is strong grounds for concluding that this text is addressed to the Levitical priests. In the law, the Levites are often first on God's list of persons deserving the tithe, because they receive no land inheritance and because they serve God in exchange of the abolished priesthood of the firstborn.

Again, the Levites are often at the top of the list. The tithing ordinances of Deuteronomy 14:27-29 and 26:12-13 both list "the Levites, strangers, fatherless, and widows" as eligible recipients of tithes. This same list is also true when the tithe was brought to the feasts (Deut. 16:11, 14). However, many texts mention the fatherless, widows and strangers and omit the Levites. (See Deut. 10:18; 24:;19-21; Ps. 94:6; 146:9; Jer. 7:6; 22:3, 7; Zech. 7:10). *If Malachi 3:5 refers to the entire nation sinning by oppressing the needy by not bringing tithes, then why are the Levites not included in the list of those who need the tithes?* Logic dictates that the Levites must be the OPPRESSOR rather than the OPPRESSED!

4. The Levitical priests have received the worst of God's rebuke throughout the book of Malachi! They have been found guilty of a wide range of sins, including theft (1:13). God does not say that the priests did not *have* suitable offerings from tithes in Malachi, but he does accuse them of keeping the good and bringing him the bad (1:14).

5. If Malachi immediately follows Nehemiah 10-13, then the evidence from Nehemiah tells us that the priests of Malachi's time actually had a *surplus* of tithes and offerings. First, the priests accompanied the Levites in collecting tithes (Neh. 10:38). Second, men were appointed to gather the tithes out of the fields (Neh. 12:44). Third, it is recorded that all Israel gave the tithes (Neh. 12:47). And, fourth, there was such an overflow that many storehouses were built to hold the tithes (Neh. 13:4-5, 12-13).

Therefore, it is very possible that the Levites were not included in Malachi 3:5 because, first, they had plenty of tithes, second, they were not giving God the best, third, they were hoarding the tithes for themselves, and, fourth, they were not using the tithes to feed the strangers, fatherless, and widows in verse 5—thus prompting verses 8-10.

6. Malachi could have been expressing God's anger and Nehemiah's anger toward dishonest priests for stealing from God. They had the tithe, but they were keeping back the best for themselves!

3:6 For I am the LORD, I change not; therefore you sons of Jacob are not consumed.

This text has often been interpreted to mean that God does not change and will always require the exact ten percent tithe from his people, whether those people are national Israel under the Old Covenant or the Christian church under the New Covenant. However, a few brief comments by several commentaries dispels this idea.

"It is because a righteous God never alters his attitude toward sin that judgment, however long delayed, will surely be carried out."[54]

"You are mistaken in inferring that, because I have not yet executed judgment on the wicked, I am changed from what I once was—namely, a 'God of judgment.'"[55]

"The new dispensation of grace and goodness, which is now about to be introduced, is not the effect of any change in my counsels; it is, on the contrary, the fulfillment of my everlasting purposes; as is also the throwing aside of the Mosaic ritual, which was only intended to introduce the great and glorious Gospel of my Son."[56]

---

54   *Wycliffe Comm.*, s.v. "Mal. 3:6."
55   *Jamieson*, s.v. "Mal. 3:6."
56   *Clarke's*, s.v. "Mal. 3:6."

In this context, "God does not change" means that he never changes about judging sin! God keeps his covenant promises of both blessings and curses. He also remembers his promises made to Abraham concerning Israel. What fallible man sees as "changes" in God's dealings with man, such as the law, types of sacrifices, and the New Covenant are, in reality, only pre-determined stages in the omniscient God's progressively unfolding plan for all mankind. Although God knows the end from the beginning, in Malachi's time, he treated national Israel in accordance with his decreed covenant promises, blessings, and curses. Just as a wise parent must change the restrictions and methods of training children as they mature, even so God adjusts the training of his people. Yet his character does not change.

Tithes: Curses and Blessings of the Old Covenant

3:7 Even from the days of your fathers you have gone away from my *ordinances*, and have not kept them. Return to me, and I will return to you, says the LORD of hosts. But you say, Wherein shall we return?

"Even from the days of your fathers...." The tithing abuse, robbery, curse, and blessings in verses 8-10 are in the context of, and refer to, "you sons of Jacob" (v. 6), "your fathers" (v. 7), and "the whole nation of you" (v. 9). While each of these phrases could refer to the nation as a whole, or especially the Levitical priests, the context is still that of national Israel, and not the church. The book of Malachi is specifically addressed to "Israel" (1:1), "Judah in Israel" (2:11), "priests" of Israel (1:6; 2:1), and "all Israel" (4:4). From Exodus to Calvary, tithing was commanded to God's special nation, Israel, and ONLY to Israel (Lev. 27:34; Num. 18:23-24; Deut. 12:5-6, 11; Heb. 7:5).

*"You have gone away from my **ordinances**, and have not kept them."* Malachi 3:14 says "It is vain to serve God: and what profit is it that we have kept his **ordinance**." Malachi 4:4 adds, "Remember the law of Moses

my servant, which I commanded to him in Horeb for all Israel, with the *statutes* and judgments."

Verses 8-10 are in the context of God's "ordinances," or "statutes," of the Mosaic Law from verse 7! The Hebrew word translated in verse 7 as "ordinances" is also translated as "statutes." Other versions translate it as "decree, due, custom, portion, and law." As previously discussed, Numbers 18 is the foundational ordinance chapter on tithing and uses "statute" and "ordinance" five times (vv. 8, 11, 19, 23). The entire Mosaic Law, or Old Covenant, consisted of commandments, "ordinances/statutes" and judgments. "Ordinances" included all instructions and duties concerning worship, including firstborn, firstfruits, food laws, health laws, holy days, offerings, sacrifices—and TITHES.

Numbers 18, not Malachi 3:8-10, is the defining tithing segment of Scripture! In its exegetical context, only the nation Israel had committed the sin of tithing abuse. Since Malachi 3 specifically refers to tithing, it is essential for any diligent Bible student to read the complete and exact wording of that "ordinance" or "statute" in Numbers 18—the "ordinance" establishing the priesthood and their assistants, the Levites. Also compare Leviticus 27:30-34; Deuteronomy 12:5-19; 14:22-29 and 26:12-13. The church has no such ordinance.

The New Testament contains numerous texts which indicate to many Christians that the Mosaic Law, especially the ordinances, have been abolished—including tithing as an ordinance. Ephesians 2:13-15 and Colossians 2:13-14 both teach that "ordinances" of the Mosaic Law have been "abolished," "blotted out." "canceled," and "nailed to the cross." There is no reason to exclude tithing from all of the other "ordinances." While Hebrews 7 is the only mention of tithing after Calvary, it clearly teaches that the "commandment" of the "law," that is, the ordinance which included tithing, was "set aside" or "disannulled" by the high priesthood of Jesus Christ (Heb. 7:5, 12, 18). This book includes separate chapters which discuss ordinances in Numbers 18, Ephesians 2, Colossians 2, and Hebrews 7. Each of these relate to the same "ordinance" in Malachi 3:7 and must be included in a correct understanding of verses 8-10.

3:8 Will a man rob God? Yet you have robbed me. But you say, Wherein have we robbed you? In tithes and offerings.

What are tithes? Tithes are only food from Israel! According to Leviticus 27:30-34, "tithes" are 10% of the *produce* of the land of Israel or of the *herds and flocks* from the land of Israel—nothing else! (See chapter one.)

Who received the tithes? According to Numbers 18:21-24, only the tribe of Levi in Israel received this 10% of the land and herds from Israel.

Why did Levites receive the tithes? Because they were assistants to the "anointed" priests and because they were not allowed to own any property in Israel or share in any property inheritance. God was their only inheritance. (Num. 18:2a, 3, 4, 8, 21-24; Deut. 12:12; 14:27-29).

What occupations did Levites have? At first Levites only performed the routine and lowly servant tasks for priests and social welfare tasks (Numbers 3, 4, 8, 18). In the temple service, Levites served in 24 divisions, each serving at the temple only a week at a time, or about two weeks per year (2 Kings 11:9; 1 Chron. 23:8; 25:6;; 27:1; Luke 1:5-8).

Beginning with King David, Levites also became political officials. Levites were the core of the king's officials, performing many governmental tasks.

Were the ministering priests supported by first tithes? No! Not from the first 10%, or first tithe. According to Numbers 18:25-29 and Nehemiah 10:38, the ministering priests only received one percent (1%) which is 10% of 10%, or a tenth of the tithe from the Levites. It must be remembered that only a small portion of Levites were priests descended from Aaron.

Many Levites who were not in government were poor. The poor Levites, widows, fatherless, and strangers (all groups who had no inheritance) were fed from tithes (Deut. 14:27-29). This is an important connection between Malachi 3:5 and the rest of the chapter.

Tithing, like other statutes was only to last while Israel occupied the land of Canaan under the Old Covenant terms (Deut. 12:1, 19).

Again, there are two possible scenarios for Malachi 3:8. The most common is that Malachi refers to the period before Nehemiah 10-13, or long afterwards, in which landowners had stopped tithing and God was rebuking the entire nation of Israel. A second possible scenario is that Malachi occurs immediately after Nehemiah 10-13 and the Levitical priests are guilty (as usual) of hoarding the tithe and neglecting the poor. Thus God was rebuking the whole nation "of you," that is, "of you priests." The priests are never the innocent party in Malachi!

What were the offerings? Remarkably, Malachi 3:8 is the only use of the Hebrew word for "heave offering" in Malachi. Every other use of "offering" is "grain offering" (1:11, 13; 2:12-13; 3:3-4). The Hebrew word used here for "heave offering" is "teruwmah" (Strong's 8641), which is also associated with "wave-offerings" and "peace offerings." Tithes, freewill-offerings, thank-offerings, and vow-offerings were all heave offerings. The NIV translates them as "contributions."

Heave offerings were waved, or presented, before the Lord. Next God, as host, symbolically presented them back to his people. Heave offerings included almost anything such as gold, silver, and man-made products from craftsmen (Exod. 25:2; 35:5, 22, 24, 25, 29). Although tithes were also heaved before God, other heave-offerings were unsolicited and no amount was specified. They were given as a free choice from a willing heart.

The original portable sanctuary in the desert, Solomon's temple, and Nehemiah's temple were all built through freewill heave offerings, given willingly from a sincere heart (Exod. 25:2-7; 31:1-14; 35:1-29; 1 Chron. 29 all). No tithes were used to pay for the buildings or furnishings.

Whereas "tithes" were received from farming and herding occupations, "heave offerings" were received from all occupations. Some heave offerings were designated for the priests and their children only (Lev. 7:13-14; Num. 5:9; 18:8-19; Lev. 22:10). However, the offerer and his household, other Levites, and the poor and needy also were allowed to eat some heave offerings (Deut. 12:11-21; 16:10-11).

Tithes and offerings. The phrase "tithes and offerings" should not be interpreted to mean that everything beyond the tithe was considered an offering. The formula is not "tithes PLUS *grain* offerings," but instead "tithes AND *heave* offerings." Tithes were only food. Therefore only landowners who were farmers or animal herders paid tithes. On the other hand, hired workers, widows, and the fatherless, who had no increase from land, only paid heave offerings (Deut. 14:27-29; 26:12-13). Although the poorest did not pay tithes (but received of them), most had no "increase" to tithe. They gave "all" they could as the "widow's mite;" they gave freely, from their heart.

Therefore, the phrase *"tithes and offerings," in context, means "tithes from landowners" AND freewill "heave-offerings" from others with other sources of income.* Of course, landowners could also bring freewill-offerings. The wealthy were expected to give more because God had blessed them more (2 Cor. 8:12-15).

Why did Malachi only use the term "heave offering" once in 3:8 (using "grain offering" 6 times)? On the one hand, grain/meal/cereal offerings were offered as a "meal" to God on his table (1:7). They represent man's best to God first. Grain offerings must accompany burnt offerings and peace offerings to atone for sin. God refused the grain offerings because of the priests' dishonesty and pretense (chapters 1 and 2). When the "messenger of the covenant" comes, he will "purify the sons of Levi" and they will then offer "grain offerings" "in righteousness" that are "pleasant to the Lord" (3:1-6).

On the other hand, heave/wave/peace offerings were offered back from God to man. They celebrated the forgiveness of sin and its resulting fellowship. Although primarily for the Levites, they were shared with the poor and needy. They were freewill and unsolicited. Any and all could contribute almost anything they wished to God. By robbing God of "heave offerings," Israel was robbing its own poor and needy. The significance of "heave" offerings in 3:8 instead of "grain" offerings is that Israel and its priests had robbed the poor of the heave offerings.

3:9 "You are cursed with a curse, for you have robbed me, even this whole nation."

This is the fifth mention of the word "curse" in Malachi. "But *cursed* be the deceiver, which has in his flock a male, and vows, and sacrifices to the LORD a corrupt thing" (1:14). "And now, O you *priests*, this commandment is for you. If you will not hear, and if you will not lay it to heart, to give glory to my name, says the LORD of hosts, I will even send a *curse* upon you, and I will *curse* your blessings: yea, I have *cursed* them already, because you do not lay it to heart" (2:1-2). Again, this author believes that Malachi 3:8-10 is a rebuke and curse primarily against the Levitical priests who had received an abundance of tithes, had hoarded them, and had not cared for the poor and needy in Israel. They are the object of God's special scorn and have already been cursed three times.

The Hebrew of verse 9 actually says, "this whole nation *of you*." The "of you" does not appear in the King James Version, but it does appear in the NAS, NIV, and RSV. The purpose of the possessive pronoun is unclear unless it distinguishes the whole nation "of you priests" from the rest of the nation. However, the author's position is not crucial for understanding verses 8 and 9. The crucial context is, first, God's address to the "sons of Jacob" verse 6, second, the nature of the "ordinances" of verse 7, and, third, the nature of the "curse" of verse 9.

The priests had already robbed God and had already received the longest and most harsh rebuke in Malachi (1:6 to 2:9). They had dishonored God, disrespected him, and despised his name (1:6). They did not offer the best of tithes and offerings received from Israel (1:7-8). Their worship was not acceptable. God desired that one of them would just stop the pretended worship and lock the temple doors (1:10). He was tired of their dishonesty (1:13-14) and cursed them as deceivers or swindlers (1:14). Specifically, the worst curse in Malachi was for the priests, the religious leaders (2:1). God would curse their blessings (2:2). Even their children would be affected by their sin and rebuked (2:3). He would spread dung in their faces during their worship services (2:3).

Deut. 27:26 *Cursed* is he who does not confirm all the words of this law to do them. And all the people shall say, Amen.

Neh. 10:29 They joined with their brothers, their nobles, and entered into a *curse*, and into an oath, to walk in God's law, which was given by Moses the servant of God, and to observe and do all the commandments of the LORD our Lord, and his judgments and his statutes.

Those guilty of robbing God were "under a curse." This can only be correctly understood as the curse of the Mosaic Covenant as found in Deuteronomy 27 and 28. In Nehemiah, chapters 8-10, Malachi's audience had again agreed to place themselves under the curse of the Mosaic Covenant for disobedience. A curse fell on any who disobeyed ANY part of the Mosaic Law. In order to "attain" righteousness, 100% obedience was expected. And, since this was impossible, a New Covenant and a new high priesthood was needed (Heb. 7:11-28).

Gal. 3:13 Christ has redeemed us from the curse of the law, being made a curse for us; for it is written, Cursed is every one that hangs on a tree.

It is sin for Christian preachers to take the curse of Malachi 3:9 out of its historical and exegetical Old Covenant context and use it to threaten church members for not paying tithes! Only the "nation" Israel was cursed because it was the only nation commanded to tithe. And only Israel had entered into the Old Covenant Mosaic Law agreement and had asked God to curse them for disobedience!

Galatians 3 discusses the "curse of the law." After quoting Deuteronomy 27:26 in verse 10, verse 12 says that the law is not based on faith. Likewise, tithing is not based on faith. As God's elect, New Covenant Christians are not under a curse for ANY reason. Scripture is clear on this (see also Rom. 8:1, 33; Heb. 10:14; Eph. 1:7). However, if there might possibly be a New Covenant application, God might indeed decide to curse churches and pastors who collect tithes under one pretense and totally ignore the poor in the congregation!

3:10 Bring all the tithes into the storehouse, that there may be food in my house, and prove me now herewith, says the LORD of hosts, if I will not open to you the windows of heaven, and pour you out a blessing, that there shall not be room enough to receive it.

"Storehouse." Israel was commanded to bring the tithes into *the* storehouse. The word "storehouse" means "armory, cellar, depository, store, treasury." Although regional storehouses may have been built in each tribe's Levitical cities, according to Deuteronomy 12:5-6 and 14:22-26, the only officially recognized "storehouse" was the area in Jerusalem at the temple.

Temple storehouses held the tithes, firstfruits, firstborn animals, and offerings that were brought to God by Israel. Heave offerings were gold, silver, or anything else. Surrounding the temple were many storehouses for wine, olive oil, grain, and stockyards of sacrificial animals. Granaries were also in nearby fields.

This giant storehouse complex became a national reserve of food and animals for times of famine and for taking care of the Levites, the fatherless, widows, and strangers (1 Chron. 27:25-28; 28:12). The storehouse also provided for sacrificial offerings to those who lived too far from

Jerusalem or those who were not herdsmen. On special occasions tithes could be converted into money at a distant location, and then reconverted back into "whatever you like: cattle, sheep, wine, or other fermented drink or anything you wish" (Deut. 14:24-26). Then the offerer would consume part of his second tithe during the festive occasions.

Originally storehouses were the sole responsibility of the Levites. However, in Malachi's historical and exegetical context, it was the responsibility of the political authority, the governor, to ensure the Levites maintained storehouses for worthy sacrificial animals and for provisions for themselves, the priests and the needy. (See 1 Kings 7:51; 1 Chron. 27:25-28; 28:12; Neh. 10:34-39; 13:12-13). Kings controlled the temple wealth. Scripture records seven times that kings gave away wealth from God's temple storehouse and from their own royal storehouse (1 Kings 14:25-26; 15:18; 2 Kings 12:18; 14:14; 16:8; 18:14-15; 20:13-19; 24:13). The royal storehouses of King David are detailed in 1 Chronicles, chapter 27.

Since a later chapter discusses the use of the word, "storehouse," under the New Covenant framework, only a few comments are necessary at this point. First Corinthians 16:1-2 does not refer to tithing. "Concerning the collection for the saints" only refers to the poor starving saints experiencing a famine in Judea. Believers in Corinth are instructed to "lay...in store" "as God has prospered." This is a clear reference to freewill offerings from the heart, not to tithing. Neither is this a reference for supporting and building churches. The food was for the poor, and only for the poor. Also, food, not money, was being collected for the famine.

For the following reasons, proper exegesis of the context of Malachi does not convert its "storehouse" into the "storehouse of the church":

1. While Old Testament storehouses were considered the property of the theocratic state, most New Covenant churches are not.

2. While Old Testament storehouses received political aid to collect its tithes, most New Covenant churches do not.

3. While Old Testament storehouses held mostly food and herd animals, New Covenant churches collect money which was never included in the definition of tithe.

4. While Old Testament storehouses provided food for the stranger, fatherless, and orphan in the land, New Covenant church members pay taxes and allow the government to do most welfare work.

5. While Old Testament storehouses provided sustenance for a national priesthood, New Covenant churches teach a priesthood of all believers.

6. While Old Covenant tithing was a separate fund from free-will offerings for buildings and maintenance, New Covenant churches should combine all needs into a total program and eliminate the Old Covenant tithing principle.

7. Theistic Jews do not handle money or collect offerings on their Sabbath. It is doubtful that early Jewish Christians would have thus defiled a holy day by handling money at a church "storehouse."

"That there may be food in my house." According to God's Word, in Israel tithes were food, and only food! "Bring tithes…that there may be food" means exactly what it says! This is very difficult for modern tithe-advocates to accept! Yet it is the only accurate biblical definition of "tithe."

The storehouses were considered part of God's house, the temple. Although silver, gold, money and other valuable items existed, NONE are ever mentioned as *direct* tithes under the Mosaic Law. Therefore, only those who owned land for farming and herd-raising paid tithes. Workers in other occupations only paid freewill heave-offerings.

Although "heave offerings" could include items other than food, the context of Malachi 3 teaches that God specifically wanted "food" to be brought—food for his "table" in the form of pure healthy sacrificial animals, food for the priests, food for the other Levites who ministered, and food for the poor (the sin of 3:5).

"And prove me now," "test me" (NAS, NIV, RSV). The tithe-advocate boldly says, "This is the only place in God's Word where he commands us to test him" as if this test to Israel under the terms of the Old Covenant somehow proves that tithing is a New Covenant doctrine. What does "testing God" mean in the context of Malachi 3:5 and the rest of the Old Testament?

> **Prov. 14:31** He who oppresses the poor reproaches his Maker: but he who honors him has mercy on the poor.

> **Jer. 22:16** He [King Josiah] judged the cause of the poor and needy; then it was well with him; was not this to know me? says the LORD.

> **Ezek. 16:49** Behold, this was the iniquity of your sister Sodom, pride, fulness of bread, and abundance of idleness was in her and in her daughters, neither did she strengthen the hand of the poor and needy.

> **Zech 7:9** Thus says the LORD of hosts, saying, Execute true judgment, and show mercy and compassion every man to his brother;
> **Zech. 7:10** And do not oppress the widow, nor the fatherless, the stranger, nor the poor; and let none of you imagine evil against his brother in your heart.

> **Mal. 3:5** And I will come near to you to judgment; and I will be a swift witness against the sorcerers, and against the adulterers, and against false swearers, and against those who oppress the hireling in his wages, the widow, and the fatherless, and that turn aside the stranger from his right, and do not fear me, says the LORD of hosts.

God tested the righteous attitude of his children in the Old Testament by the way in which they treated the poor! If the New Covenant church responds positively by testing God, is the in-gathered bounty then used in the same manner God decreed for its use in the Old Covenant, or does it keep most of the money for its own salaries? Does the church tell the congregation to "test God" by tithing and then "reproach God" by not having mercy on the poor (Prov. 14:31)? Is the church's profession of "really knowing God" shown by "judging the cause of the poor" (Jer. 22:16)? Are the churches, like Sodom, full of abundance but not helping the poor (Ezek. 16:49)? After testing God and receiving abundance of bounty, Israel was expected to take care of its poor from Malachi 3:5. How do you respond (Zech. 7:9-10)?

"I will open the windows of heaven."

Deut. 28:12 The LORD shall open to you his good treasure, the heaven to give the rain to your land in his season, and to bless all the work of your hand; and you shall lend to many nations, and you shall not borrow.

Deuteronomy, chapter 28, contains the Old Covenant blessings and curses alluded to in Malachi 3. These same blessings and curses had just been agreed to by Malachi's audience in Nehemiah. "Windows of heaven" refers to rain (Gen. 7:9; 2 Kings 7:2, 19). In a land often stricken by famine and drought, the greatest blessings to those who tithed from the land was from the "windows of heaven" in the form of rain. Israel was primarily a nation whose wealth and success depended upon its herds and farm produce. God promised that there would not be enough room in their storehouses to contain the food from a bountiful harvest.

Verse 11 discusses food with words like the "devourer" (the grasshopper), "fruits of your ground," "vine" and "your field." If tithes were other than food, then God would have promised blessings to the other "tithe-payers" such as merchants, traders, craftsmen, etc. In this economy, when farmers and herdsmen prospered, all prospered.

In verse 12, Israel, with its curses and blessings, and its priests and tithes, was to be unique compared to all other nations. God was to be blessed and Israel was to be admired as onlookers from other nations came to learn from her.

4:4 "Remember the law of Moses my servant, which I commanded to him in Horeb for all Israel, with the statutes and judgments."

The book of Malachi closes with one last reference to the Law of Moses, which is the Old Covenant. Once again its statutes/ordinances and judgments are "for all Israel" alone.

Summary

For the following reasons, tithing in Malachi, when studied exegetically, in its historical context, cannot be interpreted as a commandment for the New Covenant Christian.

1. The entire context is that of the Mosaic Law, the Old Covenant.
2. Most of the context is that of disobedient Levitical priests abusing the ordinances of the entire law and also the specific ordinances of the Levitical priesthood.
3. Tithing was a legislated ordinance of the Mosaic Law (Numbers 18).
4. Tithing was controlled, enforced, collected, and distributed under the disciplinary authority of the political ruler.
5. Tithes, as defined by the law, were only food items and were only collected from land owners, but not the poor.
6. Storehouses were under government control and could be confiscated and emptied by the government for its use.
7. The Old Covenant Mosaic Law, with all of its ordinances, ended at Calvary.
8. Christians are not under the jurisdiction or condemnation of the Mosaic Law.
9. The limited Levitical priesthood was supported by tithes because it replaced the universal priesthood of believers and was denied land inheritance rights.

10. Most Levites who received tithes only worked in the temple 1-2 weeks per year. The rest of the year many were government officials such as judges, treasurers, and social workers in the Levitical cities.

CHAPTER 15

▼

MATTHEW 23:23
LUKE 11:41-42
JESUS SUPPORTED TITHING
UNDER THE MOSAIC LAW

Matt. 23:23 Woe to you, scribes [teachers of the law: NIV] and Pharisees, hypocrites! For you pay *tithe* of mint and anise and cummin, and have omitted the weightier matters of the law—judgment, mercy, and faith; these you ought to have done, without leaving the other undone.

Luke 11:41 But rather give alms [charity: NAS; to the poor: NIV] of such things as you have, and, behold, all things are clean to you.
Luke 11:42 But woe to you, Pharisees! For you *tithe* mint and rue and all manner of herbs, and pass over judgment and the love of God; these you ought to have done, without leaving the other undone.

Matthew 23:23 and Luke 11:42 are the only New Testament texts available for those who advocate tithing. In support of tithing, Eklund says, "The New Testament does not record Jesus' practice of the tithe. However we do read about the many accusations made against Jesus by the Pharisees.... If Jesus had been guilty of neglecting the tithe, obviously the charges would have been made publicly.... Jesus could have declared the tithe invalid. In fact it would have strengthened his condemnation of the Pharisees. Yet he made it very clear that the tithe was still expected...."[57] Another pro-tithing author writes, "What do you say to people when they say that tithing is only in the Old Testament? Well, they haven't read the Bible! They need to read [quotes Matt. 23:23]."[58]

However, while it is true that Jesus taught tithing, this does not mean that he taught tithing as a New Covenant doctrine! In fact, his teaching of tithing in Matthew 23 and Luke 11 only prove that Jesus approved of tithing *while the law system was in place* and had jurisdiction over those under its tutorship (Gal. 4:4).

In rebuttal to New Covenant tithing, a seminary textbook on hermeneutics deliberately chose Matthew 23:23 to illustrate the opposite point. "The Scriptures themselves offer us a way of sorting out which commands have continuing relevance for our lives and which ones have been rendered obsolete by God's having declared their usefulness to have ended. Even though the law is one, we are taught in the Bible to distinguish at least three different aspects in that one law. Jesus authorized such a stance when he used the concept in Matthew 23:23 that some things in the law were 'weightier' than others. It is this ranking and prioritizing within the law that establishes the *moral* aspect of the law as *higher than* its civil and *ceremonial* aspects. In this verse, justice, mercy and faithfulness

---

57   Eklund, 76.
58   Clifford A. Jones, Sr., *From Proclamation to Practice, A Unique African-American Approach to Stewardship* (Valley Forge: Judson Press, 1993), 118.

are heavier and weightier than the rules for tithing spices, evidently because the *former* reflects the nature and character of God."[59]

Jesus and the Law

Gal. 4:4 But when the fulness of the time was come, God sent forth his Son, made of a woman, made under the law,
Gal. 4:5 To redeem them that were under the law, that we might receive the adoption of sons.

Jesus lived and died a Jew under the jurisdiction of the Mosaic Law. Even though uninspired persons designated the four Gospels as "New Testament" books, most thinking Christians realize that, in reality, the New Covenant did not begin until the very moment Christ died on Calvary. The blood of Christ, the blood of the New Covenant, or testament, sealed and ratified the New Covenant and ended the Old Covenant, or Mosaic Law once for all time. When Jesus cried "It is finished," the veil in the Jerusalem Temple was ripped from top to bottom exposing the formerly Most Holy Place to the view of all who peered. At that very moment, in the mind of God, the entire sacrificial system with its laws, its priesthood, and its ordinances ceased to have relevance (Heb. 9:24-26). Thus Matthew 23 and Luke 11 are events in the *context* of the Old Covenant, not the New. They cannot properly be called New Covenant examples.

Luke 11:41 But rather give alms of such things as you have; and, behold, all things are clean to you.

In the Gospel of Luke, Jesus was eating at a Pharisee's house. The Pharisee was surprised that he had not ritually washed his hands before

---

59   Kaiser, 279.

eating (Luke 11:38). The Pharisee's *interpretation and extension* of the Mosaic Law, rather than its literal meaning, was the issue! Rather than stress the law, Jesus stressed obedience to the conscience. Although tithing fulfilled the *letter* of the law, giving *alms* to the poor met the needs of the *conscience*. Giving to the poor came from within and cleansed the heart. It is important to note that, here also, Jesus made no tithing statements that extended beyond Calvary when the Mosaic Law ended.

Matt. 22:17 Is it lawful to give tribute to Caesar, or not?

Matt. 22:36 Master, which is the great commandment in the law?

The mention of tithing in Matthew 23 and Luke 11 is in the context of discussions about the Old Covenant Law. Jesus expressed his displeasure at the manner in which the scribes and Pharisees had made the Mosaic Law a burden. The Herodians had asked, "Is it lawful to give tribute to Caesar, or not?" (Matt. 22:17). In the next discussion Jesus rebuked the Sadducees by quoting from the law (Matt. 22:32 cf. Exod. 3:6.). Next, one of the Pharisees asked, "Master, which is the great commandment in the law?" (Matt. 22:36).

23:2 *The scribes and the Pharisees sit in Moses' seat;*
23:3 All therefore whatsoever they bid you observe, that observe and do; but do not do according to their works; for they say, and do not.
23:4 For they bind heavy burdens and grievous to be borne, and lay them on men's shoulders; but they themselves will not move them with one of their fingers.

Matthew 23:2-4 are crucial for understanding 23:23 because they provide its context. Jesus was the perfect law-keeper. He perfectly obeyed all of the commandments, the judgments, and the ordinances which applied to him. He obeyed all of the social and ceremonial parts of the law as taught by Moses in the Old Covenant, and he commanded the crowds and his disciples to obey the scribes and Pharisees.

> **Matt. 5:23-24 Therefore if you bring your gift to the altar, and there remember that your brother has anything against you, leave there your gift before the altar, and go your way; first be reconciled to your brother, and then come and offer your gift.**

> **Matt. 8:4 …go your way, show yourself to the priest, and offer the gift that Moses commanded, for a testimony to them.**

Again, by taking on humanity as a Jew under the jurisdiction of the law, Jesus encouraged other Jews to strictly obey the Mosaic Covenant. (He never told non-Jews to do this!) This is demonstrated in Matthew 5:23-24 and 8:4. The texts also demonstrate the Old Covenant context of what most of us call the "New Testament" gospels.

During his earthly ministry Jesus lived in strict conformity to the Mosaic Law. He was born under that law, lived under that law, and died under that law. Thus he fulfilled every minute detail perfectly. Jesus had to be sinless in order to redeem those under the curse of the law. Compare John 8:46, Romans 3:20, and Hebrews 4:15.

Tithing in Matthew 23:23

> **23:3 All therefore whatsoever they bid you observe, that observe and do; but do not do according to their works, for they say, and do not.**

Tithing in Matthew 23:23 is also in the context of the woes that began in Matthew 23:13. It is in the fifth of eight woes. Jesus placed woes on the scribes and Pharisees because they had hypocritically abused their authority and hypocritically interpreted the Mosaic Law to make it into a burden. Tithing was mentioned, not to illustrate an eternal principle for

Christians, but to illustrate their hypocrisy about the law. Concerning the scribes and Pharisees, Jesus had just said "they bind heavy burdens and grievous to be borne, and lay them on men's shoulders; but they themselves will not move them with one of their fingers" (23:4). As the recognized interpreters of the law, the scribes and Pharisees had gone to every extreme to make law-keeping a burden instead of a delight. The Pharisees were so fanatical about tithing that they even refused to eat food unless the tithe had been paid from it.

Requiring a tithe from the very smallest of garden herbs and spices was an example of making the law an extreme burden. Although Leviticus 27:30 did indeed say "of the seed of the land, or of the fruit of the tree," other tithe descriptions specifically listed grain, wine, oil and honey (Deut. 12:17; 14:23; 2 Chron. 31:5). The spirit of the tithing law referred to crops and honey which were produced for profit and sale at the local market. Many centuries would pass before the "increase of the fields" would be mis-interpreted by the Pharisees to include small garden spices for personal use. Although counting and/or weighing small amounts of garden spices went far beyond the original spirit and scope of the law, Jesus still said "these you ought to have done" out of respect for those recognized by the people as the current interpreters of the law.

It is important to restate the above conclusion. Why did Jesus say, "You ought to have done these things," that is, tithed the garden spices? Was it because the law required this extreme burden? No! It was because "the scribes and the Pharisees sit in Moses' seat and whatsoever they bid you observe, that observe and do" (23:2-3). Therefore, what Jesus said about tithing in Matthew 23:23 has absolutely nothing to do with Christian giving principles! As a good Jew living under the law, Jesus was simply buttressing the traditionally recognized authority of the scribes and Pharisees as interpreters of the law.

The Pharisees were hypocrites concerning tithing! Alfred Edersheim explains how the Pharisee actually paid *less* tithe than did others. When John Hyrcanus (135-100 B.C.) enacted a new law which required the *buyer* to pay tithes rather than the *seller*, the Pharisees vowed to only trade within their own fraternities (chabura). Thus, while others paid certain tithes every time produce exchanged hands, the Pharisees declared all except the first time to be "free" from subsequent tithing (p. 215). In addition to this, the rabbis had excluded themselves from Jewish civic taxation. Thus, while the typical citizen paid at least an extra ten percent (10%) in local Jewish taxation, the Pharisees had that much extra to pay in tithes—and boasted about tithing (p. 52). Therefore, in reality, the Pharisee paid *less* tithes in two different ways than others who did not boast.[60]

Lev. 27:30 And all the *tithe* of the land, whether of the seed of the land, or of the fruit of the tree, is the LORD's, It is holy to the LORD.
Lev. 27:32 And concerning the *tithe* of the herd, or of the flock, even of whatsoever passes under the rod, the tenth shall be holy to the LORD.

Instead of supporting the radically different definition of tithing as used in the modern church, Matthew 23:23 is a strong text which proves that tithing was still only from food of the land or herds. While approximately 1,600 years had passed since God first defined tithes in Numbers 18 and Leviticus 27, the Jews of the first century still had not expanded the definition to include money, jewelry, products from craftsmen, etc. Those items were still only included in freewill heave offerings! Contrary to our contemporary re-definition, tithes could come from grains of wheat, but not from grains of gold!

The *New Unger's Bible Dictionary* says, "The Mishnah includes everything eatable, everything that was stored up or that grew out of the earth.

---

60   Edersheim, *Sketches*, 52, 215.

The Pharisees [not God], as early as the time of Jesus, made the law to include the minutest kitchen herbs, such as mint and cummin."[61]

The New Bible Dictionary agrees, "To these comparatively simple laws in the Pentateuch governing tithing there were added [by the Pharisees] a host of minutiae which turned a beautiful religious principle into a grievous burden. These complex additions are recorded in the Mishnic and Talmudic literatures. This unfortunate tendency in Israel undoubtedly contributed to the conviction that acceptance with God could be merited through such ritual observances as tithing (Luke xi, 42) without submitting to the moral law of justice, mercy, and faith (Matt. xxiii, 23)." It concludes, like Unger, by stating, "The New Testament reference to the tithing of mint, anise, and cummin (Matt. xxiii, 23; Luke xi, 42) illustrates a Talmudic extension of the Mosaic law, ensuring that '*everything that is eaten.... and that grows out of the earth*' must be tithed."[62]

Again, when Jesus said in verse 23, "You should have practiced the latter, without neglecting the former," he was re-enforcing, not the moral law which is eternal, but the current interpretation of the ordinances of the ceremonial law of the Old Covenant.

Jesus Did Not Tithe

When Eklund says (as quoted above), "If Jesus had been guilty of neglecting the tithe, obviously the charges would have been made publicly," he reveals his misunderstanding of the definition of tithing as thoroughly explained in chapter one. The Pharisees did not accuse Jesus of not paying tithes because *he did* pay them; instead, they did not accuse him because *he did not qualify* to pay them. True biblical tithing is narrowly limited to food and clean animals from land inheritance. Also, true biblical tithing was never extended to crafts and trades. Since Jesus was neither

---

61   *Unger's*, s.v. "tithe."

62   *New Bible Dict.* (London: Inter-Varsity, 1962), s.v. "tithe."

a farmer, nor a herdsman, he was not among those who were required to tithe. Jesus was only to give freewill heave offerings.

Also, as discussed in a previous chapter about the poor, Jesus and his disciples were not required to tithe because they were poor. Again, the gleaning incident recorded three times (Matt. 12:1-12, Mark 2:23-24, and Luke 6:1-2) is important. If a tithe were required from all persons and from all kinds of food harvested, then we could have expected the Pharisees to accuse Jesus and his disciples of not paying tithe on the grain they had just harvested and eaten. The lack of such an accusation proves that no such law applied to poor persons who harvested gleanings. Compare Leviticus 19:10.

A Summary of Matthew 23

23:1 Jesus was instructing the crowds and his disciples about the Mosaic Law. As the sinless law-keeper he encouraged obedience to every ordinance of that law before Calvary. He was not setting down principles for the New Covenant church.

23:2 The scribes and Pharisees were the recognized authorities concerning the interpretation of the Mosaic Law in the first century. Jesus did not challenge their authority, but criticized their hypocrisy.

23:3 This is the KEY VERSE for correctly understanding verse 23 regarding tithing. The crowds and disciples were still under the jurisdiction of the Mosaic Law.

23:4 Their hypocritical extremes about the law became a heavy burden on the Jews. They personally did not keep the rules they set for others.

23:5 It was all for show! Their pouches for carrying verses of the law had been made extra wide. All of their legalism was just for others to see.

23:13 1st woe: You will not be saved and you keep others from being saved.

23:14 2nd woe: You abuse widows while making long prayers.

23:15 3rd woe: Your hard-earned converts will go to hell.

23:16 4th woe Your worship priorities are reversed. You are spiritually blind.

. . . .

23:23 **5th woe: Concerns tithing.** Their giving of mint, dill, and cummin was an "extension" of the principle of the Mosaic Law of tithing. It was part of the burden, the heavy load, they had put on the people as its interpreters. Tithing was emphasized to the neglect of justice, mercy and faithfulness. Verse 23 is a discussion of hypocritical extensions of "matters of the law," not post-Calvary principles of giving!

. . . .

23:25 6th woe Being ceremonially, ritually, clean is hypocrisy if one is inwardly spiritually greedy and selfish.

23:27 7th woe: It is hypocrisy to appear outwardly righteous while inwardly being wicked.

23:29 8th woe You are both the physical and spiritual relatives of those who killed the prophets.

23:33 You will be responsible for the result of your hypocrisy.

23:37-38 Jerusalem will fall because of its misuse of the Mosaic Law!

CHAPTER 16

▼

LUKE 18:12
A PHARISEE'S BOAST
ABOUT TITHING

The Self-Righteous Pharisee

Luke 18:9 And he spoke this parable to certain which trusted in themselves that they were righteous, and despised others.

Luke 18:10 Two men went up into the temple to pray—the one a Pharisee, and the other a publican [tax collector].

Luke 18:11 The Pharisee stood and prayed thus with himself, God, I thank you, that I am not as other men are, extortioners, unjust, adulterers, or even as this publican.

Luke 18:12 I fast twice in the week, I give *tithes* of all that I possess.

Luke 18:13 And the publican, standing afar off, would not lift up so much as his eyes to heaven, but smote upon his breast, saying, God be merciful to me a sinner.

Luke 18:17 I tell you, this man went down to his house justified rather than the other; for every one that exalts himself shall be abased; and he that humbles himself shall be exalted.

In the four Gospels, when one combines Matthew 23:23 and Luke 11:42, the word "tithe/tenth" appears only twice—both times as part of condemnation addressed to the Pharisees for their hypocrisy. The Pharisee in Luke 18 thought that he was more righteous and therefore despised others (v. 9). When he said, "I am not as other men are, extortioners, unjust, adulterers, or even as this publican," he was bragging about his self-righteousness through fasting and tithing (v. 11).

While the tax collector's sins included robbing God, the Pharisee sinned more by exalting himself. His mental attitude canceled out his deeds of service to God. Like many today, he foolishly thought that his large contributions would pay for sins.

However, it was the tax collector who went home justified after his sincere prayer, "God be merciful to me a sinner" (v. 13). Jesus was making neither a positive nor a negative statement about tithing. He did make it clear, though, that righteousness cannot be earned by fasting, tithing, or any other good work. This account teaches that God accepts those who humble themselves, and rejects those who exalt themselves (v. 14).

Except for his condemnation of the Pharisees, the Gospels of Matthew, Mark, Luke, and John, inspired by the Holy Spirit, did not record any other instance where Jesus mentioned tithing. Mark and John do not even use the word.

"Give All You Have to the Poor"

Luke 18:18 And a certain ruler asked him, saying, Good Master, what shall I do to inherit eternal life?

Luke 18:20 You know the commandments, Do not commit adultery, Do not kill, Do not steal, Do not bear false witness, Honor your father and your mother.
Luke 18:21 And he said, All these I have kept from my youth up.
Luke 18:22 Now when Jesus heard these things, he said to him, You still lack one thing; sell all that you have, and distribute to the poor, and you shall have treasure in heaven; and come, follow me.
Luke 18:23 And when he heard this, he was very sorrowful, for he was very rich.

Whenever the wealthy were involved, Jesus was more concerned about their treatment of the poor than he was about their tithing. Jesus told the rich young ruler, "Sell all that you have, and distribute to the poor." This saying of Jesus was quoted often and his counsel was taken literally by many of the church leaders in the first three centuries because they had no desire for salaries. Notice that Jesus did not say, "Sell all that you have, pay tithes to the priests, and give the rest to the poor." Many today would expect Jesus to say, "Give it to the church." However, rather than buttress tithing, Jesus told the rich young ruler to give ALL, not to the temple, but to the poor. For the rich ruler, whose money was his god, Jesus asked for everything.

"Give Half of What You Have to the Poor"

Luke 19:2 And, behold, there was a man named Zacchaeus, which was the chief among the publicans, and he was rich.
Luke 19:8 And Zacchaeus stood, and said to the Lord, Behold, Lord, the half of my goods I give to the poor; and if I have taken any thing from any man by false accusation, I restore him fourfold.
Luke 19:9 And Jesus said to him, This day is salvation come to this house, because he also is a son of Abraham.

A very similar account to that of the rich young ruler is found in the story of Zacchaeus in Luke 19. He voluntarily promised Jesus, "Lord, the half of my goods I give to the poor; and if I have taken any thing from any man by false accusation, I restore him fourfold." Notice again the absence of tithing. Half of his considerable wealth was promised directly *TO THE POOR*, not to the temple [or to the church].

God Expects the Wealthy to Give a Larger Percentage

2 Cor. 8:12 For if there is first a willing mind, it is accepted according to that a man has, and not according to that he has not.
2 Cor. 8:13 For I mean not that other men be eased, and you burdened,
2 Cor. 8:14 But by an equality, that now at this time your abundance may be a supply for their want, that their abundance also may be a supply for your want, that there may be equality:

These verses are quoted often in this book because they are the very heart of New Covenant giving principles. The wealthy have a greater accountability to God for their money than do the poor! God has blessed them with money-making talents and expects them to use those abilities for him. However, one cannot buy God's favor. Unlike the rich young ruler, Zacchaeus did not have a god-like problem with money, therefore, Jesus allowed him to keep at least the other half of his wealth. God blesses certain people who can handle wealth properly. We observe this in Zacchaeus, Nicodemus and Joseph of Arimathea. The church always needs God-provided funds from the wealthy to finance its mission outreach.

Whereas many churches today encourage its members to "sell all that you have" or, more often, "leave in your will much or all that you have to the church," Jesus plainly said "give it to the poor." How much of the church's income goes to the poor? Again I ask the question, "If the curse of Malachi 3:8-10 refers to those who hoarded the tithe to the neglect of the poor in 3:5, then what kind of punishment is due to the New Covenant church which becomes wealthy and neglects the poor?" "How shall we escape, if we neglect so great salvation; which at the first began to be spoken by the Lord, and was confirmed unto us by them that heard him?" (Heb. 2:3).

THE NEW COVENANT
AND
TITHING

▼

CHAPTER 17

HEBREWS 8;
2 CORINTHIANS 3
A BETTER NEW COVENANT

A Completely New Covenant

What would you think of a lawyer who tried to argue a case in a court in the United States by using the constitution and laws of, say, Iraq, or China? You would probably say, "You have got to be joking! Right?" Yet when we try to teach New Covenant doctrine using the laws and formats designed for Old Covenant national Israel, we are doing exactly the same thing! The Old Testament, especially Exodus through Deuteronomy, is the code of laws, or ordinances, for national Israel during that period of history.

Theologians Gordon Fee and Douglas Stuart wrote, "The Old Testament is not our testament. The Old Testament represents an Old Covenant, which is one we are no longer obligated to keep. Therefore we can hardly begin by assuming that the Old Covenant should automatically be binding upon us. *We have to assume, in fact, that none of its stipulations (laws) are binding upon us unless they are renewed in the New Covenant. That is, unless an Old Testament law is somehow* restated or reinforced in the New Testament, it is no longer directly binding on God's people (cf. Rom. 6:14-15)" (italics mine).[63]

Occasionally, because of necessary radical changes, a nation finds itself ready to abolish its constitution and establish a new one. When this is done, EVERY law, precept, judgment, ordinance, regulation, rule, procedure, and mandate is completely wiped off the books of the original constitution. It is as if the original constitution had never existed—both good and bad disappear. That nation then takes the BEST of the old constitution. It clarifies, simplifies, re-states, gives a new foundation, and starts all over again.

God did that! The necessary radical change occurred at Calvary. In Christ, God ended, abolished, or annulled the Old Covenant and every single law, commandment, ordinance, judgment, and precept given through Moses at Mount Sinai! Since every type, symbol, and shadow was perfectly fulfilled in Jesus Christ, the "righteousness" formerly revealed in the law is NOW revealed in Jesus Christ (Rom. 3:19-20 cf. 3:21-22). Again, the "righteousness" which was demanded by the law was fulfilled in Christ. God next took the BEST of that Old Covenant, and RESTATED it in the context of Jesus Christ and Calvary. However, the "restatement" was not in the form of "Thou shall not do." Instead, it was in the form of privileges of what "new creations in Christ will do." The *best* especially included God's eternal moral principles of love, justice, mercy, and faith (Luke 11:42; Matt. 23:23).

When we open our Bibles, we must first ask God to guide our understanding of his Word. Next, we must orient ourselves to the *position* of the

---

63   Gordon Fee and Douglas Stuart, *How to Read the Bible For All Its Worth* (Grand Rapids: Zondervan, 1980), 137.

text we are about to read. Is this Old Covenant, or New Covenant? It this *before* Calvary, or *after* Calvary? If the text is before Calvary, does it state a temporary "shadow" kindergarten teaching which has ended at Calvary, or does it contain an eternal principle which preceded creation and was restated after Calvary to the New Covenant church?

Millions of honest sincere Christians misunderstand God's Word because they fail to ground themselves in the difference between the Old and New Covenant! There is a division in the Bible for a reason! What is that reason? Even though man, and not God, decided to begin the "New Testament" with the Gospels of Matthew, Mark, Luke, and John, in God's viewpoint, the "New Covenant" was announced at the Last Supper by Christ and did not begin until his death at Calvary. Matthew, Mark, Luke, and John cover the gray connecting "interface" period; they contain flashes of the New, but are mostly Old Covenant.

At the very moment of Christ's death, when he cried out, "It is finished," the veil of the Temple was ripped from top to bottom, exposing the Most Holy Place to all mankind. At that very moment the Levitical priest lost his job (and his tithe) in the mind of God. Finally, every believer became a priest with direct access to God and the Most Holy Place of heaven. Gone were the sacrifices, temple offerings, rituals, holy days, food laws, and all of the cultic ordinances, such as tithing.

None of the three main hermeneutical approaches to theology today support tithing. First, the advocates of covenant theology divide the law into moral commandments, ceremonial statutes, and civil judgments. They, next, recognize, and dismiss, tithing as a ceremonial statute. Second, advocates of dispensational theology also divide the law into commandments, statutes, and judgments. However, they see it as an indivisible whole, dismiss the entire law, and start over again with God repeating his eternal moral principles in the New Covenant after Calvary. For example, Unger says, "To understand the Gospels one must not confuse the kingdom offered to Israel and the church of Christ. Christ fulfilled the law, died under the law, and set us free from the law.

Therefore, to understand the Gospels one must expect to be on legal ground up to the cross (Matt. 10:5-6; 15:22-28; Mark 1:44).... In understanding the New Covenant it also must be borne in mind that the full-scale revelation concerning grace is to be found in the Epistles, not in the Gospels.... The Gospels do not present the doctrine of the church."[64] Advocates of a third approach to hermeneutics between covenant theology and dispensational theology also dismiss tithing because of its cultic non-moral usage. The Apostle Paul disputed with those who wanted to add elements of the Mosaic Law back into the formula of "by grace through faith." Protestants point out that this means "by grace through faith *alone*"—plus nothing! Adding elements such as Sabbath-keeping, circumcision, unclean foods, and tithing actually weaken the gospel by adding cultic law to it. Paul boasted that he had not withheld anything important in preaching the whole gospel, yet never once mentioned tithing.

A Better Covenant with Better Promises

Heb. 8:6 But now he has obtained a *more excellent* ministry, by how much also he is the mediator of a *better covenant*, which was established upon *better promises*.

Whether one is discussing tithing, or much more important matters, the New Covenant is a "more excellent ministry," "a better covenant," and is "established on better promises." This means that grace-giving is a more excellent ministry, that grace-giving is part of a better covenant, and that grace-giving is established on better promises. God did not see fit to re-state tithing in the New Covenant documents.

---

64   *Unger's*, s.v. "New Testament."

Heb. 8:7 For if that first covenant had been faultless, then no place should have been sought for the second.
Heb 8:8 For finding fault with them, he said, Behold, the days come, says the Lord, when I will make a New Covenant with the house of Israel and with the house of Judah.

There was something wrong with the people of the Old Covenant. All Israel had vowed, "All that the LORD has spoken we will do" (Exod. 19:8). All Israel had said "Amen" twelve times as twelve curses were read to them (Deut. 27:15-26). Paul wrote, "And the law is not of faith: but, 'The man that does them shall live in them.' Christ has redeemed us from the curse of the law, being made a curse for us" (Gal. 3:12-13). As Israel failed to keep the law by self-effort they fell under the curse of God. While being under the curse of God, their only salvation would come as they placed their faith in the mercy of God, who would open the door of truth to see Jesus Christ.

"The law is not of faith" includes tithing. Tithing was a commanded ordinance. In fact, it was THE foundational ordinance of the entire Old Covenant Law! Tithing alone made possible the *very existence* of the Levitical priesthood through which God administered the rest of the law, its sacrifices, and all of its other ordinances and judgments (Numbers 3 and 18).

Heb. 8:9 Not according to the covenant that I made with their fathers in the day when I took them by the hand to lead them out of the land of Egypt, because they did not continue in my covenant, and I did not regard them, says the Lord.

The New Covenant is clearly different because it is "not according to the covenant that I made with their fathers." The law stated "Cursed is every one that does not continue in all things which are written in the book of the law to do them" (Deut. 27:26; Gal. 3:10). Failure of a qualified Israelite to tithe placed that Israelite under the curse of the Old Covenant Law (Mal. 3:9). However the Christian cannot possibly be cursed by the Old Covenant Law. When Paul said, "Christ has redeemed *us* from the curse of the law" (Gal. 3:13), he was referring to his fellow Jewish Christians who had once been under such curse.

Heb. 8:10 For this is the covenant that I will make with the house of Israel after those days, says the Lord; I will put my laws into their mind, and write them in their hearts; and I will be to them a God, and they shall be to me a people.
Heb. 8:11 And they shall not teach every man his neighbor, and every man his brother, saying, Know the Lord; for all shall know me, from the least to the greatest.
Heb. 8:12 For I will be merciful to their unrighteousness, and their sins and their iniquities I will remember no more.

God said "I will put my laws into their mind, and write them in their hearts." The New Covenant laws of God are eternal moral laws which reflect his character. Eternal laws are clearly obvious in the mind and heart of every true believer. While the "giving" aspect of tithing may be eternal, the "ten percent" is clearly cultic and not revealed by the Holy Spirit as a post-Calvary eternal principle. God's moral laws are not of the nature of tithing, which requires one person to persuade another person concerning that which is not obviously already "in the mind and heart." To restate the point, while "giving" may be moral, or natural, "ten percent" is clearly cultic and is not already evident in the mind awaiting revelation.

These texts also imply that the New Covenant will be a priesthood of believers rather than an echelon of tithe-supported priests teaching others.

Heb. 8:13 In that he says, a New Covenant, he has made the first old. Now that which is decaying [becoming obsolete: NKJ] and growing old is ready to vanish away [disappear: NAS].

Two thousand years ago it was written that the Old Covenant laws were already "becoming obsolete and growing old" (NAS); they were "obsolete and aging" (NIV); they were "out of date now" (TLB). Galatians 4:31 says that the Old Covenant had been "cast out." God's Word is clear on this subject.

From "No Glory" to "Exceeding Glory"

2 Cor. 3:6 Who also has made us able ministers of the new testament, not of the letter, but of the spirit; for the letter kills, but the spirit gives life.

Unfortunately, preaching the "letter" of the Old Covenant "kills," but the "spirit" of the New Covenant "gives life." Yet there are both Christian and non-Christian religions today which are as locked into the same "letter-exactness" of ancient law creeds as were the Pharisees of the first century. They have experienced no great revivals and lack the confidence of real spiritual freedom. Yet, Romans 8:2 says, "the law of the Spirit of life in Christ Jesus has made me free from the law of sin and death." Verse 4 adds, "The righteousness of the law [is] fulfilled in us, who walk not after the flesh, but after the Spirit." There is so much more to be gained when the letter of the Old Covenant law is abandoned and the power of the New Covenant spirit is allowed to work in our lives and in our churches. We are foolishly losing the fullness of the New Covenant blessing by teaching tithing (or any other purely Old Covenant cultic doctrine).

2 Cor. 3:7 But if the ministration of death, written and engraved in stones, *was glorious*, so that the children of Israel could not steadfastly behold the face of Moses for the *glory* of his countenance, which *glory was to be done away*,
2 Cor. 3:8 How shall not the ministration of the spirit be *rather glorious*?
2 Cor. 3:9 For if the ministration of condemnation is *glory*, much more does the ministration of righteousness *exceed in glory*.
2 Cor. 3:10 For even that which *was made glorious* had *NO GLORY* in this respect, by reason of *the glory that excels [surpasses]*.
2 Cor. 3:11 *For if that which is done away was glorious, much more that which remains is glorious*.

The impact that these verses can have on the Christian community when its replaces Old Covenant tithing with New Covenant giving principles can be astounding. Notice the progression of the word "glory" in these verses. Although the Old Covenant was "glorious" and Moses reflected "glory," that "glory" was to be done away (v. 7). Should not the ministry of the Holy Spirit be "even more glorious" (NIV) (v. 8)? The "glory" of a ministry which provides righteousness will naturally exceed the "glory" of a ministry that condemned (v. 9). While the old ministry was "glorious," the new ministry is "much more glorious" (v. 11). Actually, when the "glories" are compared, the old is so un-glorious that it has **"no glory"** in comparison to the "glory that excels" (v. 10). While using Old Covenant principles might produce "glorious" results, using clearly stated New Covenant principles is sure to produce much more exceedingly glorious results! That is what the Bible teaches! Why cannot we believe and claim the "much more exceedingly glorious" promises of God's Word when these truths are applied to tithing?

2 Cor. 3:14 But their minds were blinded; for until this day the same veil remains un-taken away in the reading of the old testament—which veil is done away in Christ.

Christian tithing falls into the trap described in verse 14. In order to teach tithing, one can only go back to pre-Calvary texts like Genesis 14, Leviticus 27, Malachi 3 and Matthew 23. Thus the tithe-advocate is still standing on Old Covenant, pre-Calvary, ground and does not see the changes brought about through viewing Christ. "The same veil remains un-taken away in the reading of the old testament."

Since Hebrews 7 teaches that "the commandment to take tithes of the people according to the law" was "disannulled" when the priesthood was changed, the veil should have been taken away by the truth of the high priesthood of Christ and the priesthood of every believer.

2 Cor. 3:16 Nevertheless, when it [a person] shall turn to the Lord, the veil shall be taken away.
2 Cor. 3:18 But we all, with open face beholding as in a glass *the glory of the Lord*, are changed into the same image *from glory to glory*, even as by the Spirit of the Lord.

The Christian church must learn to trust the New Covenant principles of grace and faith in order to prosper and be well-pleasing to God. Tithing reveals a distrust of the better principles and a reversion to dependence on outdated principles. While satellite Christian broadcasters spend an enormous amount of air-time asking for tithes, the vast majority of people channel-surf away from them. Too many lost souls stay away from church because of its money-hungry reputation and because their spiritual needs are not met.

By beholding Christ we are guaranteed to be changed from an Old Covenant no-glory status into a New Covenant glory standing. As church members feel compassion towards the lost world around them, their giving will increase spontaneously without regard to commands or percentages. The problem is that too many pastors feel secure with a set percentage to request and are afraid to remove the Old Covenant veil and take the step of faith towards other New Covenant glorious principles, as Christ desires.

CHAPTER 18

▼

THE CHRISTIAN, THE MOSAIC LAW, AND THE LAW OF CHRIST

When a preacher stands in the pulpit and insists that Christians must pay ten percent of their gross income to the church, that preacher is not grounded in Bible basics about the covenants, the law, national Israel, and the church. He is not "rightly dividing the word of truth" (2 Tim. 2:15). He is preaching "another gospel" and is "perverting the gospel" (Gal. 1:6-7). While Paul said that he had "fully preached the gospel" and that he had "kept back nothing that was profitable" (Rom. 15:19; Acts 20:20), tithing is not once encouraged by Paul! If the epistle of Hebrews is not written by Paul (as many claim), then the word "tithe" *never* appears in his writings.

These straightforward assertions are fully backed up by the following comments by the *New Scofield Reference Bible*, Lewis Sperry Chafer, Theodore Epp, and Merrill Unger. Regardless of how many years one has been preaching error, it is never too late to get back to basics, restudy the law and covenants, and preach the truth of God's Word. A blessing awaits.

Christians are not under the jurisdiction of any legal code which tells them what to do in any area of life. Yet, while many preachers will readily agree with these words, many disagree and take a different stance when the subject turns to tithing. They simply do not understand the principles of the "law of Christ" and the new creation which lead to spontaneous giving wholly from the heart, and wholly apart from law.

The New Scofield Reference Bible Notes on the Law: Galatians 3

1. Law is in contrast with grace. Under grace God bestows the righteousness which, under law, he demanded (Exod. 19:5; John 1:17; Rom. 3:21; 10:3-10; 1 Cor. 1:30).
2. The law is in itself, holy, just, good, and spiritual (Rom. 7:12-14).
3. Before the law the whole world is guilty, and the law is therefore of necessity, a ministry of condemnation, death, and the divine curse (Rom. 3:19; 2 Cor. 3:7-9; Gal. 3:10).
4. Christ bore the curse of the law, and redeemed the believer both from the curse and from the dominion of the law (Gal. 3:13; 4:5-7).
5. Law neither justifies a sinner nor sanctifies a believer (Gal. 2:16; 3:2-3, 11-12).
6. The believer is both dead to the law and redeemed from it, so that he is "not under the law, but under grace" (Rom. 6:14; 7:4; Gal. 2:19; 4:4-7); 1 Tim. 1:8-9).
7. Under the New Covenant of grace the principle of obedience to the divine will is *inwrought* (Heb. 10:16). So far is the life of the believer from the anarchy of self-will that he is "in-lawed to Christ" (1 Cor. 9:21), and the new "law of Christ" (Gal. 6:1; 2 John 5) is his delight, while, through the indwelling Spirit, the righteousness of the law is fulfilled in him (Rom. 8:2-4; Gal. 5:16-18).

"The commandments are used in the distinctive Christian Scriptures as an instruction in righteousness (2 Tim. 3:16; Rom. 13:8-10; Eph. 6:1-3; 1 Cor. 9:8-9)."[65]

To extend Scofield's comments in relation to tithing, (1) instead of demanding tithes, under grace God bestows the ability to give as we desire in our hearts; (3-4) while the law puts a curse on law breakers and non-tithers, Christ removed the curse; (5) tithe-paying neither justifies nor sanctifies; (6) the believer is dead to anything the law says; (7) the believer obeys the indwelling divine will of God.

As previously mentioned, churches that preach tithing based on texts from the Mosaic Law have missed the differences between law and grace, Old and New Covenants, and Israel and the church. First, they preach a tithing message to believers who are dead to that law. Second, they preach a weak and unprofitable law that has ended at Calvary. Third, they preach a law that has absolutely no glory and, therefore, no power to revive the church (2 Cor. 3:10). Fourth, they preach a law that has been canceled, blotted out, nailed to the cross (Col. 2:14), abolished (Eph. 2:15), annulled (Heb. 7:18), and that has long since faded away (2 Cor. 3:11), because it was obsolete (Heb. 8:13).

Tithing, as part of the Mosaic Law, is now a spiritless, revival-less doctrine. Tithing turns a good Christian into a fearful legalist who is afraid of the wrath and curse of God if He/she does not "pay up." It drives many away from church because they are too poor to give ten percent of their gross income. It also deprives well-qualified poor members from holding church leadership positions. On the other hand, churches that preach gospel principles of grace-giving thrive financially under the freedom of the gospel.

---

65   *Scofield*, s.v. "Gal. 3."

The Christian and the Law: Theodore Epp

The following are excerpts about the law from a very excellent book by Theodore Epp, *Moses, Volume III, Great Leader and Lawgiver.* The Scriptures between the quotations are omitted. Epp was the founder of the radio broadcast, *Back to the Bible.*

"It is clear from these scriptures (Gal. 5:18; Rom. 6:14-15) that the Mosaic Law, as law, has *absolutely nothing* to contribute in accomplishing sanctification. On the contrary, being free from the bondage of the law, makes it possible for the Holy Spirit to operate effectively in the believer."

"So the evidence from Scripture is that the Christian is not under the Mosaic Law. All this has been accomplished because Christ fulfilled every demand of *both the moral and ceremonial law.*"

"*The Christian is not under the Mosaic Law in any sense.* But the whole law is an essential part of the Scriptures, and as such is profitable to believers of all ages."

"But although we are to profit from all the scriptures in that we learn valuable lessons from them, not all Scripture passages were written to us specifically."

"*The Christian's standard of living is not the law.* If the Christian is not under the law, what is his standard of living? Basically, the standard for a Christian is to do the will of God by the enabling grace that is supplied in Christ Jesus our Lord through the Holy Spirit."

"The proper formula for getting to know Christ as a believer is presented in Romans 8:1-4. This is a reference to the law of Moses which revealed the awfulness of sin, made sin a transgression and pronounced death as the penalty for sin."

"Now that we have Jesus Christ as Savior, we have a new life principle—'the law of the Spirit of life in Christ Jesus.' Because God has set a new principle into operation within the believer, the believer is enabled to live a life of victory. Therefore, even though the believer is delivered from the Mosaic Law, the righteousness of that law is really fulfilled in him through Christ (8:4)."

"Believers are commanded to 'fulfill the law of Christ.' 'Bear you one another's burdens' indicates the nature of the law of Christ. The law of Christ is really the law of love."

"So even though a person in this age is not bound by the Mosaic Law, there are definite commandments of God that are in force today.... 'that we should believe on the name of his Son Jesus Christ, and love one another.' This law of love is not a new law in itself because it was at the heart of the Old Testament law system...but...to love as Christ loved is a new principle" (italics mine).[66]

To summarize my understanding of Epp, if tithing, taken only from the law, contributes to neither justification nor sanctification, then it has no benefit at all in the Christian life! It is only when the believer is released from the commanded obligations of the law (the exact ten percent) that the Holy Spirit is able to work effectively. If we love as Christ loved, and give as Christ gave, it should be totally unnecessary even to mention tithing. Tithing was based on God's command to support the Levites for their service in exchange for property inheritance. Tithing was not based on any great loving example which the other tribes wanted to demonstrate to the Levites. In fact, history reveals that the Levitical priests were often despised (and deserved to be despised).

The New Covenant "Law" of Christ

"Law" in the New Testament does not always refer to the Mosaic Law. Failure to understand the many uses of the word "law" confuses many Christians who do not seriously study the Bible. For example, the "new" "Law of Love" is NOT the Mosaic Law of the Old Covenant!

Scofield says, "The new 'law' of Christ is the divine love, (1) as wrought into the renewed heart by the Holy Spirit (Rom. 5:5; Heb. 10:16), (2) and

---

66   Theodore H. Epp, *Moses, Vol. III, Great Leader and Lawgiver* (Lincoln: Back to the Bible, 1976), 178-87.

out flowing in the energy of the Spirit, (3) unforced and spontaneous, toward the objects of the divine love (2 Cor. 5:14-20; 1 Thess. 2:7-8), (4) the law of liberty (Jas. 1:25; 2:12), (5) in contrast with the external law of Moses: a) Moses' Law demands love (Lev. 19:18; Deut. 6:5; Luke 10:27); b) Christ's 'law' "IS" love (Rom. 5:5; 1 John 4:7, 19-20), c) and so takes the place of the external law by fulfilling it (Rom. 13:10; Gal. 5:14), d) the law written in the heart under the New Covenant (Heb. 8:8)."[67]

Unger says, "(1) This category includes the doctrines and precepts of grace, addressed to the redeemed child of God in this age. It must be carefully noted that the Christian is not under law. (2) Grace has imparted to him all the merits that he could ever need (John 1:16; Rom. 5:1; 8:1; Col. 2:9-10). (3) Being "in-lawed" to Christ (1 Cor. 9:20-21) does not mean that the Christian is without law. (4) But it does mean, as one redeemed by grace, he has the duty, or rather the gracious privilege, of not doing what is displeasing to God and fully discharging that which is well-pleasing to him on the basis of manifestation as *spontaneous gratitude* for his salvation in grace" (italics mine).[68]

Concerning tithing, something cannot be both "spontaneous" and "commanded" or an "expectation" at the same time. The New Covenant "law of love" is not comparable to the Old Covenant concept of law.

Zodhiates' Hebrew-Greek Key Study Bible

"The Gospel, or gospel-method of justification is called (1) The 'Law of Faith' opposite the 'Law of Moses' (Rom. 3:27). (2) The 'law of the spirit of life' opposite the law, i.e., power, dominion of sin and death (Rom. 8:2). (3) The 'royal law' (Jas. 2:8) because (4) it is the law of Christ, our King, (5) 'the perfect law of liberty' (Jas. 1:25 cf. 2:12) *freeing believers from the yoke of ceremonial observances* and slavery of sin opposite the

---

67   *Scofield,* s.v. "2 John 5."
68   *Unger's,* s.v. "Law of Grace."

Mosaic Law, which made nothing perfect (Heb. 7:19; 10:1)" (italics mine).[69]

It is illogical to teach tithing when a better law, or principle, has replaced the legalistic Mosaic Law—that is, LOVE! There are no "Thou shall nots," but the out flowing, spontaneous, response of living FAITH. This is because the true believer is filled with, the Holy Spirit. Giving, like everything else in the believer's life, is intended to be a purely faith response, and not of law!

From Shadow Laws to Christ the Word

Rom. 3:21 But now the righteousness of God, without the law, is manifested, being witnessed by the law and the prophets;
Rom. 3:22 Even the righteousness of God, which is by faith of Jesus Christ, to all and upon all them that believe; for there is no difference.

The Old Covenant "shadow" law states, "Your word I have hid in my heart, that I may not sin against you" (Ps. 119:11), and "Your word is a lamp to my feet, and a light to my path" (Ps. 119:105). In the Old Covenant God's Word, or the Mosaic Law, represented his standard of righteousness, that is, his standard of judgment. His Word best represented his perfect character and wisdom. That Word was most closely related to the Mosaic Law in all its commandments, statutes, and judgments.

However, the New Covenant "substance" reveals that the "Word" is actually "Jesus Christ," and not the Mosaic Law! "In the beginning was the Word, and the Word was with God, and the Word was God" (John 1:1). "For in him dwells all the fulness of the Godhead bodily" (Col. 2:9). "[God] has in these last days spoken to us by his Son, whom he has appointed heir of all things, by whom also he made the worlds" (Heb.

---

69   *Zodhiates' Hebrew-Greek Key Study Bible*, 1984 ed., s.v. "nomos: law 3, lexical aids 3551."

1:2). Jesus Christ, the Living Word, not the Mosaic Law, is now hid in the heart of the believer (Gal. 2:20; Col. 1:28). Christ is now the believer's lamp (John 1:9), not the law. The greater glory of God's "Law of Love," in the Person of the indwelling Holy Spirit, has superseded the written law (Heb. 8:8-13; 2 Cor. 3:3-6; John 16:13-15). God's standard of judgment is now Jesus Christ! This means that judgment is now determined, not by how we respond to the law, but how we respond to Jesus Christ (John 16:8-9; 2 Cor. 3:18; Heb. 9:26-28). The Mosaic Law, good as it was, only served as a shadow truth in comparison to Jesus Christ (Heb. 10:1; Col. 2:17). The revelation of God in Christ was the totality of God's revelation of himself to man. Therefore, only by reading the Old Covenant Law with New Covenant insight can one correctly understand it (2 Cor. 3:13-14). What God wants New Covenant man to know, he now reveals in and through Jesus Christ (Heb. 1:1-2).

▼

RELEVANT POST-CALVARY TEXTS

▼

CHAPTER 19

HEBREWS 7
CHRIST'S HIGH PRIESTHOOD
ABOLISHED TITHING

The Importance of Hebrews, Chapter 7

Hebrews, chapter 7, is extremely important because it is the only New Testament mention of tithing after Calvary! Although this chapter is not primarily a discussion of tithing, it draws heavily from Numbers 18, which is the ordinance establishing the priesthood and tithing. It contrasts the Aaronic priesthood, which was established by tithing, with Christ's Melchizedek priesthood, which is eternal and is based on the unlimited eternal power of God.

While "tithe/tenth" is found in verses 2, 4, 5, 6, 8, and 9, beyond this chapter the word does not appear after Calvary in the New Testament! It is difficult to understand how and why biblical researchers of the subject of New Covenant giving, as a group, ignore this important chapter. By ignoring this chapter in a study of tithing, the most fundamental rules of sound exegesis are set aside. Therefore, for the reasons stated in the previous paragraph and for the sake of honesty to the Word of God, this chapter's use of tithing must be thoroughly researched and included in *any* legitimate exegetical discussion about tithing.

Three Pivotal Texts Involving Tithing

It is the goal of this chapter to accurately, and honestly, correlate Hebrews 7:5, 12 and 18 into the logical and exegetically correct conclusion that the New Covenant teaches that tithing is not a valid doctrine for the Christian. The purpose is to reveal biblical truth and move believers from a legalistic approach of giving towards the surpassing principles of the New Covenant.

The Historical Context of Hebrews

The epistle of Hebrews was written to prepare Jewish Christians in Jerusalem for the severe religious culture shock which was approaching. Soon after the epistle was written, in A.D. 70, a Roman army under Titus destroyed the city. The temple was destroyed and its sacrifices ceased. Jews were not allowed to enter the ruins and rebuild. Consequently, the high priest and other priests were not allowed to perform any sacrificial services.

The Root of the Problem in Jerusalem

Acts 21:17 And when we came to Jerusalem, the brothers received us gladly.
Acts 21:18 And the day following Paul went in with us to James, and all the elders were present.

Acts 21:19 And when he [Paul] had saluted them [the church at Jerusalem], he declared particularly what things God had done among the Gentiles by his ministry.

Acts 21:20 And when they heard it, they glorified the Lord, and said to him, *You see, brother, how many thousands of Jews there are which believe, and they are all zealous of the law.*

Acts 21:21 *And they are informed of you, that you are teaching all the Jews which are among the Gentiles to forsake Moses, saying that they ought not to circumcise their children, neither to walk after the customs.*

Acts 21:22 What should be done? The multitude will certainly come together, for they will hear that you are come.

Acts 21:23 Therefore, do this that we say to you. We have four men which have a vow on them.

Acts 21:24 *Take them, and purify yourself with them, and pay their expenses, that they may shave their heads, and all may know that those things, whereof they were informed concerning you, are nothing; but that you yourself also are walking orderly, and are keeping the law.*

Acts 21:25 *Concerning the Gentiles which believe, we have written and concluded that they observe no such thing, except only that they keep themselves from things offered to idols, and from blood, and from strangled, and from fornication.*

Acts 21:26 *Then Paul took the men, and the next day purifying himself with them, entered into the temple, to signify the accomplishment of the days of purification, until that an offering should be offered for every one of them.*

The particular problem concerned the many Jewish Christians who still considered themselves Jews first, and Christians second. It is evident from the activities recorded in Acts 15; 18:18 and 21:17-26 that there was no lessening of law-observances for the Jewish Christians. As a historical fact, most Jewish Christians in Jerusalem *never* did abandon the Mosaic Law; they later established their own Christian sect, and rejected Paul as a heretic. The full impact of the meaning and shift of the gospel away from the Mosaic Law never did come to many Jewish Christians. Such realization and changes of over a thousand years of tradition could not possibly occur quickly as far as Jewish Christians were concerned. Paul's letters to the Romans, Galatians, Ephesians, Philippians and Colossians especially tried to explain the shift away from the law.

Concerning tithing, there is no legitimate reason to believe that Jewish Christians had ceased paying tithes to their temple priesthood at this time. In fact, history records that these Jewish Christians continued to observe the law's holy days, feasts, rituals and continued to honor the high priest. Therefore, it is also logical to assume that they, as obedient Jews, also felt obligated to keep on paying tithes to the Levitical priesthood!

Church historian, Williston Walker, agrees, "The early Jerusalem company were faithful in attendance at the temple, and in obedience to the Jewish law, but, in addition, they had their own special services among themselves, with prayer, mutual exhortation, and 'breaking of bread' daily in private houses. *This 'breaking of bread' served a twofold purpose. It was a bond of fellowship and a means of support for the needy*" (italics mine).[70] Notice that he does not say, "for the support of the clergy."

The Problem the Epistle Must Solve

It was essential for the writer of Hebrews to convince the church in Jerusalem that their current earthly city of Jerusalem with its temple, high priesthood, sacrifices and support structure were no longer a necessary part of God's plan for the church! They must immediately break away from their immature faith in, and mistaken dependence upon, the city of Jerusalem, the temple and the high priesthood. Otherwise, when all of these soon disappeared, within a few years at most, their spiritual lives would suffer severe devastation.

---

70   Williston Walker, *A History of the Christian Church*, 3rd ed., (Charles Scribner's Sons: New York, 1970), 22.

In order to break this connection, the Jewish Christians must stop going to the temple for festivals, vows and sacrifices. They must also immediately stop accepting the Levitical high priesthood as legitimate and stop paying tithes to support it. The precise wording of the letter of Hebrews was necessary because of the inaccurate theology of the Jewish Christians. Again, since they still accepted the legitimacy of the Jewish temple and priesthood, they must have also continued to pay their law-commanded tithes to it. Thus tithing plays an important part in the refutation of the Jewish priesthood in Hebrews, chapter 7.

How Christ's High Priesthood Solves the Problem

Jesus Christ is presented in the Epistle of Hebrews as the answer to all of their imminent problems. *"In Christ"* the believer has a better country, a better city, a better sanctuary, a better high priesthood, a better priesthood, and better sacrifices. The better country, city and sanctuary are heavenly for the church. The better high priest is Christ. The better priests are all believers (not pastor-teachers). The better sacrifices from believers are those of praise, thanksgiving, service and financial support spurred by the love of Christ and desire to seek and to save the lost. Only by understanding these truths could the Jewish Christian survive the culture shock which occurred after A.D. 70.

Melchizedek Was the Key to Understanding the High Priesthood of Jesus Christ

7:1 For this Melchisedec, king of Salem, priest of the most high God, who met Abraham returning from the slaughter of the kings, and blessed him.

"Historically" speaking, Melchizedek was the "king of Salem" (considered by most commentators to be Jerusalem) approximately 2000-1970

B.C. However, the writer of Hebrews uses Melchizedek "typically," not "historically." For a detailed discussion of the historical Melchizedek, see the previous chapter of this book which discusses Genesis 14.

As detailed in the Genesis 14 discussion, "the Most High God" (El Elyon; Strong's 5945) and the Aramaic equivalent (Strong's 5943) was a common non-Hebrew title for one of the "gods" who occupied the high places. The most important revelation of Genesis 14 is that the Canaanite concept of the "Most High God" was, in reality, the "LORD (Yahweh) the Most High God." Perhaps the writer of Hebrews was inspired to use the Gentile version of the title (rather than Abraham's) in order to strengthen the argument that God, and Christ's high priesthood, are not exclusively Hebrew, which required "Yahweh" as a qualifier. This difference is lost by many while discussing tithing from Genesis 14.

7:2 To whom also Abraham gave a *tenth* part of all; first being, by interpretation, King of righteousness, and, after that, also King of Salem, which is, King of peace.

After rescuing Lot and recovering the goods stolen from the region around Sodom, Abraham offered Melchizedek a tenth of the spoils of war (also verse 5).

"First of all," Melchizedek's identity was "being by interpretation" only, not in reality. In Hebrew, "melchi" means "king," "zedek," means "righteousness," and "salem," evolved to mean "peace." Therefore Melchizedek was, typically, by interpreting his name, the "King of Righteousness" and also the "King of Peace." Both of these titles are appropriate for the Messiah in the Old Testament.

Historically, though, Melchizedek was not actually "the" King of Righteousness or "the" King of Peace (that is, Christ); he was only that person "typically," "by interpretation." The emphatic "the" before the titles is absent in the Greek.

Abraham gave a tenth *"of all"* to Melchizedek. Verse 4 limits this to the "spoils of war." Actually, according to Genesis 14, Abraham kept absolutely nothing from these spoils of war. Except for what his private militia had consumed, the rest was freely returned to its owners in Sodom and Gomorrah via the king of Sodom. God had blessed Abraham so that he required nothing else. Neither did he want to give the king of Sodom an opportunity to brag that he had made Abraham rich.

7:3 Without father, without mother, without descent, having neither beginning of days, nor end of life, but made like to the Son of God, abides a priest continually [perpetually].

Melchizedek was *"without father, without mother, without descent."* Historically, this was negative; he possessed no recorded genealogy. In the ancient world, this term could merely mean the parents were "obscure," "of no importance," or even "slaves." To an Israelite, one who applied to serve as a priest and had Gentile parents or wife was considered to be "without father, and without mother." Both Ezra 2:61-62 and Nehemiah 7:63-64 say that some claiming to be priests were not "reckoned by genealogy" because they had become "polluted" and were "put from the priesthood." No records identify Melchizedek's father, his mother, or any ancestors. Therefore, because of this lack of genealogy, the Israelites would never have accepted him as either king or priest.

"Having neither beginning of days, nor end of life" must be understood "typically," but not literally. Why? Because Melchizedek was not Jesus Christ living in the flesh before his virgin birth. Jesus had family trees in both his deity and humanity! As God, he always existed. As the God-man, he often declared that the Father sent him. As the Son of David, his physical genealogy is recorded in Matthew and Luke. There is no doubt concerning the descent, or genealogy, of Jesus Christ. Therefore, legally (through the law), Jesus Christ would never have been accepted as high priest without Aaronic credentials. However, "typically," these non-credentials of Melchizedek

make him eternal, not limited to death as was Aaron's priesthood, and superior to the law.

"Made like the Son of God." Melchizedek was not THE Son of God, but was "made LIKE the Son of God." His name, title, and lack of genealogy all make him into a type of Christ—not his person! Christ is "after the order of," "like" (v. 3), or "after the similitude" or "likeness" of Melchizedek (v. 15). The Christ-event, not Melchizedek's rule as priest-king, is the time when God took on flesh and personally lived among his created beings. However, occasionally someone will use the description from Hebrews 7:1-3 to teach that Melchizedek was actually Christ in a pre-incarnate form. Such a claim destroys the meaning of the incarnation of Christ. Jesus Christ, the God-man, clothed himself in humanity as a baby, lived and suffered among men as their kinsman-Redeemer, and before many witnesses was crucified, buried, and resurrected for our salvation!

We must realize the difference between the "historical" Melchizedek of Genesis 14, and the "typical" "prophetic" Melchizedek of Psalm 110 and Hebrews 7. "Out of Egypt I have called my Son" "historically" means "national Israel," but "typically" and "prophetically" it means Jesus Christ (Hos. 11:1 cf. Matt. 2:15). "A virgin shall be with child" "historically" referred to Isaiah's wife and child, but "typically" and "prophetically" it refers to Mary and Christ (compare Isa. 7:14-16 and Matt. 1:23). First, the "historical" Melchizedek appeared in Genesis 14. Second, Melchizedek appeared "prophetically" when David mentioned him in Psalm 110 almost a thousand years later. And, third, Hebrews 7 uses him both "prophetically" and "typically."

"Negative" features about Melchizedek are actually reversed to become "positive" features of Christ in Psalm 110 and Hebrews 5-7. Negatively, Melchizedek only worshiped the Gentile concept of a god called "El Elyon, God Most High." He did not know God as "Yahweh, the LORD," the God of Abraham's household. Also negatively, his family record did not exist. Without a proven genealogy, he would never qualify later under the Old Covenant, either as a Levitical priest, or as a legitimate king from one of the twelve tribes of Israel. The genealogies of Genesis do not link him to Abraham, nor anybody else.

Psalm 110 and Hebrews use Melchizedek's "negatives" as "positives." Whereas, the LORD (Yahweh) was the exclusive covenant God of Abraham and Old Covenant Israel, in the New Covenant, God expanded special knowledge of himself beyond national Israel. When God reached out as "God Most High" to all nations, Melchizedek's unrecorded family tree is used to illustrate that Christ was eternal, pre-existed his incarnation, and was superior to the law.

First Evidence That Melchizedek is Greater: Abraham Paid Tithes to Melchizedek

7:4 Now consider how great this man was, to whom even the patriarch Abraham gave the *tenth* of the spoils.

The first evidence that Melchizedek was superior to Abraham and the Mosaic Law is that Abraham gave tithes to him. With *"now consider"* the author of Hebrews begins laying the groundwork for his crucial declaration in verse 18 that the entire Levitical system of worship, including its high priesthood and tithing, has been "set aside," or "disannulled." "Now consider" begins a list of evidences which prove to the Hebrew mind that Melchizedek's priesthood replaced that of Aaron. This list of evidences is found in verses 4-10 and the conclusions begin in verse 11.

It is important to note that the "tithe" is a vital part of every evidence used! Melchizedek was greater than the Levitical priests because Abraham "gave a tenth of the choicest spoils" to him. While Abraham's pre-law tithe was the first mention of tithing *before* the law began, this chapter in Hebrews is the only mention of tithing *after* the law ended at Calvary.

Although an entire chapter is given to Genesis 14, a short review is appropriate:

1. Abraham's tithe to Melchizedek consisted of only the "spoils of war" (Greek: *akrothinion*). *Thayer's Greek-English Lexicon* says this means "the top of the heap, the first fruits: the best of the spoils."[71] It was not from the holy land of Canaan.

2. Abraham kept nothing, but also returned the remaining 90%; therefore, this was not an example of God blessing Abraham "because" he tithed.

3. Abraham tithed, not because of any Mosaic Law requirement, but because of a mandatory centuries old pagan tradition. Even the king of Sodom recognized this.

4. Abraham did not tithe because he thought that Melchizedek was Yahweh's priest. Melchizedek's "Most High God" was probably the Canaanite "El" or "Baal."

5. Abraham's spoils-of-war tithe is never used or quoted in the Mosaic Law, Gospels, or Epistles as a proof-text for tithing.

6. Abraham freely gave the 90% to the king of Sodom. Certainly we are not to follow his example and give the 90% to Satan. Nobody would use this as an example of free-will offerings before the law!

7. The Mosaic Law, in Numbers 31:26-31, specified 1/50th (or 2%) of the spoils to be returned to God, not 10% as the pagans required.

8. Genesis 14:20 should be compared to the spoil-taxes in Numbers 31, but not to the Law-tithes in Numbers 18 and Leviticus 27.

9. If Melchizedek in Genesis 14 could be used to demonstrate that pre-Law tithing existed, then Melchizedek in Hebrews 7 can be used to demonstrate that post-Law tithing should not exist!

In Hebrews 7, tithing is merely used as a means of understanding Melchizedek, both before and after the Mosaic Law. As seen in Genesis

---

71   Joseph Henry Thayer, *Thayer's Greek-English Lexicon of the New Testament* (Grand Rapids: Zondervan, 1962), CD-ROM (Seattle: Biblesoft, 1999), s.v. "*akrothinion*."

14, Abraham acknowledged Melchizedek's authority when he offered the tithe-tax of the spoils. Melchizedek's rule may have reached to Mamre and Hebron where Abraham lived. Since it is evident that no Mosaic Law of tithing existed, Abraham was following established pagan custom. He was paying a mandatory tribute to his pagan king.

The First Key Verse Involving Tithing

7:5 And truly they that are of the sons of Levi, who receive the office of the priesthood, *have a commandment to take tithes of the people according to the law,* that is, of their brothers, though they come out of the loins of Abraham.

This is a crucial verse for understanding the remainder of the chapter, because all other references to "tithe" and "law" refer back to this verse!

"Sons of Levi" reminds the readers that the Levitical priests owed their existence and authority to their authority to collect tithes. The writer of Hebrews first reminds his readers where the authority of the Levitical priesthood originated before he proves that Christ's authority is greater and replaces the former!

"According to the law" establishes the connection between "tithing" and the Mosaic Law. Whereas, in Hebrews, neither the word "tithe" nor "law" occurs before chapter 7, in this chapter "tithe" occurs 7 times (vv. 2, 4, 5, 6, 8, and 9), and "law" occurs 7 times (vv. 5, 11, 12, 16, 19, and 28). Tithing does not occur anywhere else in the New Testament after Calvary! Since the first use of legal terms often determines their exact definition, this aspect of the chapter cannot be ignored. A primary purpose of this chapter in Hebrews is to demonstrate the change of the legal law which established the Levitical priesthood.

As already mentioned, both the first and last Scriptural occurrence of tithing involve Melchizedek! Therefore, in order to correctly understand this chapter, one must observe the vital connection between tithing and the Old Covenant Mosaic Law. *From the context, the word "law," first used in verse 5, definitely must, though not exclusively, refer to tithing!*

"A commandment" refers specifically to Numbers, chapter 18. Those who study Numbers 18 in order to support New Covenant tithing are compelled to discard it and concentrate on more obscure texts. However, one who takes the time to study Numbers 18 will soon discover why tithing is not suitable for New Covenant believers. Since Numbers 18 actually contains the "commandment," "ordinance" or "statute" of tithing, it should be carefully studied by every serious Bible student with the goal of discovering exactly what the Bible says.

Even in our own society, any law which creates a job position must first include the "provision," that is, the source of revenue for paying that person for services rendered. Therefore, the "provision" is the very heart, the foundation, and the enabler of the person in the position being created by law. Again, Numbers 18 *is* the "chair," or "provision ordinance," of the Mosaic Law which established the Levitical priesthood and its support through tithing. The connection explains why tithing is mentioned so often in Hebrews, chapter 7. This "ordinance" or "statute" of tithing which provided sustenance for the Levites had abolished the centuries-old tradition which had designated the male head of the household as the family priest. The tithing ordinance forced Israel to support the Levitical system through tithes and offerings. It also applied a death penalty on anyone trying to "draw near" to worship God directly.

Second Evidence That Melchizedek Is Greater: Melchizedek Received Tithes and Blessed Abraham

7:6 But he whose descent is not counted from them received *tithes* of Abraham, and blessed him that had the promises.
7:7 And, without all contradiction, the less is blessed of the better.

The second evidence that Melchizedek was superior to Abraham and the Mosaic Law is that Melchizedek received tithes from Abraham and blessed Abraham. Using accepted Hebrew logic, the writer of Hebrews states that, because the historical Melchizedek received tithes from Abraham, such reception proves that the typical Melchizedek (Christ) was greater than Abraham.

Melchizedek was greater than Abraham because Melchizedek blessed Abraham. Yet he was neither an Israelite, not a Levite, and was not descended from Abraham (v. 6). The one bestowing the blessing is greater than the one being blessed.

Third Evidence That Melchizedek Is Greater: Melchizedek Received Tithes and Is Eternal

7:8 And here men that die receive *tithes*; but there he received them, of whom it is witnessed that he lives.

The third evidence that Melchizedek was greater than Abraham and the Mosaic Law is that Melchizedek received tithes while being eternal, but Levites receive tithes and die. Melchizedek was greater than Levi because Levi is mortal, while the typical Melchizedek is eternal and is still living. The "mortal" men are those of the Levitical priesthood. Typically, Melchizedek was eternal and had no beginning. Whereas the Genesis account says nothing about his lack of genealogy or eternal attributes, Psalm 110 "witnessed" that he lives on. The Melchizedek of Psalm 110:4 is clearly the "Messiah."

Historically speaking, whereas the Levitical priesthood received its authority to receive tithes from the Mosaic Law, Melchizedek received tithes from his own inherent authority as a Canaanite priest-king. However, the author of Hebrews ignores the *historical* "Canaanite priest-king" aspect and builds his argument on the fact that Melchizedek's *typical* authority was inherent and eternal. The focus is on the eternal-ness and superiority of Jesus Christ.

Fourth Evidence That Melchizedek Is Greater: Levitical Priests Paid Tithes to Him

7:9 And, as I may so say, Levi also, who receives *tithes*, paid *tithes* in Abraham.
7:10 For he was still in the loins of his father, when Melchizedek met him.

The fourth evidence that Melchizedek was superior to Abraham and the Mosaic Law is that the Levitical priests, through Abraham, paid tithes to Melchizedek. Levi's great-grandfather was Abraham. What Abraham did represented all of his promised seed, including Levi. This evidence is stronger in the eastern mind-set of the Bible than in western society.

Conclusions from Evidence Presented: Melchizedek's Priesthood Replaced Levi's Priesthood

7:11 If, therefore, perfection were by the Levitical priesthood (for under it the people received the law), what further need was there that another priest should rise after the order of Melchisedec, and not be called after the order of Aaron?

"If therefore" begins drawing conclusions from the evidence presented in verses 4-10, which began with "now consider." On the basis of the Levitical priesthood Israel "received the law," that is, all of the Mosaic Law! Since this is a discussion of tithing, one must conclude that "the law" must also include tithing. A compound Greek noun-verb here means that the law was "legislated" and "enacted" through them. After being initiated by God, the "legislated" law of tithing and other offerings provided for the

very existence of the Levitical priesthood, and, in turn, the Levitical priesthood gave the whole law to Israel.

"If therefore perfection were" (or could have been achieved) through the Levitical priesthood implies that something was lacking. The problem was that *nothing, absolutely nothing,* in the system of laws that established their priesthood, or that resulted from the ministry of their priesthood, had been able to produce the perfection required by God! This included tithing! *All the financial support in the world cannot, and will not, produce a moral priesthood (or clergy).* Therefore, there was need for another greater priesthood.

In Acts 15:5-22, the apostles in Jerusalem, being Jewish Christians, had not required Paul to teach the Gentiles to observe the Mosaic Law and temple-tithing. However, due to a lack of spiritual insight, they still required themselves and other Jewish Christians to continue observing all of the law. This error caused a multitude of problems which Paul faced and tried to correct in his letters, especially Romans, Galatians, Ephesians, Colossians, and 2 Corinthians, chapter 3. This failure to understand the impact of the gospel on the Mosaic Law also caused the situation in the church that was being addressed by this letter to the Hebrews.

Since all four "evidences" in verses 4-10 involved tithing, it is therefore logical to conclude that the "law" being discussed in verse 11 must also include the law of tithing in Numbers 18. This is especially true since the first use of both "law" and "commandment" in Hebrews refers to tithing. In verse 5, tithing was singled out of the entire law because it best enabled the Levitical priesthood to exist. The Levitical priesthood, like human organizations, began with the means to support it.

"Order of Melchizedek." The writer of Hebrews returns again to Psalm 110 to discuss the consequences of understanding and applying Christ's Messianic high priesthood to the order of Melchizedek, instead of to the order of the Levitical ordinance.

The Second Key Text

7:12 For the priesthood being changed, there is made of necessity a change also of the law.

"Being changed" begins this Greek sentence for emphasis. The Greek word *"metatithemenees"* (metatiqeme/nh$) is a present passive participle. It is a metamorphosis, a transposition, a change from one to another (Strong's 3346). As used in Scripture, it means a great change. The word describes Jacob's bones moving from Egypt to Canaan (Acts 7:16), the Galatians' apostasy from the gospel (Gal. 1:6), Enoch's translation (Heb. 11:5) and apostates (Jude 4). The following verses make it clear that this great "change" in the priesthood was its total abolishment and replacement.

"There is made of necessity" (comments at verse 18).

"A change also of the law." This is an interesting phrase because the Greek omits the article "the." While most versions insert the article, the New American Standard omits it. The Greek article appears with "law" in verses 5, 11, 19, and 28, but is missing in verses 12 and 16. Since the Mosaic Law does not govern both sides of the "change," it is probably best to omit the article and let the word "law" refer to a "principle." Context leads to the conclusion that the "principle" being changed *"from"* is *the* Mosaic Law. On the other hand, the "principle" being changed *"to"* is an eternal one which is not governed by any mortal or man-made set of laws. The following texts expand on this principle.

The instant that Christ died, "the priesthood" was changed by being abolished. The veil in the temple was ripped open and the Passover lamb's blood was replaced by Christ's blood. The result changed the history of the world. The high priesthood of Aaron was replaced by the Melchizedek high priesthood of Jesus Christ and the regular priesthood of the other priests was replaced by the New Covenant doctrine of the "priesthood of all believers." (See 1 Pet. 2:5, 9; Rev. 1:6; 5:9.)

Exactly what was "changed"?—the law, or ordinance, which established the Levitical priesthood—especially the primary law of tithing! Neither the change in the high priesthood nor the change in the regular priesthood were taught in the Mosaic Law. The "law" or "principle" which now establishes the office of Jesus Christ (and also believer-priests) is not derived from any kind of written or engraved law whatsoever, and this includes tithing! Instead, the principles of grace and faith are linked to the eternal nature of God which supersedes the law.

Any change in the priesthood itself would make necessary changes in *all* the laws governing and supporting the priesthood, especially tithing.

7:13 For he of whom these things are spoken pertains to another tribe, of which no man gave attendance at the altar.
7:14 For it is evident that our Lord sprang out of Judah—of which tribe Moses spoke nothing concerning priesthood.

In the phrase, *"For he of whom these things are spoken,"* the writer of Hebrews begins pulling all of the evidences and conclusions together into the person of Jesus Christ. This "change of the law" was not minor, but catastrophic to the entire Levitical system! Jesus was from the tribe of Judah which was forbidden by the law to officiate as priests. Finally, the author makes it clear that he was speaking about Jesus Christ, and not the historical Melchizedek.

"Moses spoke nothing" about a change of the priesthood from Levi to another tribe. Whereas large portions of Exodus, Leviticus, Numbers, and Deuteronomy describe Levi's financial support structure, authority, and duties, *absolutely nothing* is said in the law about how a priesthood from Judah should be financially supported and serve! The reasons are, first, Christ's priesthood is completely new and beyond the law. Second, tithing to support a "priesthood of every believer" does not require tithing at all. And, third, the New Covenant structure of pastor-teachers, evangelists, and deacons is foreign to the Old Covenant system. Therefore, by logic

and extension concerning tithing, neither can anything in the law be legitimately used to dictate how the New Covenant structure should operate! The idea of grace-giving is even superior to the basic Old Covenant idea of free-will offerings.

7:15 And it is yet far more evident [that], when another priest arises after the similitude of Melchisedec,
7:16 Who is made, not after the law of a carnal [physical] commandment, but after the power of an endless [indestructible] life.

While it was *"evident"* that Moses spoke nothing in the law about a priest from Judah, it "is yet far more evident" that Moses in the law spoke nothing about a priest after the likeness of Melchizedek, who was—of all things—a Gentile! While it would be difficult enough trying to explain financially supporting an Israelite Judaic-priesthood from the Mosaic Law, it would be far more difficult trying to explain supporting a Gentile priesthood with roots *outside* of the heritage of Israel, for instance, that of Melchizedek. This dilemma can be solved only by doing away with the entire Mosaic Law, or, at the very least, that part of the law relating to the establishment of the priesthood.

"Not after the law of a carnal [physical] commandment" must, in its context, include the commandment of tithing mentioned in verse 5. This reinforces the statement that "Moses spoke nothing concerning [the] priesthood" beyond Levi, and especially not beyond Israel itself. The author of Hebrews has now taken the reader *outside* of the confines of the Mosaic Law for an answer to the legitimacy of Christ's high priesthood! Clearly, Christ's priesthood, the priesthood of believers, and the ministry of pastor-teachers and other church workers are NOT governed by instructions in the Mosaic Law!

"But after the power of an endless [indestructible] life." What a statement! The "commandment," "law," or (better) "principle," that authorizes and

makes Christ's priesthood work, comes from his divine eternal character which preceded the law. This remark is drawn from Psalm 110:4's statement about Melchizedek being a priest "forever." Because of this, he cannot fail! Because of this, we, as priest-believers cannot fail! The church will be victorious!

Again, in its basic context, this primarily refers to "the priest's office [which has] commandment in the law to collect a tenth," from verse 5 (which refers back to Numbers 18:19-28)! In extension, however, it applies to every aspect of the Levitical priesthood, including dress code, ritual anointing, how to offer sacrifices, etc. Whereas Levi had the ordinance of Numbers 18 from the law establishing his priesthood and support by tithing and other sacrifices, Christ's greater priesthood needs neither! Christ has the power, the authority of God!

"Grace" principles of support, motivated by love for God, out-give legalistic forced principles of support such as tithing. Christ is the high priest of the church, which means every believer. Now every believer is personally a priest—not giving tithes to other priests, but, as priests themselves, offering sacrifices of praise and thanksgiving. Christ is the head and the priesthood of believers is his body, this means his "power" flows into us and becomes our power. Therefore, the church does not need to use the weak Mosaic Law-power of tithing to further its goals; it has the eternal "indestructible" life-power of grace and faith from Jesus Christ!

7:17 For he testifies, You are a priest forever after the order of Melchisedec.

Psalm 110:4, again quoted here, is the key point of the entire book of Hebrews. It is directly quoted, or referred to, five (5) times in chapter 7 alone, and eight (8) times in Hebrews (5:6, 10; 6:20; 7:11, 17, 20, 21, 28).

The Most Important Text

7:18 For [on the one hand: NAS] there is truly a disannulling of the commandment going before for the weakness and unprofitableness [uselessness] thereof.

"On the one hand" (Greek: *men...de...*construction) God removed something that had been around since the time of Moses. He removed the ordinances of the Levitical priesthood in order to establish the greater eternal priesthood of Jesus Christ.

"There is a setting aside of a former commandment." The correct exegetical context of this chapter can *only* point to Numbers, chapter 18, as the "former commandment" being discussed and first mentioned in verse 5! The conclusive statement of this verse is the key statement of this chapter. Whether or not one cherishes tithing is totally irrelevant. What does the Scripture say? What does this verse mean in its context? These questions must be answered honestly. If tithing is indeed included in this verse, then the New Covenant Christian must deal with such conclusion in an honest manner.

Again, Numbers 18 is "the" "commandment in the law" from 7:5 which established the support structure and described the broad duties of the Levitical priesthood. Numbers 18 is the basic statute/ordinance which details the fundamental use of the first tithe by both the Levites who served in the tabernacle and the priests who offered sacrifices before the altar. As mentioned in the discussion of verse 5, the definitive first use of both "law" and "commandment" in the book of Hebrews are both in the context of tithing.

It is unsound biblical exegesis to claim that 7:18 abolished every ordinance pertaining to the Levitical priesthood, except tithing! In reality, by *first* abolishing tithing (its chief financial support) the priesthood would end. The domino effect from abolishing tithing knocks down every other authority and function of Levitical priests. This is exactly why tithing has such an important role in Hebrews 7.

Comments from Noted Biblical Scholars on Hebrews 7

Consider what some well-known Bible commentators and expositors say about the scope of Hebrews 7:5; 7:12; and 7:18. They agree that Christ abolished the *entire* paraphernalia, structure, or apparatus, of the Levitical priesthood, that is, everything remotely connected to it! After reading this chapter and the conclusions below, it is difficult to understand how any logical person, intent on preaching God's truth for the New Covenant church, can still say that tithing is a New Covenant doctrine!

William Barclay:

The law of tithes is laid down in Numbers 18:20-21. There Aaron is told that the Levites will have no actual territory in the promised land laid down for them but that they are to receive a tenth part of everything for their service.... From beginning to end the Jewish priesthood was dependent on physical things.... The *whole* paraphernalia of the ceremonial law was *wiped out* in the priesthood of Jesus (italics mine).[72]

Albert Barnes:

But the meaning is, that since a large number of laws—constituting a code of considerable extent and importance—was given for the regulation of the priesthood, and in reference to the rites of religion, which they were to observe or superintend, it followed that when their office was superseded by "one of a *wholly different order*," the law which had regulated them vanished also, or ceased to be binding (italics mine).[73]

---

72   William Barclay, *Daily Study Bible Series: The Letter to the Hebrews* (Philadelphia: Westminster, 1976), s.v. "Heb. 7:5-19."

73   *Barnes*, s.v. "Heb. 7:12-18.

Adam Clarke:

There is a *total abrogation*, of the former law, relative to the Levitical priesthood (italics mine).[74]

Louis H. Evans Jr.:

The sacrifices were to be provided for by the people by means of tithes brought to the priests. An interesting comparison is implied between the Levites and the Son. *Whereas the dependency of Levites is upon the obedient tithe-giving of the Israelites, the Son is dependent upon no human resource.* This is one more factor of superiority of the Son over the Levitical priests (italics mine).[75]

Matthew Henry:

Changing the Levitical priesthood also means changing the whole economy with it. There being so near a relation between the priesthood and the law, the dispensation could not be the same under another priesthood; *a new priesthood must be under a new regulation, managed in another way, and by rules proper to its nature and order* (italics mine).[76]

Jamieson, Fausset and Brown:

These presuppose a transference of the priesthood; this carries with it a change also of the law which is *inseparably bound up with the priesthood: both stand and fall together.* And, as the Levitical priesthood and the law are inseparable, a repealing of the law also (italics mine).[77]

---

74   *Clarke's,* s.v. "Heb. 7:18."
75   Louis H. Evans, Jr., *The Communicator's Commentary: Hebrews* (Waco: Word, 1985), s.v. "Heb. 7:18."
76   *Henry,* s.v. "Heb. 7:18."
77   *Jamieson,* s.v. "Heb. 7:18."

A. M. Stibbs:

Also, the priesthood was so fundamental to the Old Covenant between God and His people (the whole relationship was constituted in dependence upon its ministry), that *any change in the order of priesthood must of necessity imply and involve a change in the whole constitution;* i.e. it implies nothing less than an accompanying new, and indeed better, covenant (italics mine).[78]

"Setting aside" (Greek: *atheteesis;*) (Strong's N.T. 115), is the first word in this Greek sentence for emphasis. According to *Thayer's Greek Lexicon,* it has stronger meanings such as "disannulling," "annulling," "putting away," "cancellation," "abolition," and "rejection."[79] In Hebrews 9:26, *atheteesis* means that Christ appeared once to "put away" sins by the sacrifice of himself.

"For the weakness and unprofitableness thereof" (Greek: asthenes kai anoopheles). The Bible clearly states that *all* of the laws concerning the Levitical priesthood (including tithing) had proven to be "without strength and without profit, or advantage." The NAS and RSV read "because of its weakness and uselessness"; the NIV says "because it was weak and useless"; and the TLB paraphrases "because it didn't work." For other texts using this word for "profit," see 1 Cor. 15:32; 1 Tim. 4:8; 2 Tim. 3:16; Tit. 3:8; 5:9; Jas. 2:14, 16.

Simply stated, the laws which established the Levitical priesthood and detailed its functions, including tithing, did not accomplish the spiritual maturity which God had intended them to provide. Yet it is strange how many fundamental conservative Christians set aside the first 27 chapters and 29 verses of Leviticus as being Old Covenant, but keep the last five verses on tithing (27:30-34) as applicable to the New Covenant church.

---

78   *New Bible Comm.,* s.v. "Heb. 7:18."

79   *Thayer's,* s.v. "*atheteesis;*"

Yet, it is as if the last few verses do not exist within the context of the last chapter and the entire book of Leviticus. As one reads all of Leviticus, chapter 27, in context, everything said about tithing is also said about the other items in chapter 27 which New Covenant Christians almost always set aside.

It is also strange how so many theologians can agree that Hebrews 7:18 refers to *all* of the ordinances relating to the Levitical priesthood, and then resurrect tithing as a "strong," "profitable," and "necessary" New Covenant doctrine.

Tithing Had Become a Powerless and Profitless Doctrine

1. Tithing, along with all of the other Levitical ordinances and statutes, had failed to produce the spiritual perfection and maturity within believers which God required (7:11, 19; 9:9, 11; 10:1).

2. Since the Levitical ordinances (including tithing) had proven weak and unprofitable, there was an inherent need of a New Covenant (7:19, 22; 8:7-13; 10:1-9).

3. Old Covenant tithing was not motivated by grace, love, or the burden for lost souls. Under the Mosaic Law, it did not matter whether one paid tithes out of sincere desire, paid grudgingly, or paid without being cheerful. One must pay, regardless of attitude or the condition of the heart.

Exod. 23:32 You shall make no covenant with them, nor with their gods.
[Also Deuteronomy 7:2.]

4. Tithing was not oriented towards evangelism. As a matter of biblical truth, national Israel was commanded not to share its covenant with any other nation; the covenant was their distinction which set them apart (Num. 18:19-21; Lev. 27:34; Mal. 3:6-9). Even today Jews do

not deliberately evangelize or attempt to convert others.

5. Tithes limited the priesthood. Only one part of one family in one tribe could "draw near" into the presence of God—Aaron's house. Levites and priests were not encouraged to establish independent outposts for evangelism of other nations. Today, too many churches totally ignore the clear implication of verse 18. In practice, they replace the tithe-receiving aspect of the Levitical priesthood, not with the priesthood of believers, but with tithe-receiving pastor-teachers. Too many ignore New Covenant giving principles of grace and insist that pastors be paid a tithe according to the commandment of the Mosaic Law. The pastors then keep more than ten percent of the total tithe, and also own and inherit property—all contrary to the law itself. In doing so, both churches and pastors "set aside" better giving principles of grace, based on God's "indestructible power," and return to the "weak" and "unprofitable" principles of tithing.

6. Tithing too often receives a greater priority than evangelism. I have personally known pastors who preach on tithing at least monthly, yet the members do not have a burden for souls, are not trained in soul-winning, and the churches are weak, dying, or dead. Preaching tithing is not the Scriptural ingredient that guarantees successful church growth!

7. The New Testament clearly shows that tithing, along with circumcision, Sabbath-keeping and adherence to food laws became profitless marks of boastful self-righteousness among the legalistic Pharisees and scribes.

8. It is not by accident that the only three uses of the words "tithe" and "tithes" recorded in the Gospels record the hypocrisy and failure of legalistic Jews who boasted of their tithing achievements.

9. Even in the church, tithing does more harm than good. First, church leaders tend to be wealthier tithe-payers, while better spiritual leaders who cannot give as much because of family sickness and other legiti-

mate losses are left out of leadership roles. *The Bible does not teach that the financially competent are also the best spiritual leaders.* Neither does the Bible teach that an inability to give disqualifies one from a church office. There is no justification in adding to the Bible a requirement that church officers are required to give ten percent of their income. Excluding the financially less-fortunate deprives the church of their God-given gifts and competent leadership abilities. The resulting unbalanced leadership is spiritually weak.

10. A second reason that tithing is more harmful than good in the church relates its abuse of tithing and the public reputation of the church. Frankly, the legalistic strict preaching of tithing has given many churches a bad reputation and a weak witness.

11. The most important reason that tithing does more harm than good relates to the gospel. Teaching tithing to meet financial needs actually robs the church of God's blessing available from using the Spirit-approved New Covenant approach. Those pastors and churches that teach tithing will never experience the greater success they will enjoy from God's hand when they replace tithing sermons with sermons about soul-winning. The success of the New Covenant church proves that the first century poor, women, children and slaves were motivated by the desire to see souls won to the Lord.

12. Great evangelistic movements, great revivals and great growing churches (whether tithe-advocates or not) occur only when church members are burdened for the lost. The power is in gospel principles, not in principles of the law. Sincere believers, burdened for lost souls, will give out of a love response for the lost without recourse to any legal prodding. Churches that are not growing are churches without a burden for the lost.

13. Since tithing is included within the scope of Hebrews 7:18, one must conclude that teaching tithing is equivalent to teaching a spiritually "weak" and "unprofitable" doctrine.

7:19 For the law made nothing perfect, but the bringing in of a better hope did, by which we *draw near* to God.

7:25 Therefore he is able also to save them to the uttermost that come to [draw near: NAS] God by him, seeing he ever lives to make intercession for them.

"The law made nothing perfect." It is clear that neither a perfect sacrifice, nor a perfect fellowship, nor a perfect system of giving were accomplished under the terms of the Mosaic Law, or Old Covenant.

"But, on the other hand," concluding the thought introduced in verse 18, God replaced the old with the better; he took away all weak unprofitable legalistic principles and replaced them with better principles of grace. Accepting the truth of Christ's high priesthood brings in a "better hope" than tithing and the Levitical priesthood could ever bring in. That "better hope" is the person of Jesus Christ (6:19; 9:24).

If and when the Jewish Christians in Jerusalem realized this fact, they could look beyond the physical temple to Christ. They could finally be free from, and forget, the Levitical priesthood and its ordinances. The author of Hebrews was trying to stop his readers from supporting and depending on the temple services. They must stop Old Covenant homage, sacrifices, and tithes and offerings to that priesthood. They must accept their own priesthood as believers, and accept Jesus Christ as high priest. That was the key to success. Sadly, however, history records that they never accepted the truth and eventually self-destructed.

"Draw near" (also 7:25) is another direct reference to the original tithing law in Numbers 18 which uses similar terminology four time (vv. 3, 4, 7 and 22). The Hebrew term (Strong's O.T. 7126) is common and can mean "approach, come near, draw near, or present as offering." The abolition of the Levitical priesthood, with its prohibitions about "drawing near" to God, opened the way again to the priesthood of every believer.

Before Calvary, only Levitical priests could "draw near" to God; the penalty for disobedience was death! Now each believer-priest "comes boldly to the throne of grace" (4:16). We "draw near" because of our "better hope." God saves us forever because we "draw near" as believer-priests (7:25). We draw near, not with a tithe and a real sacrificial lamb, but with the blood of Jesus Christ and a committed and victorious lifestyle. Through Christ's blood we "draw near" in full assurance of faith, having a clean conscience (10:22).

7:20 And inasmuch as, not without an oath, he was made priest.
7:21 (For those priests were made without an oath, but this with an oath by him that said to him, The Lord swore and will not repent, You are a priest forever after the order of Melchisedec).

7:28 For the law makes men high priests which have infirmity, but the word of the oath, which was since the law, makes the Son, who is consecrated for evermore.

The "oath" refers back to the discussion of 6:13-20. Christ's priesthood will succeed because God is able to perform his oath and fulfill his needs. And, since Christ is the high priest of the church, and its members are priest-believers, then the church is assured of its success. Therefore, the church is not dependent on any "commandment in the law" (like tithing or otherwise) to assure its continued success. Success was assured by the oath of God the Father to God the Son! What a marvelous thought! Preaching Christ has produced many successful churches, schools, and ministries which do not find it necessary to teach tithing. They have found better principles of grace.

"The Lord has sworn and will not change his mind" (NAS) is from Psalm 110:4 yet another time. However, for the first time, the first part of the text is included, and the last part is omitted. This emphasizes that God has

no intention of ever going back to the ordinances of the Levitical priest-hood or any part of them for success. His promises to Christ are forever.

7:22 By so much was Jesus made a surety of a better testament.

Concerning Melchizedek, the detailed discussion now concludes. After chapters 5, 6 and 7 he (and tithing) are not mentioned again in Hebrews. The post-Calvary discussion of both Melchizedek and tithing both begins and ends in the book of Hebrews.

The point has been made and proven with Scripture and deductive rea-soning from Scripture. Since the Levitical priesthood was limited, weak, and mortal, it could not possibly bring in perfection concerning sin and salvation. Therefore, it was "fitting," or "perfectly suited," that Jesus, the Melchizedek-high priest, prophesied in Psalm 110, would of necessity replace it and laws governing it (including tithing). That is the only way he could "bring in" the perfection of salvation that the law could not do.

Summary:
1. Tithing is inseparable from "the commandment in the law" that pro-vided for, appointed, and set apart the Levitical priesthood (7:5).
2. Tithing is used in each of four evidences to prove that Christ's priest-hood is superior to that of the Mosaic Law (7:4-10).
3. The Old Covenant methods of worshiping God through tithes, offerings, sacrifices and Levitical priests failed (7:11).
4. Failure of the old system implied a need for a totally new system of service and worship (7:11).
5. The change of priesthood must also bring in entirely new principles of service and worship (7:12).
6. Since Christ came from Judah, it is evident that nothing in the law that related to the Levitical priesthood (including tithing) could be carried over to the new priesthood of Christ (7:13-14).

7. Psalm 110 patterned the new priesthood after a non-Jewish Melchizedek. This fact makes it far more evident that nothing in the law regarding the Levitical priesthood (including tithing) should be carried over to the priesthood of Christ (7:15).

8. Therefore one must conclude that Christ's Melchizedek priesthood is not governed by any set of laws given to men. His priesthood is governed by the power of Eternal God (7:16-17).

9. The old commandment which financed, established and described the Levitical priesthood's duties has been set aside. It was inherently weak and unprofitable (7:18).

10. Man can become spiritually perfect only through applying the principles of the better hope (7:19).

11. Since the Levitical priesthood has been replaced by the high priesthood of Christ and the priesthood of all believers, all believers, as priests who do not require tithes, can draw near to God in worship (7:19).

12. The success of Christ's priesthood and his church is as sure as God's oath to him (7:20-27).

▼

CHAPTER 20

EPHESIANS 2: 14-16; COLOSSIANS 2:13-17 ORDINANCES OF THE LAW ENDED AT CALVARY

Tithing Was a Statute and Ordinance of the Mosaic Law

Num. 18:23 But the Levites shall do the service of the tabernacle of the congregation, and they shall bear their iniquity; it shall be a *statute [ordinance]* forever throughout your generations, that among the children of Israel they have no inheritance.

Num. 18:24 But the *tithes* of the children of Israel, which they offer as a heave offering to the LORD, I have given to the Levites to inherit;

therefore I have said to them, Among the children of Israel they shall have no inheritance.

Mal. 3:7 Even from the days of your fathers you have gone away from my *ordinances [statutes]* and have not kept them....

As previously discussed in the chapters on Numbers 18, Deuteronomy 12 and Malachi 3, tithing was a statute, or ordinance, of the Mosaic Law. The exact wording of the tithe statute itself, Numbers 18, uses the word, "statute," in verses 8, 11, 19, and 23. Numbers 18:23-24 contains the most accurate wording of the purpose of tithing found in the entire Bible. Tithes were food products from the land of Israel which were to compensate the Levites for their service to God as a replacement for their lost land inheritance rights in Israel. Tithes are included in the "statute" found in Deuteronomy 12, as seen in verses 1, 6, 11 and 17. Those who often quote Malachi 3:8-10 usually omit God's rebuke of Israel for violating the "ordinances," or "statutes," in 3:7.

Ephesians 2:12-16 Abolished Law Ordinances

Eph. 2:12 That at that time you were without Christ, being aliens from the commonwealth of Israel, and strangers from the covenants of promise, having no hope, and without God in the world.
Eph. 2:13 But now, in Christ Jesus, you who sometimes were far off are *made near* by the blood of Christ.
Eph. 2:14 For he is our peace, who has made both one, and has broken down *the middle wall of partition* between us—
Eph. 2:15 Having abolished in his flesh the enmity, even *the law of commandments contained in ordinances,* to make in himself of two one new man, so making peace.
Eph. 2:16 And that he might reconcile both to God in one body by the cross, having slain the enmity thereby.

Concerning the abolishment of Mosaic Law ordinances, including tithing, Ephesians, chapter 2 plainly teaches:

1. Gentiles had been far off from God (vv. 11-12).
2. The blood of Christ brought them near (v. 13). As believer-priests, they could "come near" and approach God directly.
3. Christ made Jew and Gentile one (v. 14).
4. However, he did not make us one by forcing Gentiles to observe ordinances of the law (v. 14).
5. Instead, he made us one by breaking down the wall which divided the two groups of believers (v. 14).
6. The wall which divided us was "the law of commandments contained in ordinances" (v. 15).
7. Again, Christ destroyed the separating enmity (v. 16).

The Jewish temple had a series of walls which subdivided its people, created inequalities, and created culture differences. The first wall distinguished between the high priest and other priests; the second wall separated priests from Levites; a third wall separated Levites from other Hebrews; a fourth wall separated Hebrew men from Hebrew women, and a fifth wall separated all Hebrews from Gentiles. A prominent warning sign promised death to any Gentile who dared to pass beyond their wall into the confines of the temple to worship Yahweh.

The "ordinances" of the law defined at least the two most important of these walls; Solomon's temple arrangement established other walls; and the law itself even served as a partition (Mark 12:1; Neh. 9:13; Ezek. 20:11-12). Various ordinances restricted worship for women, sick persons, persons with missing body parts, persons of mixed genealogies, persons with ceremonial defilement, plus many more who were excluded from full worship and acceptance.

The tithing ordinance was one of the many ordinances which made sharp distinctions between Jew and Gentile, and, of necessity, must be abolished if the church were to be united into one spiritual organism.

Tithes were only received from Jewish landowners and from the sacred land of Israel. Ordinances defined the daily lives of every Jewish person and ordinances defined everything the priest was and did.

Tithing, and its associated offerings, was included in the very *first* ordinance of the Levitical priesthood. Financially speaking, tithing "created" the priesthood by enabling it to exist! In turn the priesthood received, enacted, controlled and enforced other ordinances such as circumcision, holy days, food laws, and every other distinctly Hebrew custom.

Gentiles did not qualify under the ordinances as tithe-payers. Under the Old Covenant, Gentiles could never be fully considered as God's people; they could not inherit God's land and, thus, had no holy land from which to pay tithes. Even Gentiles who had been circumcised as proselytes were always considered "at the gate," rather than full Jews. A Jewish priest would never accept a supposed "tithe" from a person who was not a Jew or from land which was considered defiled pagan dust. Therefore, tithing must be included among those ordinances which were walls between Jews and Gentiles.

Colossians 2:13-17 Abolished Law Ordinances

Col. 2:13 And you, being dead in your sins and the uncircumcision of your flesh, he has quickened together with him, having forgiven you all trespasses—
Col. 2:14 Blotting out the handwriting of *ordinances [statutes]* that was against us, which was contrary to us, and took it out of the way, *nailing it to his cross.*
Col. 2:15 And having spoiled principalities and powers, he made a show of them openly, triumphing over them in it.
Col. 2:16 Let no man therefore judge you in food, or in drink, or in respect of a holy day, or of the New Moon, or of the Sabbath days—
Col. 2:17 Which are a shadow of things to come, but the body is of Christ.

Colossians discusses a Gnostic-like heresy that had combined some pagan practices with restrictions already existing under the Old Covenant Mosaic Law. False Jewish-Christian teachers (and possibly others) were attempting to force those practices on Gentile Christians. This perverted the gospel.

In its discussion on tithing, the *Wycliffe Bible Dictionary of Theology* says, "The silence of the N.T. writers, particularly Paul, regarding the present validity of the tithe can be explained only on the ground that the dispensation of grace has no more place for a law of tithing than it has for a law on circumcision."[80]

Concerning the abolishment of Mosaic Law ordinances, Colossians, chapter 2 teaches:

1. The Christian who has been re-created anew in Jesus Christ has been forgiven of all trespasses (v. 13).
2. God's forgiveness included the "blotting out the handwriting of *ordinances* which was against us." The NAS reads "having canceled out the certificate of debt consisting of *decrees* against us." The NIV reads, "having canceled the written code, with its *regulations*, that was against us, that stood opposed to us." The RSV reads, "having canceled the bond which stood against us with its *legal demands*" (v. 14).
3. Jesus metaphorically "nailed" these "ordinances," "decrees," "regulations," or "legal demands" to the cross (v. 14).
4. By doing so, he triumphed over our adversaries (v. 15).
5. As a result of Christ's actions, we are not to judge one another, specifically regarding the ordinances of unclean food and holy days (v. 16).

---

80   Everett F. Harrison, Geoffrey W. Bromiley, and Carl F. Henry, editors., *Wycliffe Dictionary of Theology*, Orig. *Baker's Dictionary*, 1960 (Peabody: Hendrickson, 1999), s.v. "tithe."

6. These ordinances were only mere imperfect and temporary shadows of future things (v. 17) (Heb. 10:1).
7. The reality and substance to which the ordinances pointed is Jesus Christ (v. 17).

While it is certain that unknown Gnostic-like heresies contributed to the problems of the church in Colossae, it is equally clear that some Jewish mixture of Mosaic Law principles with grace principles was also involved. Jewish and Gentile Christians were most likely accusing one another of violating each other's traditional food laws and holy days. We must remember that each culture had its own set of ordinances, and not just the Jews.

This problem plagued the early church because it had not decided what to do with all of the ordinances of the Mosaic Law in light of Calvary. This problem is faced in Acts 10, 15, 21, Romans 14, 1 Corinthians 8, Galatians 2-4, Ephesians 2, Colossians 2, and all of Hebrews. Again, it is important to note the double standard and confusion over law ordinances which existed in the Jerusalem at least thirty five years after Calvary.

Acts 21:21 And they are informed of you, that you are teaching all the Jews which are among the Gentiles to forsake Moses, saying that they ought not to circumcise their children, neither to walk after the customs [ordinances and traditions].

Acts 21:24 Take them, and purify yourself with them, and pay their expenses, that they may shave their heads; and all may know that those things, whereof they were informed concerning you, are nothing; but that you yourself also are walking orderly, and are keeping the law.

Acts 21:25 *Concerning the Gentiles who believe*, we have written and concluded that they observe no such thing, except only that they keep themselves from things offered to idols, and from blood, and from strangled, and from fornication.

Luke correctly preserved the erring words of the leaders of the Jerusalem church. The original church decision is found in chapter 15. However, Paul was right! The Jewish-Christian church leaders, including James and Peter, at Jerusalem were wrong! This church squabble over ordinances, by forcing Paul to go to the temple, indirectly caused Paul's imprisonment in Caesarea and later imprisonment in Rome.

Why were Jewish-Christians still going to the temple? Because at least until the temple was destroyed in A.D. 70, most Jewish Christians continued to observe ALL of the ordinances of the Mosaic Law—including tithing. They continued to worship at the temple and support the Levitical priesthood.

Acts 15:19 Therefore my sentence is, that we do not trouble, which from among the Gentiles are turned to God;
Acts 15:20 But that we write to them, that they abstain from pollution of idols, and from fornication, and from things strangled, and from blood.

The Jews at the Jerusalem Christian church only understood half of the truth concerning the Mosaic Law after Calvary. They correctly understood that no Gentile was ever to be placed under any ordinance of the Mosaic Law which was only applicable to Old Covenant Jews. Therefore they completely released Gentile Christians from the necessity of keeping any ordinance of the Mosaic Law—*including tithing*. The four restrictions all relate to pagan worship which was especially offensive to sensitive Jews.

For the following reasons, tithes must be included in the list of abolished ordinances in Colossians.

1. Both covenant theology and dispensational theology interpret law ordinances as abolished at Calvary; the middle theological approach also discards it as cultic, instead of an eternal principle. *The New*

Scofield Reference Bible comments at Colossians 2:14-17 include "law observances were abolished in Christ."[81]

2. The second "festival tithe" was essential for the food and drink offerings at the "festivals" of verse 16. There would be no food and drink offerings without tithing.

3. Just as circumcision was included in Colossians 2:8-11, ALL ordinances are included in the "shadows" of verse 17 and Hebrews 10:1.

4. Dispensational theology teaches that the Mosaic Law, the Old Covenant, the commandments, ordinances, and judgments are all part of ONE indivisible revelation which belonged to Old Covenant Israel. Only those laws which are restated in the principles and wording of the New Covenant have been passed on to the Christian church.

5. None of the ordinances, including tithing, could be kept perfectly and resulted in the "handwriting of ordinances which was against us." This was an open admission in one's own handwriting of guilt. Nobody (but Christ) could spiritually, or physically, obey every sacrificial law, every food ordinance, every festival ordinance, or every minute ordinance of giving. All of these ordinances were only "a shadow of things to come" (2:17; Heb. 8:5; 10:1).

6. The Greek word, "*dogma*," translated in Ephesians and Colossians as "regulations" (NIV) and "decrees" (NAS) is translated "ordinances" in the King James Version. The King James translators could have given the word its more common meaning of "doctrine," but recognized its context and relationship to the Old Covenant "ordinances."

7. Tithing was not mentioned as an "exception" to the rule decreed by the Jerusalem church leaders in the book of Acts.

---

81   *Scofield*, s.v. "Col. 2:14-17."

Summary

Ephesians 2:15 says that Christ "abolished" ordinances. Colossians 2:14 says that he "canceled" or "blotted out" ordinances. Since tithing was the key foundational ordinance that made possible the practical everyday operation of the sanctuary service and its festivals, it must be included in that part of Israel's religious life that Christ ended. This is a logical hermeneutical principle. Whether or not one understands the abolished ordinances as including all of the Mosaic Law, or just part of it—even abolishing the one ceremonial or cultic part of it makes New Covenant tithing hard to explain.

Finally, wherever tithing is found in God's Word, it is usually surrounded by other religious "ordinances" that almost all Christians readily understand as being "nailed to the cross" and not applicable in the New Covenant.

CHAPTER 21

1 PETER 2: 9-10
THE PRIESTHOOD OF BELIEVERS
ELIMINATES THE PURPOSE OF TITHING

[Original purpose of God]

Exod. 19:5 Now therefore, if you will obey my voice indeed, and keep my covenant, then you shall be a peculiar treasure to me above all people, for all the earth is mine.

Exod. 19:6 And you shall be to me *a kingdom of priests*, and a holy nation. These are the words which you shall speak to the children of Israel.

[Temporary amended purpose]

Num. 18:7 Therefore you and your sons with you shall *keep your priest's office* for every thing of the altar, and within the veil; and you shall serve: I have given your priest's office to you as a service of gift: and the stranger that *comes near* shall be put to *death*.

[Re-established original purpose]
1 Pet. 2:9 But you are a chosen generation, a royal priesthood, a holy nation, a peculiar people, that you should show forth the praises of him who has called you out of darkness into his marvelous light—
1 Pet. 2:10 Which in time past were not a people, but are now the people of God, which had not obtained mercy, but now have obtained mercy.

The New Covenant doctrine of the "priesthood of believers" is yet another important doctrine that abolishes tithing practices. In order to verify this statement, it is necessary to retrace the history of the concept of priesthood. Each of the following italicized quotations is from the *New Scofield Reference Bible* notes at 1 Peter 2:9.

"Until the law was given the head of each family was the family priest (Gen. 8:20; 26:25; 31:54)."

The patriarchs were nomadic herdsmen who moved wherever pasture was good. They would live under the jurisdiction of any number of pagan warlords such as the Egyptians, Philistines, Ammonites, Moabites and other Canaanites. Although they might occasionally have to pay taxes to the local priest-king, the family head was also the family priest. Each man built his own altar and offered sacrifices directly to God for himself and for his family. Since there was no social structure by which to help the poor, each family priest took it upon himself to aid those who were less blessed than himself.

"When the law was proposed the promise to perfect obedience was that Israel should be to God a 'kingdom of priests' (Exod. 19:6); but Israel violated the law, and God shut up the priestly office to the Aaronic family, appointing the tribe of Levi to minister to Israel, thus constituting the typical priesthood (Exod. 28:1)."

In order words, the Levitical priesthood, like the entire Old Covenant, never was God's ultimate purpose for Israel. Even before the Ten Commandments, the ordinances, and the judgments of the law were given, God declared his ultimate desire for Israel to become a kingdom of priests (Exod. 19:5-6).

However, instead of *progressing* from the family-head priesthood to the priesthood of every believer, Israel proved itself unworthy and forfeited its universal priesthood aspirations. This means that the Levitical priesthood was actually a *digression* because of Israel's sin in making idols to worship while Moses was away receiving the Ten Commandments. This sad story is found in Exodus 32. The result of Israel's sin was the limited Levitical priesthood with its death decree on any who would dare to sacrifice to God directly.

Exod. 25:2 Speak to the children of Israel, that they bring me an offering; of every man that gives it willingly with his heart you shall take my offering.

Exod. 30:16 And you shall take the atonement money of the children of Israel, and shall appoint it for the service of the tabernacle of the congregation.

What would have happened if Israel had not sinned in making and worshiping the golden calves? The scenario is not difficult to imagine.

1. Israel would have immediately become a "kingdom of priests," per Exodus 19:5-6.
2. All twelve tribes, including Levi, would have received land possession and inheritance rights.
3. Since there would be millions of priests to assist Aaron and his family, none would be gone from home long enough to require sustenance from tithing.

4. *The tithing ordinance of Numbers 18 would have never needed to be enacted.*

5. The servant duties later performed by the non-priestly Levites would be shared by all priests from all of the people.

6. Freewill offerings and the census-atonement shekel would provide funds for the sanctuary and temple. This was the plan before the Levites where chosen to substitute for all of their brothers.

"In the Church Age, all Christians are unconditionally constituted a 'kingdom of priests' (l Pet. 2:9; Rev. 1:6), the distinction which Israel failed to achieve by works. The priesthood of the Christian is, therefore, a birthright, just as every descendant of Aaron was born to the priesthood (Heb. 5:1)."

Tithing is not mentioned in the book of Exodus which assigned priestly duties only to Aaron and his sons, but did not detail the system or assistants. Since three priests could not possibly handle millions of worshipers, logic dictates that a more involved priesthood would follow. In God's original plan, this "more involved priesthood" was a priesthood of every believer (Exod. 19:5-6) to draw near to him. However, when Israel sinned, this plan was replaced by the Levitical priesthood and the tithing ordinance of Numbers 18 was enacted to support them. Therefore, tithing was only enacted as an ordinance of the law *after* God replaced the national priesthood with the very limited priesthood of the Levites.

Consequently, since tithing was not an ordinance of God *until* the Levites replaced the universal priesthood concept, there is no valid reason to believe that tithing should exist under the Christian concept's return to God's plan for the universal priesthood of believers! The believer-priest now stands in the same position today in which God originally wanted all Israel to stand in Exodus 19:6.

"The chief privilege of a priest is access to God. Under the law only the high priest could enter 'the holiest of all,' and that but once a year (Heb. 9:7);

but when Christ died, the veil, a type of Christ's human body (Heb. 10:20), was rent, so that now the believer-priests, equally with Christ the High Priest, have access to God in the holiest (Heb. 10:19-22). The High Priest is corporeally there (Heb. 4:14-16; 9:24; 10:19-22)."

Not only does the believer-priest replace the Levitical priests, he has the same privileges as the Aaronic high priest. The Aaronic priesthood definitely preceded the Levitical priesthood and the tithing ordinance. Although the extension of this concept to abolish tithing seems odd to most of us, this is because we have constructed a system of salaries, buildings, and dependencies beyond that which is taught or implied in the New Covenant. While the Apostle Paul was a very great evangelist who established many house churches, he worked as a tentmaker for his sustenance and never seriously complained. In fact, he preferred it that way. (See the chapters on 1 Corinthians 9 and Acts 20.)

"In the exercise of his office the N.T. believer-priest is a sacrificer who offers a fourfold sacrifice: (1) his own living body (Rom. 12:1; Phil. 2:17; 2 Tim. 4:6; Jas. 1:27; 1 John 3:16); (2) praise to God, "the fruit of our lips giving thanks to his name to be offered continually (Heb. 13:15; cf. Exod. 25:22, 'I will commune with you from above the mercy seat' (3) his substance (Rom. 12:13; Gal. 6:6, 10; Tit. 3:14; Heb. 13:26; 3 John 5-6); and (4) his service, i.e. 'to do good' (Heb. 13:16). Second, the New Testament priest is also an intercessor (Col. 4:12; 1 Tim. 2:1)."[82]

It is important to realize that, in the New Covenant, Christ is the high priest, and every believer is a priest (1 Pet. 2:9-10; Heb. 10:19-22; Rev. 1:6). The primary teacher of the church is neither priest nor preacher, but the Holy Spirit (John 14:15-17; 16:12-14). God said "I will put my laws

---

82   *Ibid.*, s.v. "1 Pet. 2:9."

into their mind and write them in their hearts" and "no longer will a man teach his neighbor" because "all shall know me" (Heb. 8:10-11).

The believer-priest is at the heart of the New Covenant! Instead of priests being responsible for teaching the Mosaic Law, every believer is responsible for his or her own spiritual seeking after God's will. **Every function performed by the Old Covenant priest who received tithes is NOW performed by every believer-priest.** Again, the believer-priest, and NOT the pastor-teacher, replaced the Old Covenant priest! What this truth does to the Mosaic Law ordinance of tithing should be self-evident.

The "pastor-teacher" of the New Covenant church fills an entirely new office not found in the Old Covenant rules for priests (Heb. 7:14-15). This office does NOT exist because of Mosaic Law provisions, but ministers under principles of grace and faith (Heb. 7:16). Since the connection is not linear (straight-line), there is no Scriptural justification for shifting law-tithing from Old Covenant priests to the pastor-teachers. In fact, there is Scriptural justification for *not* transferring the tithe obligations from Old Covenant priests to New Covenant pastor-teachers (Heb. 7:14-19).

The New Covenant pastor-teacher has more in common with the Old Covenant prophet, and, later, the rabbi, than its priest. Many Old Covenant prophets were not Levites. They ministered by faith, depending on God's provisions and their own hands at a trade. Therefore, it is erroneous to act as if the New Covenant pastor took up where the Old Covenant Levitical priest left off and is, therefore, due the priest's tithe.

One final important comment must be made about the doctrine of the priesthood of believers. The earliest church fathers and church historians give ample evidence that there was no distinction between the laity and clergy for almost two hundred years in the early church. When this non-distinction was lost, when the clergy evolved into a superior hierarchy, when the local bishop was transformed into a 'bishop-priest,' when this doctrine was pushed out of the way—then full-time paid clergy emerged in church history, which opened the way for tithing to re-enter much later in support of an unscriptural exclusive priesthood in the church. While there is nothing inherently wrong with a full-time paid clergy, the original advocates of tithing in the church (such as Cyprian) did so on the false premise that the priesthood of believers had been replaced by an Old Testament equivalent of the priesthood and its rituals.

CHAPTER 22

▼

1 CORINTHIANS 9: 1-19
PAUL REFUSED
HIS "RIGHT" OF SUPPORT

First Corinthians, chapter 9, is very important for those seeking to know the truth about New Covenant tithing. Why? Because it focuses on the "right," "power, or "authority" (Greek: *exousia*) of gospel workers to compensation. If tithing were a New Covenant law for support of the gospel worker, then this would be the most appropriate chapter to discover the doctrine.

This letter was written near the middle of the first century between 20-30 years after Calvary. As long as the Jewish synagogues allowed Christians to worship with them on their Saturday Sabbaths, the Roman authorities considered them merely as an offshoot of Judaism. However, those Christians who refused to be connected to Judaism were considered to be an "illegal" religion, but were not generally hunted and persecuted until

Christianity became an "outlaw" religion around A.D. 80. Until approximately A.D. 260 the church meeting places would be hiding places in homes, abandoned places, catacombs, or caves—wherever meetings could be held without discovery by the Roman Empire, which was constantly searching for those guilty of sedition and urging its overthrow.

This historical data is important because our contemporary mind-set wants us to picture "churches" as we know and recognize churches today, which is not true. Except for the state-approved synagogues for Jewish worship, early Christians had no signs on the door and no buildings to proclaim as their own. At first they found some safety blending in and appearing to be a Jewish offshoot, and by not trying to be too obviously different.

The subject of full-time support for the gospel minister centers on verse 14. While theologians and full-time gospel workers usually argue for their tithe support from this text, church historians usually disagree concerning tithing. Church historians, regardless of denomination, often agree that it is highly unlikely that early Christian leaders received full-time compensation for ministering to churches. First, like Paul, many of the Christianized scribes and lawyers would have refused total sustenance for teaching God's word because of their traditional Jewish prohibitions against it. These, like Paul, would have insisted on having trades to sustain themselves. Likewise, the Christianized former-priests considered the tithes as belonging only to purely Jewish Temple worship services.

Second, the Roman government made it their business to know the occupational status of its citizens in order to assess taxes and to identify revolutionaries. They would have become suspicious of someone who had no obvious legal trade and did not appear to be a beggar. One could not tell the Roman authorities that his sustenance was provided by Christian church members; he must have a legitimate and evident trade in order to keep from being held in suspicion!

As evidence of both of these points, *The Lion Encyclopedia of the Bible* says, "It is likely that some form of trade guilds came into being fairly early, especially in the cities, where the different crafts seem to have had their special quarters. The Bible mentions the carpenters' quarters, the potters', the goldsmiths', and the perfumers' sections."

"In New Testament times trade guilds were well-known in the Roman Empire. But they had to have a *license* to make sure they were not simply a cover for undesirable political activities."[83]

How does this discussion fit into tithing? Much indeed! First, Scripture does not record any post-Calvary tithing to support a full-time clergy. Second, if such full-time support did exist, Roman authorities would arrest them for leading an illegal religion. As it was, many were arrested and put to death after A.D. 80 for leading an outlaw religion and for defending the faith. Third, although Cyprian (A.D. 250) loosely used the word, "tithe," and advocated tithing, he did so as a strong admirer of Tertullian, the great ascetic. Cyprian actually renounced his worldly possessions when he was baptized and was extremely strict about sharing all tithes and offerings with the poor. None of the earliest church fathers ever said that exact tithing was used to support full-time ministry. Even Cyprian also said that bishops received according to their dignity and merit.

1 Thess. 2:9 For you recall, brothers, our labor and hardship, how working night and day so as not to be a burden to any of you, we proclaimed to you the gospel of God.

2 Thess. 3:8 Neither did we eat any man's bread for nothing, but worked with labor and travail night and day, that we might not be a burden to any of you.

Acts 20:34 You yourselves know, that these hands have ministered to my necessities, and to them that were with me.

---

83   Pat Alexander, ed., *Lion Encyclopedia of the Bible*, Orig. *Eerdman's Family Encyclopedia of the Bible*, 1978, 3rd ed. (Batavia: Lion Publishing, 1987), 218.

First Corinthians, chapter 9, is a good example of the previous discussion. While working at his trade as a tentmaker (Acts 18:3) and receiving occasional help from other churches, Paul arrived at the contentious church in Corinth.

9:1 Am I not an apostle? Am I not free? Have I not seen Jesus Christ our Lord? Are you not my work in the Lord?
9:2 If I am not an apostle to others, yet doubtless I am to you, for you are the seal of my apostleship in the Lord.

Immediately Paul and his company were challenged about their lack of credentials. Having been sent forth from Antioch instead of Jerusalem, he and Barnabas had picked up other helpers such as Timothy and Titus. The question of proper credentials was evidently not resolved because it is again mentioned in 2 Corinthians, chapter 3. "Am I not free," he later clarified, refers to his freedom to accept or reject partial compensation for his work of ministry.

9:3 My answer to them that examine me is this,
9:4 Have we not power [a right] to eat and to drink?
9:5 Have we not power [a right] to lead about a sister, a wife, as well as other apostles, and as the brothers of the Lord, and Cephas?
9:6 Or is it only Barnabas and I who have not power [a right] to stop working?

It appears that Paul was answering false accusations that he wanted enough sustenance to stop working for a living and live wholly from church support. Evidently some of the apostles from the Jerusalem church had received some amount of sustenance for their mission efforts. In verses 3-6 Paul was merely asserting (not asking for) his equal privilege, or right, to receive sustenance just as the others had their rights (which he would have refused).

9:7 Who goes to war any time at his own charges [expense]? Who plants a vineyard, and does not eat of the fruit thereof? Or who feeds a flock, and does not eat of the milk of the flock?

When Paul asserts that the soldier, farmer, and shepherd are all somehow paid for their services, he is merely demonstrating the self-evident "privilege" due the worker without regard to the worker's "right" to refuse such payment. While Paul often refers to himself as a bond-slave (Greek: *doulos*), for the sake of this argument at least, he compares himself to a hired servant in comparison to hired servants of other callings.

9:8 Am I saying these things as a man, or does not the law say the same also?
9:9 For it is written in the law of Moses, You shall not muzzle the mouth of the ox that treads out the grain [Deut. 25:4]. Does God take care for oxen?
9:10 Or does the law say this also for our sakes? For our sakes, no doubt, this is written, that he that plows should plow in hope; and that he that threshes in hope should be partaker of his hope.
9:11 If we have sown to you spiritual things, is it a great thing if we shall reap your carnal things?

Paul progresses from the literal interpretation to the spiritual application which was widely accepted by Jews. If the ox can choose to eat grain while it is grinding, then the gospel worker should be able to choose whether or not he wants to accept sustenance *while* that worker is performing God's work.

9:12 If others are partakers of this power [right] over you, are not we also? Nevertheless, we have not used this power, but endure all things, unless we should hinder the gospel of Christ.

Having established his right to receive sustenance for gospel ministry, Paul then concludes with his great "nevertheless" statement which is so often ignored by those who insist that gospel workers should expect full-time support through tithes or otherwise. For Paul, at least, the freedom to preach the gospel unhindered superseded his right to expect full-time support.

9:13 Do you not know that they which minister about holy things live of the things of the temple? And they which wait at the alter are partakers with the alter?

Having completed his argument that he deserved sustenance as a gospel worker, and, having declared his decision not to accept it from the Corinthian church, Paul begins the argument all over again by using religious examples instead of secular ones.

Concerning this study on tithing, *if Paul had believed that tithing were a valid doctrine for the New Covenant church, then why does he not mention tithing at this critical point of his discussion?* If he believed in tithing, he has missed his "golden opportunity"! In all of Paul's writings, *this* is *the passage* at which he is finally in the midst of discussing monetary support for gospel ministers. After progressing from soldiers, farmers, shepherds, and a grinding ox, Paul finally compares gospel workers to the Levitical priests who minister in the temple. At this point many would expect Paul, inspired by God, to come right out and boldly say, "The priests who serve God deserve and receive tithes and offerings from the people they serve. Therefore, gospel workers also deserve tithes and offerings from the people they serve." However, while affirming the general *principle* of due recompense, Paul did not affirm a legalistic percentage. Paul supported the eternal moral principle of giving while rejecting the cultic principle of ten percent.

Today, while many gospel workers desire to follow Paul's examples in soul-winning, few today want to follow his example in self-sacrifice for the sake of the gospel. Indebted to no man, and obligated to no man (except to preach the gospel), Paul had no intention of teaching tithing for himself or others! He simply did not see tithing as part of God's New Covenant plan of freedom and liberty.

The Key Verse

9:14 Even so has the Lord ordained that they which preach the gospel should live of the gospel.

This text is quoted quite often by gospel workers to prove that they deserve full-time support for their ministry. However, while this may be a valid application, it ignores the greater gospel principle found in verses 12 and 15. Also, verse 14 itself prompts questions which need to be properly answered before ultimately deciding upon its proper application.

What is the origin of this quotation? Since verse 14 has no definite parallel in Scripture, any clear application is impossible. The cross-referencing in many Bibles from the *Treasury of Scripture Knowledge* sends the reader to Matthew 10:10 and Luke 10:7, which end by Jesus saying "for the workman/laborer is worthy of his hire."[84] Many other reference works also agree that this verse probably alludes to Matthew 10 and Luke 10. For example, this is also the cross-reference in *Adam Clarke's Commentary, Barnes' Notes, Jamieson, Fausset, and Brown Commentary, Robertson's Word Studies,* and the *Wycliffe Bible Commentary.*

If the quotation from Jesus is indeed from Matthew 10:10 and Luke 10:7, then what impact does this have on tithing to support gospel ministers? Tithing is nowhere seen or even implied in Matthew 10 or Luke 10! Matthew 10 contains instructions to the twelve as Jesus sent them out and Luke 10:1-17 contains similar instructions to the seventy. Both passages describe

---

84   Jerome Smith, *Treasury of Scripture Knowledge,* CD-ROM (Seattle: Biblesoft, 1999), s.v. "1 Cor. 9:14."

temporary evangelistic efforts just as modern evangelistic crusades send out (predominantly unpaid) workers to canvas cities before the crusade arrives. Both accounts also describe the life of those gospel workers in terms of food-less, shelter-less, and penny-less workers dependent entirely on the grace of God to daily supply their needs from freewill charity from those who are being served. Also, sustenance for the gospel workers of Matthew 10 and Luke 10 compares to that of the Old Covenant prophets rather than to the Old Covenant priests and law-tithing.

At least while the disciples and seventy were serving with Jesus, their lives were exactly as described in Matthew 10 and Luke 10. This was an even *lower* standard than that by which Paul lived during his years of mission service. Tithing definitely does not enter this picture for full-time gospel support.

What is meant by the phrase, "they which preach the gospel should live of the gospel"? When this phrase is taken out of its context, it is applied as a proof-text for full-time support of gospel workers. However, this phrase is obviously the conclusion of the immediate preceding phrases. Therefore, if the preceding phrases do indeed refer to Matthew 10 and Luke 10, then it cannot possibly be used to support tithing.

The KJV phrase, "they which preach the gospel should *live* of the gospel," is translated "get their *living* from the gospel" (NAS); "receive their living from the gospel" (NIV); "by the gospel" (RSV); and "should receive their *livelihood*" (Phillip's). The Greek is literally ho kurios (the Lord) dietaxen (ordained) tois (those) to (the ones preaching the gospel) ek tou euangeliou (from the gospel) zeen (to live)." Many translations of the Greek word, "*zoee*," give the impression that this word exclusively refers to a sustaining occupation, which is very far from being its real meaning. This key Greek word is parsed as a present active infinitive verb. "*Zoee*" (Strong's 2198) occurs over 140 times in the New Testament and is most often translated as the verbs "live" and "alive," the noun "life," and the participle "living." "*Zoee*" is most often "life" itself, the opposite of "death." (Compare 1 Cor. 7:39; 15:45; 2 Cor. 1:8; 3:3;

4:11; 5:15; 6:9, 16; 13:4.) In researching the 140 plus uses of this word in Scripture, there is no justification evident for insisting that the word must only be interpreted in this text as equivalent to "livelihood," "occupation," "profession," "trade," "craft," "labor," or "work."[85]

As a matter of biblical fact, "*zoee*" is far from the best word to use for "livelihood." If Paul had intended to *unquestionably* convey the idea of "livelihood," or "occupation," he had many much better words to choose from. "*Bios*" (Strong's 979) occurs 11 times and means "livelihood" in Luke 15:12. The verb, "*ergazomai*" (Strong's 2038), occurs 37 times and is the kind of work Jesus and the Father perform in John 5:17. "*Ergasia*" (Strong's 2039) occurs 6 times and means "craft" or "occupation" in Acts 19:25. "*Ergates*" (Strong's 2040) occurs 17 times and is translated "laborers" and "workers." "*Technee*" (Strong's 5078) occurs 3 times and means "trade, skill, or occupation" in Paul's tentmaker text of Acts 18:3. "*Meros*" (Strong's 3313) means "craft" in Acts 19:27. Again, several of these Greek words much better convey the idea a of full-time profession, occupation, trade, or craft in which to earn a living. "Living," at least in 1 Corinthians 9:14, best refers to gospel principles of grace and faith, rather than to a lifestyle occupation.

First Corinthians 7:20 is an extremely interesting text to look at in this discussion of tithing. "Let every man abide in the same *calling* (Strong's 2821) wherein he was called." In its context, Paul was teaching that, unless our job or life situation is immoral or unjust, we should remain where we are! This makes sense when viewed from the tradition that one's vocation was a calling from God. The author of this statement, Paul, makes it even more interesting, because Paul remained in his secular "calling" as a tentmaker while pursuing his spiritual calling as a gospel evangelist. Such an attitude would certainly preclude tithing.

"Gospel" is the most important word in 9:14, not "live." Those who preach from "gospel" principles should depend on "gospel" principles to

---

85   *Strong's*, s.v. "zoee, N.T. 2198."

sustain themselves. "From the gospel" means "from faith," but not from law! This is yet another reason to exclude law-tithing from the formula for supporting gospel workers. They are not "law workers," but "gospel workers!" The gospel, not the law, is "*ek pisteoos eis pistin*", that is, it comes "out of faith" and goes back "into faith" (Rom. 1:17). The gospel contains no part of the law. It is purely of faith from beginning to end. Yet, it is astounding how many "gospel" churches correctly insist on basing every New Covenant gospel doctrine on post-Calvary texts—except tithing. However, God did not say that "everything in the gospel is from faith to faith—except tithing." The disciples in Matthew 10 and the seventy in Luke 10 did not depend on tithing and principles of law for sustenance. Instead they depended entirely on gospel principles and freewill offerings. The better they served God's people, the better God's people responded out of love and appreciation to them.

9:15 But I have used none of these things; neither have I written these things, that it should be so done to me, for it were better for me to die, than that any man should make my glorying void.

Probably all commentaries, systematic theologies, and books on biblical hermeneutics are written by gospel ministers who are receiving full-time compensation as gospel workers. Therefore, one can logically expect almost every commentator to interpret verse 14 as support for full-time gospel workers. True objectivity is lost. For example, one commentator says, "Has the Lord appointed, commanded, 'arranged' that it should be so '*dietaxe*.' The word here means that he has made this a law, or has required it."[86] A second says, "Just as God gave orders about the priests in the temple, so did the Lord Jesus give orders for those who preach the gospel to live out of the gospel. Evidently Paul was familiar with the words

---

86   *Barnes*, s.v. "1 Cor. 9:14."

of Jesus in Matthew 10:10 and Luke 10:7 either in oral or written form. He has made his argument for the minister's salary complete for all time."[87] And a third says, "The same Lord Christ 'ordains' the ordinances in the Old and in the New Testaments (Matt. 10:10)."[88]

There are two reasons to question the previous three conclusions. First, if Matthew 10 and Luke 10 constitute an unchanging "commanded" covenant and the "ordained" "law" or "ordinance" for gospel workers, then New Covenant gospel workers are commanded to live day by day, as paupers, in total dependence on the charity of those they serve in obedience to gospel (not law) principles. The 12 and 70 were all Jews. Jewish tradition quoted elsewhere from the *Didache* and other sources in this book indicates that evangelists were only permitted to depend on charity for two or three days at each place before moving on or taking up a trade.

Second, if verse 14 is the "chair" verse for the support of New Covenant gospel workers, then Paul deliberately disobeyed the direct ordained command of Jesus in verse 15. "For you remember, brothers, our labor and travail: for laboring night and day, because we would not be chargeable to any of you, we preached to you the gospel of God" (1 Thess. 2:9). "Neither did we eat any man's bread for nothing; but worked with labor and travail night and day, that we might not be chargeable to any of you" (2 Thess. 3:8). Paul did exactly the opposite of what Jesus *supposedly* commanded in Matthew 10 and Luke 10 in order to preach unhindered.

Instead, Paul placed his total faith in the gospel principle of "freedom" rather than "privilege." For Paul, the gospel principle of "freedom" outweighed his gospel "right" to receive sustenance for gospel service. He refused his legitimate right in order to win more souls for Christ. Paul would rather be dead than to have somebody think that he served Christ for worldly gain.

---

87   *Robertson's*, s.v. "1 Cor. 9:14."

88   *Jamieson*, s.v. "1 Cor. 9:14."

Neither was Paul disobeying a direct command from Christ in refusing his right to support. In reality, Christ "ordained" gospel workers to live every day from "gospel" principles which greatly supersede law principles. Those who make verse 14 say anything beyond gospel principles, like law-tithing, are simply ignoring its context.

9:16 For though I preach the gospel, I have nothing to glory of; for necessity is laid upon me; woe to me if I do not preach the gospel!
9:17 For if I do this thing willingly, I have a reward; but if against my will, a dispensation of the gospel is committed to me.

For Paul, the previous discussion about the "right" to be paid for serving Christ, including verse 14, totally misses the reason for his compulsion and drive. After arguing and proving that he had a "right" to be paid if he desired to pursue such a "right," Paul then declined to exercise that right. Paul had a lot of accusers in Corinth. Proving his point, or winning the argument, was more important that the "content" of the argument.

Paul had no intention of receiving full-time support and only accepted limited partial assistance from other churches. For Paul, the former Jewish rabbi, tithing was as foreign as all of the other law principles which he had rejected for gospel principles. He did not serve God because he viewed himself as a soldier, farmer, herdsman, grinding ox, or Levitical priest (vv. 7-13). No! He said "necessity is laid upon me." The NAS says "I am under compulsion." His calling to preach was a "dispensation, a sacred trust, a stewardship" which is reflected in Paul's more familiar terms of a bond-slave to Christ. In Paul's perspective, the more free he was from obligations, the more unhindered he could preach the gospel in all of its power.

9:18 What is my reward [pay, wage] then? Truly that, when I preach the gospel, I may make the gospel of Christ without charge, that I do not abuse my power in the gospel.
9:19 For though I am free from all men, yet I have made myself servant [bond-slave] to all, that I might gain the more.

Although Paul is not eliminating the possibility of full-support for all gospel workers, he is certainly not emphasizing it either. Just as they were for Paul, verses 15-19 should be the mountain top shout of most gospel workers today. We need less complaining about "rights" and more action motivated by "liberty" and what can be accomplished when hindrances are removed.

Paul did not preach because he was paid a salary and was obligated as a steward to an earthly master (9:17). Read verse 18 again. "What then is my reward? That, when I preach the gospel, I may offer the gospel without charge, so as not to make full use of my right in the gospel." His reward, or pay, WAS the ability of preaching FOR FREE, without charge! *His reward WAS "not using" his "right" to receive wages!* What a profound statement!

Why did Paul refuse a salary? First, because his culture and tradition as a rabbi would never allow a teacher of God's Word to accept money for such purposes. Second, his culture and tradition as a Jew expected all men to learn a trade and be self-sufficient. Third, he wanted to serve and provide for others—not have others serve and provide for him (9:19). Fourth, he wanted to be a more effective soul-winner. Being free from asking others for a salary "that I might win the more" (9:19) was Paul's motivation. Whatever sacrifice or effort it might take to win others to Christ, even refusing his right of a salary, Paul was prepared to make that sacrifice or effort (9:20-27).

The Living Bible is sharper, *"And this [refusal of support] has as real advantage; I am not bound to obey anyone just because he pays my salary; yet I have freely and happily become a servant of any and all so that I can win them to Christ."* While we may have far less large churches, we would have many more thousands of house churches.

In 1 Corinthians 9 Paul affirmed that he would not let money become an issue that would hinder his preaching the gospel. Although his "rights" as an apostle and gospel minister did indeed include receiving some support for service for Christ as a poor person, tithing was not mentioned as one of those "rights"—nor was it wanted. Paul would have certainly refused a tithe just as he refused regular offerings as contrary to his freedom in Christ.

What about tithing? "Do you not know that those who perform the sacred services eat the food of the temple, and those who attend regularly to the altar have their share with the altar (9:13)?" Again, this would have been the ideal time to teach tithing! If tithing were legitimate, then *why* did not Paul seize the opportunity? No tithe-supporter would have ignored such an open door! Neither was there an appeal to Abraham's pre-law tithe in Genesis 14! Instead Paul says, "In the same way, the Lord has commanded that those who preach the gospel should receive their living from the gospel" (9:14). While the principles that supported the Levitical priesthood flowed from the law, the principles that provide for the gospel ministry flow from the gospel—faith, grace, love, and the guidance of the Spirit! Tithing was not mentioned because it is simply not a principle of grace!

Additional Comments on Matthew 10 and Luke 10

Many gospel workers will quote 1 Corinthians 9:11-14 and "the laborer is worthy of his wage" from Matthew 10:10, Luke 10:7, or 1 Timothy 5:18 to prove that they should be totally supported by the church. However, the entire context of Matthew 10:10 and Luke 10:7 is impossible to work into such a simple conclusion.

Matt. 10:8 Heal the sick, cleanse the lepers, raise the dead, cast out devils; freely you have received, freely give.
Matt. 10:9 Provide neither gold, nor silver, nor brass in your purses,

Matt. 10:10 Nor scrip for your journey, neither two coats, neither shoes, nor yet staves; *for the workman is worthy of his food* [support: NAS] [Greek: *trophees*].

Matt. 10:11 And into whatsoever city or town you shall enter, inquire who in it is worthy; and there abide till you go from there.

Luke 10:4 Carry neither purse, nor scrip, nor shoes; and salute no man by the way.

Luke 10:5 And into whatsoever house you enter, first say, Peace to this house.

Luke 10:6 And if the son of peace is there, your peace shall rest upon it; if not, it shall turn to you again.

Luke 1:7 And in the same house remain, eating and drinking such things as they give; for the laborer is worthy of his hire [reward] [Greek: *misthos*]. Go not from house to house.

Concerning Matthew 10:8-9, the *Wycliffe Bible Commentary* agrees with the two-three day statement of as found in the *Didache*. "These ministrations were to be *performed freely, without charge,* for their authority had been received in this manner. *These instructions apply only to this specific mission of limited duration*" (italics mine).[89] If this is true, then how can tithe-advocates say that 1 Corinthians 9:14 alludes to Matthew 10:8-11 and Luke 10:4-7? Also, according to Jewish tradition, after this "limited duration," even gospel workers were expected to either leave or take up a craft, as did Paul. Yet how many evangelists or preachers follow more than two of the instructions in Matthew 10 and Luke 10? Is one honest to the context by ignoring the other points? The context neither teaches tithing nor full-time support for the ministry!

Concerning 1 Corinthians 9:14 the following quotations predominantly from church *historians* from many denominations should not be

---

89   *Wycliffe Comm.*, s.v. "Matt. 10:8-9."

ignored. Difficult as it may be, theologians must admit that the historians are correct in asserting that tithing was neither taught nor practiced in the early church. These quotations certainly do not allow room the doctrine of tithing, as seen in many Christian churches today.

Robert Baker, *A Summary of Christian History*

This Southern Baptist textbook states, "*The leaders [before A.D. 100] usually worked with their hands for their material needs.* There was no artificial distinction between clergy and laity." He later added, "*The earliest bishops or presbyters engaged in secular labor to make their living and performed the duties of their church office when not at work*" (italics mine).[90]

The *Code of Jewish Law*

The *Code of Jewish Law* says that a poor sage who studies the law is to be established in a business and given superior treatment to assure that he is successful. "Even if an honored sage becomes poor, he should find some occupation, even of a menial kind, rather than depend on men."[91]

H. E. Dana, *The New Testament World*

This Southern Baptist textbook states, "Among the Jews professional life was limited. The one widely extensive profession was that of rabbi, if profession it might be called, *for most rabbis followed some trade or secular pursuit for a livelihood*, while devoting all the time possible to the study and teaching of the law…. Every Jewish boy was expected to learn some trade. Rabbinic tradition declared that 'whoever does not teach his son a trade is as if he brought him up to be a robber'" (p. 149) (italics mine).

"Those who worked at a common trade frequently organized themselves into a trade-union, comparable to our modern labor unions. Thus

---

90   Robert A. Baker, *A Summary of Christian History* (Nashville: Broadman, 1959), 11, 43.

91   *Code*, 1-114.

there were guilds of bakers, of smiths, of fullers, and of practically every trade known to the period.... It is probable that there was a tent-makers guild, and it may be reasonably assumed that Paul was a member of it (p. 217)."

"The prevalent use of tents [by travelers] made the tent-making trade a lucrative occupation. One belonging to the same trade-guild, religious cult, or having any other personal relationship to any resident of the locality could nearly always find welcome more or less genuine in a private home.... *This was the prevailing manner in which the first Christian missionaries were provided for,* though likely the entertainment was tendered them without cost (cf. 2 John 10-11; 3 John 5-8)" (p. 221) (italics mine).[92]

The *Didache,* or *The Teaching of the Twelve*

Paragraph XI:..."Now, as concerning the apostles and prophets according to the teaching of the gospel, so do; and let every apostle that comes to you be received as the Lord; and he shall stay but one day, and, if need be, the next day also; but if he stay three days he is a false prophet. When the apostle goes forth, let him take nothing but bread, till he reach his lodging: *if he ask money he is a false prophet....* But whosoever shall say in spirit, 'Give me money, or other things,' you shall not listen to him; but it he bid you give for others that are in need, let no man judge him."[93]

Alfred Edersheim, *Sketches of Jewish Social Life*

"Thus...to come to the subject of this chapter...we now understand how so many of the disciples and followers of the Lord gained their living by some craft; how in the same spirit the Master Himself condescended to

92   H. E. Dana, *The New Testament World,* 3rd. ed., rev. (Nashville: Broadman, 1937), 149, 217, 221.
93   Henry Bettenson, ed., *Documents of the Christian Church,* 2nd ed. (New York: Oxford UP, 1963), *"Didache,"* or *"Teaching of the Twelve,"* 64-65.

the trade of his adoptive father; and how the greatest of his apostles throughout earned his bread through the labor of his hands, probably following, like the Lord Jesus, the trade of his father. For it was a *principle*, frequently expressed, if possible 'not to forsake the trade of the father'" (p. 169) (italics mine). Furthermore, although its origins is unknown, Roman law required that a son should follow in the trade of his father (per the life of Martin, an early monk).

"And this same love of honest labor, the same spirit of manly independence, the same *horror of trafficking with the law*, and using it either as a 'crown or as a spade,' was certainly characteristic of the best Rabbis" (p. 172) (italics mine).

"For, in point of fact, with few exceptions, all the leading Rabbinical authorities were working at some trade, till at last it became quite an affectation to engage in hard bodily labor..." (p. 173).[94]

The *Jamieson, Fausset, and Brown Commentary*

"The stipends of the clergy were at first from offerings at the Lord's supper. At the love feast preceding it every believer, according to his ability, offered a gift; and when the expense of the table had been defrayed, the bishop laid aside a portion for himself, the presbyters, and deacons; and with the rest relieved widows, orphans, confessors, and the poor, (Tertullian, d. 220, 'Apology,' 1 Cor. 3:9). Again, the stipend was in proportion to the dignity and merits of the bishops, presbyters, and deacons (Cyprian, A.D. 250, c. iv. ep. 6)."[95]

George E. Ladd, *Wycliffe Bible Commentary*

[Acts 20:34] "Paul reminded the Ephesians of his custom of making tents not only to support himself but to provide for the needs of others with him. He quoted a saying of the Lord which is not recorded in any of

---

94   Edersheim, *Sketches,* 169, 172, 173.
95   *Jamieson,* s.v. "1 Cor. 9:14."

the Gospels, about the blessedness of giving…. *The main objective of giving in the early church was to provide for the needs of the poor brothers rather than to support the preaching of the gospel as is the case today.*"

[Acts 18:1-4] "It was customary for Jewish rabbis *not* to receive pay for their teaching, and therefore, Paul, who had been raised as a rabbi, had learned the trade of tent-making. The apostle did not at once launch into the evangelization of Corinth, but joined Aquilla and Priscilla in practicing his trade during the week. The Sabbaths he devoted to preaching in the synagogues." [96]

The Lion Encyclopedia of the Bible

"Crafts were held in high regard by the Jews at this time. Craftsmen were exempt from the rule that everyone should rise to his feet when a scholar approached. *Most of the scribes probably had a trade. The writings of the rabbis mention a nail maker, a baker, a sandal maker, a master builder, and a tailor.*"[97] Remember, Paul was a rabbi!

The *New Bible Commentary*

[Acts 18:1-4] "Even rabbis were expected to earn their living by manual labor and not to make the teaching of the law a means of gain; thus Paul maintained himself by leather."

[2 Thess. 2:9] "His policy [working night and day] not only reflected a desire to be financially independent of those among whom they ministered, but it also marked them off from the ordinary religious traffickers of the day, and showed the converts a good example."

[2 Cor. 11:8] "Paul is really indicating that he did not receive wages *at all* for preaching the gospel. If what was given him for his support by other churches was to be regarded as 'earnings,' then he had in effect 'robbed'

---

96   *Wycliffe Comm.*, s.v. "Acts 20:34" and "Acts 18:1-4."
97   *Lion*, 218.

them since the service given was not to them but to the Corinthians" (italics mine). [98]

Philip Schaff, *History of the Christian Church*, Volume II

"In the apostolic church preaching and teaching were not confined to a particular class, but every convert could proclaim the gospel to unbelievers, and every Christian who had the gift could pray and teach and exhort in the congregation. The New Testament knows no spiritual aristocracy or nobility but calls all believers "saints," though many fell short of this vocation. Nor does it recognize a special priesthood in distinction from the people, as mediating between God and the laity. It knows only one high-priest, Jesus Christ, and clearly teaches the universal priesthood, as well as universal kingship, of believers. It does this in a far deeper and larger sense than the Old; in a sense, too, which even to this day is not yet fully realized. The entire body of Christ is called 'clergy,' a peculiar people, the heritage of God" (p. 124).

"With the exaltation of the clergy [in the third century] appeared the tendency to separate them from secular business, and even from social relations...They drew their support from the church treasury, which was supplied by *voluntary contributions* and weekly collections on the Lord's Day. *After the third century* they were forbidden to engage in any secular business, or even to accept any trusteeship" (p. 128).

On pages 387-427 Schaff discusses asceticism. In the universal church, the ascetics received the highest regard and sought with enthusiasm a martyr's death (p. 391). "The ascetic principle, however, was not confined, in its influence, to the proper ascetics and morals. *It ruled more or less the entire morality and piety of the ancient and medieval church*" (p. 392). "The orthodox or catholic asceticism starts from a literal and over-strained construction of certain passages of Scripture" (p. 393). "Among these works [of supererogation] were reckoned martyrdom, *voluntary*

---

98   *New Bible Comm.*, s.v. "Acts 18:1-4," 2 Thess. 2:9," and "2 Cor. 11:8."

poverty, and voluntary celibacy. All three, or at least the last two of these acts, in connection with the positive Christian virtues, belong to the idea of the higher perfection, as distinguished from the fulfillment of regular duties or ordinary morality (p. 395).

"The ground on which these particular virtues were so strongly urged might be easily understood. *Property,* which is so closely allied to the self-ishness of man and binds him to the earth, and sexual intercourse—these present themselves as the firmest obstacles to that perfection, in which God alone is our possession, and Christ alone is our love and delight"(p. 395). "The [Jewish Christian] Ebionites made poverty the condition of salvation." (Even the name, "Ebionite," is Hebrew for "poor.")

"*The recommendation of voluntary poverty* was based on a literal inter-pretation of the Lord's advice to the rich young ruler…. To this were added the actual examples of the poverty of Christ and his apostles, and the community of goods in the first Christian church in Jerusalem. Many Christians, not only of the ascetics, but also of the clergy, like Cyprian, accordingly gave up all their property at their conversion, for the benefit of the poor" (italics mine) (p. 396).[99]

---

99 Schaff, 118, 128, 391, 392, 393, 395, 396.

CHAPTER 23

▼

1 CORINTHIANS 16
GIVING TO NEEDY SAINTS

First Corinthians 16:1-3 is quoted as often as any other New Testament text to demonstrate that Christians should support their church through tithes and offerings. Yet, the context of these verses does not contain a single word about tithes, money to "support" the local church, pay salaries, or sustain an organization.

16:1 Now concerning the collection for the saints, as I have given order to the churches of Galatia, even so do.

"Now concerning." "Now" means that Paul is changing to yet another problem area faced by the Corinthian church. He has previously dealt with a different problem in almost every chapter. It is not surprising, therefore, that the Corinthians also had problems regarding freewill offerings for the needy. Those who argue that tithing was not mentioned in the

New Testament because it was not a problem simply underestimate the problems in the Corinthian church. It is highly unlikely that the problems Paul addressed in each chapter would exist if the church was as faithful in giving as the argument from silence assumes.

"Concerning the collection for the saints." The "saints" are specifically the needy in "Jerusalem" (v. 3). Famine was a common occurrence in Palestine throughout Bible history. Acts 11:27-30 tells of a "great famine through-out all the world, which came to pass in the days of Claudius Caesar," at approximately A.D. 47. The Christian congregations decided to help those hit hardest by the famine in Judea. Acts 11:29-30 says, "Then the disciples, every man *according to his ability*, determined to send relief to the brothers which lived in Judea: which also they did, and sent it to the elders by the hands of Barnabas and Saul." Acts 12:25 recorded that Barnabas and Saul delivered this first collection personally.

Paul probably brought famine relief on several return trips to Jerusalem. In Romans 15:25-26 he wrote, "But now I go to Jerusalem to minister to the saints. For it has pleased them of Macedonia and Achaia [Corinth] to make a certain contribution for the poor saints which are at Jerusalem." Galatians 2:9-10 mentions a collection, "And when James, Cephas, and John, who seemed to be pillars, perceived the grace that was given to me, they gave to me and Barnabas the right hands of fellowship, that we should go to the heathen, and they to the circumcision. Only they would that we should remember the poor; the same which I also was eager to do."

Second Corinthians 8:4 describes the Macedonian church's strong com-mitment, "Praying us with much entreaty that we would receive the gift, and take upon us the fellowship of the ministering to the saints." Second Corinthians 9:1 continues the subject, "For as touching the ministering to the saints, it is superfluous for me to write to you." Therefore, every "giv-ing" principle in 2 Corinthians, chapters 8 and 9 relates to this "collection for the saints" who were experiencing famine conditions in Judea. The

Christians in Macedonia had begged Paul "for the favor of participation in the support of the saints" even "beyond their ability" (2 Cor. 8:1-6).

At least three of Paul's companions, Stephanus, Fortunatus, and Achaicus, had "devoted themselves for ministry to the saints" (1 Cor. 16:15-18). Clearly, the "saints," or "fellow believers in Judea," is the ONLY focus in the context of 1 Corinthians 16:1! This burden, shared by the leaders in Jerusalem, and Paul, is either in the foreground, or background, of much of the book of Acts, and most New Testament letters.

To summarize the problem, the situation in Jerusalem was very serious indeed. Many Jews (especially the Sadducees) had reacted to Christianity with hostility, cruelty, and depravation of basic necessities to Christians whenever possible. It is also very possible that the early resources from Acts 2:46 had been exhausted and the church needed to rebuild its financial foundation. Paul was instructing the churches that it was their duty to help fellow believers in need. The discussion in 1 Corinthians 16 does not relate to local church fund-gathering except as it might apply to aid for the poor.

"*The collection (tees logeias;).*" Paul's readers knew exactly what he was referring to by "the collection," thus, he did not need to explain himself (2 Cor. 9:1). However, almost 2,000 years later, verse 2 often gets separated from its context of verses 1 and 3. The needs of the poor have therefore been overshadowed by the needs of the local church. Yet such is contrary to Old and New Covenant priorities.

Exactly what was being collected "for the saints"? Was it "money," "food," or "money and food"? The Greek word, *logeia* (Strong's 3048), only occurs twice in the Bible, as "collection" in verse 1 and as "gathering" in verse 2. It could be a gathering of almost anything. Paul and Luke (in Acts) never specify exactly what the "collection" contained. Acts 11:29 calls it "relief"; Acts 24:17 says "alms" and "offerings"; Rom. 15:25-28 reads "contribution," "material things," and "fruit" (non edible). Second Corinthians 8 and 9 uses terms such as "gift" (8:4); "their want" (8:14);

"this grace" (8:19); "this abundance" (8:20); "this service" (9:12); "this ministration" (9:13); and "distribution" (9:13).

However, for the following reasons, the "collection" was probably food, and not money:

1. Paul never used any term for "money" while describing the "collection." In fact, Paul's writings never refer to "money," or "silver," in a positive sense! Except for Luke's quotation of Paul in Acts 20:33, his letters do not even contain the basic word itself! First Timothy 3:3 uses the word *"aphilarguros,"* "without covetousness," and 1 Timothy 6:10 uses *"philarguros"* (covetousness). Neither did Paul ever use any of the "currency" terms for money! One must conclude that Paul had a strong aversion concerning money. [See *argurion* (Strong's 694), *aphilarguros* (866), *kerma* (2772), *nomisma* (3546), *philarguria* (5365), *chalkos* (5475), and *chrema* (5536). Paul never used any of the "specific" words for money. See *lepton* (3015); *kodrantes* (2835); *assarion* (787); *drachma* (1406); *mina* (3414); *talanton* (5007).

2. Money does not purchase enough survival food in a famine. The men accompanying Paul would have to protect food-supplies much more than money. Revelation 6:6 reads, "A measure of wheat for a penny, and three measures of barley for a penny; and see you hurt not the oil and the wine." In our terms, this means that a day's wages will buy enough for one person to eat." (Also see 2 Kings 6:25; 7:1)

3. There are direct and indirect allusions to food in several verses referring to the "collection."

   a. Acts 11:29 "relief" (Greek: *diakonia*) was originally "deacons," or "servants" of food.

   b. Acts 24:17 "Now after many years I came to bring alms to my nation, and offerings." "Alms," is a call for "mercy" by the hungry poor who will accept anything given to them. Compare Luke 11:41.

   c. Acts 24:17 "offerings" could be food or otherwise.

    d. 2 Cor. 8:15 "As it is written, He that had gathered much had nothing over; and He that had gathered little had no lack." This is a quotation of Exodus 16:18 in reference to food.

    e. 2 Cor. 9:6 "But this I say, He who sows sparingly shall reap also sparingly; and he who sows bountifully shall reap also bountifully."

    f. 2 Cor. 9:9 "As it is written, He has dispersed abroad; he has given to the poor: his righteousness remains forever." This could be a reference to sowing.

    g. 2 Cor. 9:10 "Now he that ministers seed to the sower both minister bread for your food, and multiply your seed sown, and increase the fruits of your righteousness."

    h. Paul's journey by ship would have been delayed much longer for food collection than for money.

    I. the collection is never called money.

4. Religious Jews do not handle or collect money on their Sabbath even today. The earliest Christians who recognized Sunday as a holy day might have had a similar reluctance.

16:2 Upon the first day of the week let every one of you lay by him in store, as God has prospered him, that there may be no gatherings when I come.

"On the first day of the week." Although Christians traditionally bring contributions for local church support on Sunday, this text, in its exegetical and historical context, does not command it! It does exhort believers to set aside *at home* contributions "for the poor" every Sunday! Nothing, however, is stated about bringing tithes or offerings to support the church budget! Paul did NOT say "On the first day of every week let each one of you bring your tithes and offerings for the local church budget." Such manipulation of the text ignores its context.

"*Lay by him* (*para heautooi tithetoo,*)." This phrase does not have an exclusive translation. The NAS says "put aside and save;" the NIV reads "set aside a sum of money;" and the RSV says "put something aside." "Lay by him" (literally "by himself to place") has been variously understood as either "by himself," or "personally." However, either interpretation is totally irrelevant if local church support is not included in the original context. There is no conclusive reason to presume that corporate worship, rather than personal action, is meant here. Instead, the believers are being instructed to make provision for the poor their top priority for the week's schedule. Whatever is to be "put aside" could be very heavy, or very light.

"*In store*" (thee-sau-ri-zoon,) is a present active participle of the verb, "*thesaurizo*" (Strong's 2343) which simply means "storing up." The participle is translated "*in store*" in the KJV, "*and save*" in the NAS, "*saving it up*" in the NIV, and "*store it up*" in the RSV. Its noun form is "*thesauros*" (Strong's 2344). The noun occurs eleven (11) times in the New Testament, but only three times outside of the Gospels. They are the "gifts" of the wise men (Matt. 2:11); the treasures of the heart (Matt. 12:35; 6:19, 21; Luke 6:45); the treasures in heaven (Matt. 6:20; 19:21; Mk. 10:21; Luke 12:33); and all the wisdom and knowledge of Christ (2 Cor. 4:7; Col. 2:3). In its eight New Testament occurrences, the verb form refers to "*laying up* earthly wealth" (Matt. 6:19); "*laying up* things of heavenly value" (Matt. 6:20), "*laying up* whatever is important to a person, like food stored in barns" (Luke 12:21), "*storing up* wrath" (Rom. 2:5), "parents' *provision* of care of children" (2 Cor. 12:14), "*storing up* gold and silver for the last days" (Jas. 5:3), and God's "*reservation* of the heavens and the earth for the day of judgment" (2 Pet. 3:7).

The important point of this word study is that, although the two forms of the word used in 1 Corinthians 16:2 are usually translated "treasure" in the KJV, they are most often NOT money. Yet some scholars dogmatically declare that "*thesauros*" here only refers to the church as a treasury, or storehouse for money. They deduce this, not from context and accepted principles of interpretation, but from pagan Greek worship practices where the temple was a banking, or safe-keeping place secure from theft. A wide range of interpretation exists in commentaries, for example:

Adam Clarke's Commentary

He was then to bring it on the first day of the week, as is most likely, to the church or assembly, that it might be put in the common treasury.[100]

Matthew Henry Commentary

The manner in which the collection was to be made: Every one was to lay by in store (v. 2), have a treasury, or fund, *with himself*, for this purpose. The meaning is that he should lay by as he could spare from time to time, and by this means make up a sum for this charitable purpose.... Some of the Greek fathers rightly observe here that this advice was given for the sake of the poorer among them. They were to lay by from week to week, and *not* bring in to the common treasury, that by this means their contributions might be easy to themselves, and yet grow into a fund for the relief of their brothers (italics mine).[101]

The New Bible Commentary

Either put on one side at home a sum proportionate to what one has received, or else bring it to the central treasury of the church.[102]

Wycliffe Bible Commentary

"By him" is probably a reference *to the home*; giving was to be private giving.... This system would revolutionize present church customs! Paul's carefulness in money matters should be noted. *He never appealed*

---

100   *Clarke's*, s.v. "1 Cor. 16:2."

101   *Henry*, s.v. "1 Cor. 16:2."

102   *New Bible Comm.*, s.v. "1 Cor. 16:2."

for money for himself and did not even desire to handle money for others if there could be the slightest question about it" (italics mine).[103]

The pagan Greek temples were safe "treasure houses" where pagans kept their valuables, but did not *give* them to the gods. The premise behind using the temples as holding places, or banks, was that the gods would bring vengeance on anybody stealing from their temples. In no way should the Christian church be used as a temporary storage place, or bank, for God to protect our financial wealth so that we can withdraw it later for our own personal use. Although neither concept is New Covenant, calling the church a "treasury-storehouse" places more of a pagan Greek connotation on *thesauros* than an Old Testament storehouse connotation. See comments on Malachi 3:10.

Matt. 27:6 And the chief priests took the silver pieces, and said, It is not lawful to put them into the *treasury [corban: 2878]*, because it is the price of blood.

Mark 12:41 And Jesus sat over against the *treasury [gazophulakion: 1049]*, and beheld how the people cast money into the treasury....

John 8:20 These words Jesus spoke in the *treasury [gazophulakion: 1049]*, as he taught in the temple....

The Greek New Testament does not call the Hebrew temple in Jerusalem or the Christian church a "treasury"—perhaps to avoid the pagan connotation. If Paul had wanted to convey the idea of a treasury in the church like that in the Jewish temple, he would have used either *"corban"* (Strong's 2878) (as per Matt. 27:6) or *"gazophulakion"* (Strong's 1049) (as per Mark 12:41, 43; John 8:20) for "treasury." This was the

---

103   *Wycliffe Comm.*, s.v. "1 Cor. 16:2."

room in the temple where the priests stayed, public records were kept, and thirteen chests for collections of money for temple service and the poor were kept. It would have been a simple matter to remind Christians that the church now served such function. However, Paul did not make such a comparison.

Therefore, since "*thesauros*" does not "exclusively" mean "treasury" or "storehouse," theologians should not insist that it *must* mean "the treasury, or treasurer, of the local church." It must be remembered that this is the first century early church that usually met in homes and later in caves and catacombs. It did not have separate church buildings, nor did it yet have an organized system of salaried leadership. While it may be true that pagan Greeks used their worship centers to store wealth, the Greek worship centers were secure and protected by soldiers! Secure Christian worship structures did not exist when Paul wrote 1 Corinthians. The church could not even agree on leadership authority, much less other church offices (1 Cor. 1:12; 9:1-3; 2 Cor. 3:1-6). Those practices which evolved in later centuries when the church was a political and social establishment should not be read back into the original text.

> 2 Cor. 12:14 Behold, the third time I am ready to come to you, and I will not be burdensome to you for I seek not yours, but you; for the children ought not to *lay up [thee-sau-ri-zein]* for the parents, but the parents for the children.
> 2 Cor. 12:15 And I will very gladly spend and be spent for you; though the more abundantly I love you, the less I be loved.

In 2 Corinthians 12:14-15 Paul used the phrase, "lay up," in exactly the *opposite* meaning from the way some interpret 1 Corinthians 16:2. Paul is definitely NOT referring to a treasury in the church here. While Paul and other church elders are the "parents," church members and new converts are the "children." The passage, from 12:10 to 12:21, includes the underlying problem of payment for services rendered. It reflects his same thoughts expressed in 1 Corinthians 9:15-18 and Acts 20:33-35. For Christ's sake, Paul considered it a "pleasure" to be in need (necessities); among other things it made him "strong" (12:10). Admittedly, other churches had helped Paul with the bare necessities, even when he served others (12:13), but that does not mean that they continued to do so. As we shall see in a later chapter, the early church fathers, like Paul, considered it an honor to be poor for Christ's sake and many greatly valued an ascetic lifestyle.

In three trips to Corinth, Paul refused any help whatsoever from that large congregation. In 2 Corinthians 12:14-15 "laying up" means that, instead of receiving money *from* the church, Paul would "spend" everything he had on church members—money, health and vitality! With tongue in cheek, Paul said that his approach to the Corinthians was "crafty" and "with guile, deceit, trickery, or cunning" (12:16). He meant that, by refusing to "make a gain" of them by accepting wages (the Greek means daily rations) (12:17-18), he had disarmed his accusers (12:20). Likewise, it is obvious that Paul did not intend for "lay by in store" in 1 Corinthians 16 to include any pastoral support.

"Set aside a sum of money" (NIV). Why does the NIV read "set aside a sum of money" instead of "lay up in store"? "Money" is a rather poor paraphrase rather than a translation! Surely Paul, who was well-educated, and, inspired by the Holy Spirit, knew all of the common words for "money" and would have used one of them if he indeed meant money! See the previous discussion under "collection." While *"argurion,"* the most common word for "money," occurs twenty-one times in the New Testament, Paul used none of the terms for "money" in this text!

"As God has prospered him" (KJV); "as he may prosper" (NAS, NKJ); "in keeping with his income" (NIV); (*ho ti ean euodootai;*), literally, "that which he may be increased."

Exod. 25:2 Speak to the children of Israel, that they bring me an offering. Of every man that gives it willingly with his heart you shall take my offering. (See also Exod. 35:5, 21; 1 Chron. 29:9; Ezra 3:5.)

Deut. 15:11 For the poor shall never cease out of the land. Therefore I command you, saying, You shall open your hand wide to your brother, to your poor, and to your needy, in your land.

Acts 11:29 Then the disciples, every man according to his ability, determined to send relief to the brothers which lived in Judea.

2 Cor. 8:12-14 For if there is first a willing mind, it is accepted according to that which a man has, and not according to that which he has not. For I do not mean that other men be eased, and you burdened; but by an equality, that now at this time your abundance may be a supply for their want, that their abundance also may be a supply for your want, that there may be equality.

2 Cor. 9:7 Every man according as he purposes in his heart, so let him give—not grudgingly, or of necessity; for God loves a cheerful giver.

This simple phrase, *"as God has prospered him,"* includes the Greek conditional particle, *"ean,"* which means "in case that," and suggests uncertainty. The word, *"eu-odontai,"* literally means "good journey" and refers to those whom life has treated well. Therefore every person should store up for the poor to the extent that they may have been blessed in life.

The idea of freely giving as one had been prospered is common in Scripture. However, contrary to common application, this phrase has no contextual reference to tithing, nor to support of local churches and salaries. It is perfectly clear that "as he may prosper" is not a command concerning how much to give to the CHURCH, but to POOR SAINTS! Yet those who teach tithing ignore the context and include compulsory tithing in this text along with freewill offerings to support the church. *In fact, under New Covenant principles, the vast majority of contributions should go first to the poor, and not merely the leftovers.* Also, under New Covenant principles, the amount given is a freewill faith response.

A seminary textbook, *Introduction to Biblical Interpretation*, says, "Just as poor people could offer less costly sacrifices in those days (Lev. 12; cf. Luke 2:24), so *Christians should not require identical levels of giving from all believers today. In fact the N.T. does not promote a fixed percentage of giving.* We may better capture the spirit of N.T. giving through what R. Sider calls 'graduated tithe,' by which the more one makes, the higher percentage one ought to give to the Lord's work, and especially to helping the poor (1 Cor. 16:2; 2 Cor. 8:12-15)" (italics mine).[104]

The preceding statement probably reflects the majority of biblical books on the subject of tithing. In *1001 Things You Always Wanted to Know about the Bible*, J. Stephen Lang says that "the New Covenant urges generous giving proportionate to one's income. Wealthy Christians were expected to give generously to aid the less fortunate brother in the faith."[105]

In *The Complete Book of Bible Answers*, Ron Rhodes says, "I do not believe that Christians today are under the ten percent tithe system. *We are not obligated to percentage tithe at all.* There is not a single verse in the New Testament where God specifies that we should give ten percent of their income to the church.... We are to give as we are able. For some this will mean less than ten percent, but for others whom God has materially blessed, this will mean much more than ten percent" (italics mine).[106]

---

104   William W. Klein, Craig L. Bloomberg, and Robert L. Hubbard, Jr., *Introduction to Biblical Interpretation* (Dallas: Word Publishers, 1993), 415.

105   J. Stephen Lang, *1001 Things You Always Wanted to Know About the Bible* (Nashville: Nelson, 1992), 321.

106   Ron Rhodes, *The Complete Book of Bible Answers* (Peabody: Harvest, 1997), 296.

Baker's Evangelical Dictionary of Biblical Theology agrees, "Paul's vocabulary and teaching suggest that giving is voluntary and that there is no set percentage. Following the example of Christ who gave even his life (2 Cor. 8:9), we should cheerfully give as much as we have decided (2 Cor. 9:7) based on how much the Lord has prospered us (1 Cor. 16:2), knowing that we reap in proportion to what we sow (2 Cor. 9:6) and that we will ultimately give account for our deeds (Rom. 14:12).[107]

In Acts 3:6 Peter said, "Silver and gold I have none; but such as I have I give to you; In the name of Jesus Christ of Nazareth rise up and walk." Gone are the days that most clergy can say with Peter, "I have no silver and gold." Also gone is their ability to say "in the name of Jesus Christ of Nazareth, rise up and walk." It is past time that the church returned to New Covenant basic attitudes towards the poor. The early church's attitude towards giving and the poor is drastically different from the modern concept. Priorities have been reversed! Too often the lion's share of contributions must go to pay unnecessary building expenses and large salaries, while the poor are ignored. And too often newspaper headlines reveal church financial scandals rather than works of charity for the poor.

Compulsory giving cannot possibly produce the level of giving which is prompted spontaneously by the Holy Spirit when the gospel is preached with power and authority! When Peter and John were "filled with the Holy Spirit and began to speak the word of God with boldness, and the congregation was of one heart and soul," they gave and shared all, "for there was not a needy person among them (Acts 4:31-34)." Yet Peter did not preach on tithing here, nor anywhere else in the records of the New Testament; he preached the gospel of Jesus Christ!

History proves that many centuries of compulsory legalistic tithing failed to produce moral and spiritual blessings in Old Covenant Israel. On

---

107   Walter A. Elwell, ed., *Baker's Evangelical Dictionary of the Bible* (Grand Rapids: Baker, 1996), s.v. "tithe."

the other hand, while the first century church was composed mainly of women, children, and slaves, it still flourished and grew. The giving principles of the New Covenant, which are freewill offerings, revert back to God's original plan before the Levites were temporarily inserted to replace the priesthood of believers.

"Each one of you, on the first day of each week, should set aside a specific sum of money in proportion to what you have earned and use it for the offering."[108]

The preceding translation of 1 Corinthians 16:2 currently appears on an offering envelope provided by Lifeway Envelope Services for Southern Baptist churches. It is sad that, while the denomination preaches conservative adherence to a literal correctness of the Word of God, this kind of alteration of God's Word has crept onto its offering envelopes. This translation is not found in any legitimate version of the Bible. It is an obvious reference to specific tithing of money, which the text does not teach.

16:3 And when I come, whoever you shall approve by your letters, them I will send to bring your liberality to Jerusalem.

Again, the famine context of the "collections" most likely means that the contributions were "food," not money. "Preservation" of the food was a greater concern for the contributing churches than was theft. Each church was asked to send persons along with the "collections." Titus and another "brother" volunteered to help in the collection (2 Cor. 8:16-18). This unnamed "brother" had been chosen by the churches to travel with them (8:19). In 2 Corinthians 8:20-24 there was some problem of trust

---

108   Offering Envelope, *Lifeway Envelope Service*, Nashville, TN (still available in 2000).

involved because Paul chose his words carefully and had to assure the others of his traveling companions.

Paul had discreetly rebuked the Corinthians about the consequences of not giving as much as other churches. He had sent the brothers to prevent other representatives from finding them unprepared (2 Cor. 9:1-6). If the collection were only money entrusted to Paul, then those from Macedonia would not know how much was given. However, if the collection were food supplies, then a visual check of ship stores would reveal the quantity.

Most likely, each church sent representatives for several purposes. First, they insured that the food supplies were kept watertight and secure on board the ship. Second, each protected its own supplies from general theft. Third, the Gentile converts became "samples" of Paul's work among the Gentiles when he arrived in Jerusalem. Also, there may have been some mistrust between the Macedonian churches and the Corinthian church.

CHAPTER 24

▼

1 TIMOTHY 5: 17-20
WORTHY OF DOUBLE HONOR

5:17 Let the elders that rule well be counted worthy of *double honor*, especially they who labor in the word and doctrine.
5:18 For the Scripture says, You shall not muzzle the ox that treads out the grain, and, The laborer is worthy of his reward.
5:19 Against an elder do not receive an accusation, except before two or three witnesses.
5:20 Rebuke them that sin before all, that others also may fear.

Verses 17 and 18 have been quoted by many commentaries as the strongest texts in God's Word that discuss pay for gospel ministers. The correct interpretation, they claim, is "worthy of double *pay*," or *"double salary."* However, this author strongly disagrees with such conclusion for the following reasons:

1. *Greek scholars who translated the most respected versions refused to translate "double honor" as "double pay."* Although the Greek word can mean "price," the best translations of the Bible read "honor." For example, "honor" is found in the KJV, NAS, NIV, RSV, NKJ, and Catholic New American. Paraphrased versions take more liberties; Phillips says "worthy of respect and of adequate salary"; The Living Bible says "should be paid well and should be highly appreciated"; the Amplified Bible says "doubly worthy of honor [and of adequate financial support]."

   Again, it is strange that, while many scholars of the Greek language claim in their written literature that "pay" is meant, they still refuse to commit to that word in the reputable translations they co-translate. They fully realize that, in its *context*, "honor" is the correct translation.

2. The context of "double honor" in 5:17 is that of *rebuking wrongdoers* in the church, and not "salary." Verses 1-16 and 19-20 are clearly discussions of discipline. Context must be the primary determining factor.

   5:1 Do not *rebuke* an elder [older man] [remember their honor].
   5:3-16 **Honor** widows [honor is greater than rebuke].
   5:17-18 Give double **honor** to elders who labor in the word.
   5:19-20 *Rebuke* [ministering] elders openly that sin.
   5:21 Do not be impartial [honor first; rebuke last resort].
   5:22 Do not be hasty in discipline [remember their honor].
   5:24 God will judge sins.

The disciplinary honor sequence begins with "Do not rebuke an elder" (v. 1) and ends with "rebuke an elder who sins before all" (v. 29). The "elder" of verse one is probably an older church member who is due honor because of his age and experience. After discussing the cautious approach to rebuking fellow church members (vv. 1- 2) and special rules for honoring widows (vv. 3-16), the writer next takes up the unpleasant, but necessary, rebuke of the church's spiritual leaders (vv. 19-20). First, however, he reminds all of the double-honorable position of the person he is about to discuss (vv. 17-18). While an ordinary elder (older person) is due single "honor," an elder who leads in the Word of God is worthy of "double honor"—the first honor because of his age and the second, or double honor, because of his ministry in the Word.

To restate the previous conclusion, since all church members are "honorable" (1 Cor. 12:23-24), they are all worthy of honorable and cautious rebuke. Older persons are to be rebuked with an honor which respects their age and experience. However, ruling and teaching elders are worthy of double "honor," that is, of a *"double-cautious rebuke."* Such is the context, not salary! Because elders are worthy of double honor, those wishing to rebuke them must be "twice" as careful and should not rebuke them on a one-to-one basis, but in front of two or three witnesses (v. 19). Those elders who continue in their sin are to be rebuked before the whole church (v. 20). In rebuking church leaders, it appears that the one-to-one first stage is omitted. Compare and contrast these principles with those of Matthew 18:15-17.

3. If "wages," or "salary," were the intended meaning for "honor" in verse 17, then the inspired writer would have certainly used the word *"misthos"* (as he did in verse 18) instead of *"timees."*

4. The Greek word for "honor," *as used in verse 17 and in the rest of the New Testament,* does NOT mean "salary" or "wage." As just mentioned, the noun in 5:17 is *"timees"* (Strong's 5092). It occurs 38 times in the KJV New Testament: 28 times as "honor," 8 times as "price," once as "sum," and once as "precious," but NEVER as "wage." When used as "price," it does not mean "wage" or "salary," but "value." *"Timees"* is the "price of blood" (Matt. 21:6, 9), the "prices of things sold" (Acts 4:34), the "price of land" (Acts 5:2-3), the "price of Sarah's sepulcher" (Acts 7:16), and the "price of books" (Acts 19:19). Redeemed believers are "bought with a price" (1 Cor. 6:20; 7:23). In NONE of the occurrences is *"timees"* "pay" for work

performed. "*Timees*" is the "price," "worth," or "value" of a person or thing bought or sold.

The verb form of "honor" (Strong's 5091) occurs 21 times in the New Testament. With the lone exception of Matthew 27:9, when Judas received the "price" (noun) of Jesus according to the way Israel "valued" (verb), the word merely means "honor" or "respect." Therefore, of the 59 total occurrences of this word in the KJV New Testament, it is never translated as "wage" or "salary." Thus, it is inaccurate to insist that it *must* be interpreted as "salary" or "wage" in 1 Timothy 5:17.

5. Consequently, the Greek word for "honor" is not used elsewhere in Timothy to mean "pay" or "wage." Timothy's Greek name is a combination of "honor" and "God." God and Paul saw Timothy as very honorable and valuable to God. In his pastoral letter to Timothy, Paul used the noun, "*timees,*" four (4) times. "Now to the King eternal, immortal, invisible, the only wise God, be *honor* and glory forever and ever" (1:17). "Let as many servants as are under the yoke count their own masters worthy of all *honor*, that the name of God and his doctrine be not blasphemed" (6:1). "Who only has immortality dwelling in the light which no man can approach to; whom no man has seen, nor can see; to whom be *honor* and power everlasting" (6:16). The verb form is used once in 5:3, "Honor widows."

6. To expand on point 3, if the writer of 1 Timothy had wanted to clearly convey the meaning of "wage," or "salary," there are much better words he could have used. The Greek word for "labor" in 5:17 is the verb "*kopiao*" (Strong's 2872) and does not implicitly mean "labor for a living." The word merely means "grow tired, become weary." "*Ergazomai*" (Strong's 2038, 2039, 2040) is the common verb for "work to acquire" and occurs 41 times in the New Testament. Without a modifier, such as "hired," even its noun form for laborer, "*ergates*," does not necessarily mean one who is paid. "*Misthos*" (Strong's 3408) is the more common word for "reward,

wages, hire" and would have been the preferable word to use in 5:17, if "salary" were intended.

7. Why would Paul tell the church to give Timothy a double salary when he himself refused any at all (1 Cor. 9:12, 15)? Was not his companion, Timothy, included in the injunction, "I have shown you all things, how that so laboring you ought to support the weak, and to remember the words of the Lord Jesus, how he said, It is more blessed to give than to receive" (Acts 20:35)?

8. Both phrases in 5:18 refer to extreme poverty, and not to well-paid salaried professionals receiving tithes. "The laborer (*ergates*) is worthy of his reward (*misthos*)." It is because of this verse, and not because of verse 17, that paraphrasers and commentaries often render "*timees*" as "salary" and "pay" rather than "honor."

Why were the two examples of 5:18 given? We must remember that the context relates to discipline. Paul used this same example of the "ox" in 1 Corinthians 9:9-10. Although he concluded in 1 Corinthians 9:12 and 9:15 that he and others had certain legitimate "rights" of compensation for their work in the ministry, he did not say that he meant double salaries for all. That would have been the very last thing Paul would have said about wages! Also, although in 2 Corinthians 11:8 Paul admitted to receiving "wages" (*opsonion*; Strong's 3800), this Greek word merely means "a soldier's ration," or daily bare necessities of life, while continuing his trade as a tentmaker.

The real emphasis of 5:18 is on the "double worthiness" of the ox. While it was normally unmuzzled *while not working*; it was double-worthy of not being muzzled *while working*. Thus the ox "plowed in hope" that its needs would be met. The "ox" illustration has no reference to salary unless the gospel worker works in double hope that God will give a double blessing. If Paul had wanted to teach tithing at this point, he would have quoted Numbers 18:20-26 and compared Christian workers to the Aaronic priests instead of referring to a grinding ox.

9. "The laborer (*ergatees*) is worthy (*axios*) of his reward (*misthos*)," again, in its context, refers to double honor, and not double pay. Why would a discussion of honorable discipline (vv. 1-16 and 19-20) be interrupted by a reminder of how much salary a minister should get (vv. 17-18)? Such an idea is absurd! It is true that, even the word "wage" is not the only definition which can be assigned to "*misthos*" in verse 18 (Strong's 3048)! Of the 29 occurrences, only 5 could possibly be "wages," or "salary," while the remainder simply mean "reward." In fact, Paul used "*misthos*" twice in 1 Cor. 9:17-18 as "reward" in his refusal of a wage! "*Misthos*" is the believer's "reward" in heaven and the "reward" which Christ brings with him.

In the context of 1 Timothy 5:17-18, the ministering elder's "reward" is the "double-honor," or double-cautious *discipline* due him! The minister is first worthy of single honor while being disciplined because he is a Christian, and he is worthy of double honor while being disciplined *because he is a laborer* in the church. These are the words of Jesus in Matthew 10:10 and Luke 10:7. "*Misthos*" appears in Luke, but "*trophee*" (Strong's 5160) which basically means "food" appears in Matthew. While "food" is the basic definition, "support," "rations," and "wages" are extensions. This is also discussed in the chapter on 1 Corinthians 9. When Jesus made this statement, he told his disciples NOT to carry any money, extra shoes, or stay anywhere except in the first homes which invited them (Matt. 10:9-11). This meant living as a pauper day by day, without receiving a salary, or accumulating any goods at all. Old Covenant prophets usually followed this pattern. When his disciples healed the sick, raised the dead, and cast out devils, they were giving freely, because they had received freely (Matt. 10:8). Compare also Luke 12:22-40; especially 33-34.

Deut. 24:14 You shall not oppress an hired servant that is poor and needy, whether he is of your brothers, or of your strangers that are in your land within your gates.

Deut. 24:15 At his day you shall give him his hire, neither shall the sun go down upon it; for he is poor, and sets his heart upon it: unless he cry against you to the LORD, and it is sin to you.

Many commentaries and cross-references say that Paul's reference to "Scripture" in 1 Timothy 5:18 must have meant Deuteronomy 24:14-15. Yet, here again, these verses also refer to the poorest farm workers who lived from meager earnings day by day and were required to be paid at the end of each working day. They do not refer to financially secure merchants worthy of double pay. Compare Leviticus 18:13; Matthew 29:8; and James 5:4.

10. If Paul had meant "double-pay" in 1 Timothy 5:17, then why did he quote references to paupers who owned or accumulated nothing? How can one refer to penniless paupers to prove that one should receive double salary?

6:1 Let as many servants as are under the yoke count their own masters *worthy of all honor*, that the name of God and his doctrine will not be blasphemed.

11. If "worthy of *double* honor" in 5:17 means "worthy of double pay," then what does "worthy of *all* honor" mean only nine verses later in 6:1? Certainly Paul is not saying that a Christian slave should give his master ALL the money he accumulates! Thus the *context* and word usage in 1 Timothy does not support the translation of "double pay."

6:5…[those who are] destitute of the truth, supposing that gain is godliness—from such withdraw yourself.

12. Timothy is told to "withdraw" from those who think that religion, or godliness, is a means of gaining wealth (6:3-5). This is a strange command to follow-up "worthy of double salary" with!

6:6 But godliness with contentment is great gain.
6:7 For we brought nothing into this world, and it is certain we can carry nothing out.
6:8 And having food and raiment let us therewith be content.

13. Paul told ministers to be content with bare necessities. This also is inconsistent to the "double pay" interpretation of 5:17. Their "great gain" is not double salary, but "godliness which brings contentment."

6:9 But they that want to be rich fall into temptation and a snare, and into many foolish and hurtful lusts, which drown men in destruction and perdition.
6:10 For the love of money [covetousness] is the root of all evil, which while some coveted after, they have erred from the faith, and pierced themselves through with many sorrows.
6:11 But you, O man of God, flee these things, and follow after righteousness, godliness, faith, love, patience, meekness.

14. Paul warned Timothy against accumulating wealth. Yet today many ministers of wealthy churches are themselves very wealthy.

6:12 Fight the good fight of faith...
. . . .
6:14 That you *keep this commandment* without spot, unrebukeable, until the appearing of our Lord Jesus Christ.

15. Paul encouraged Timothy to "fight the good fight of faith" and be "un-rebuke-able" (6:12-14). From the context, this "fighting" at

least includes the warning, "don't get caught up in money matters and a desire for wealth." Unfortunately, all too often, ministers need to be rebuked about money matters.

6:17 Instruct them that are rich in this world, that they should not be high-minded, nor trust in uncertain riches, but in the living God, who gives us richly all things to enjoy.
6:18 That they do good, that they be rich in good works, ready to distribute, willing to communicate.

16. The "rich in this world" (6:17-19) are referred to as "them," but not "us," or gospel ministers.
17. Paul instructed that the gospel minister is "to do good, to be rich in good works, to be generous and ready to share" (1 Tim. 6:18 NAS). His "richness" is in sharing with others.

6:19 Storing up for themselves the treasure of a good foundation for the future, so that they may take hold of that which is life indeed.

18. The gospel minister "stores up," or "treasures up," not worldly wealth, but "a good foundation for the future. This is the same *"thesaurizoon"* discussed in 1 Corinthians 16:2!
19. Tithing is not even implied in these passages. The author did not tell the church that the pastor is due full-time support through tithing. As in 1 Corinthians 9:14, another "golden opportunity" to teach tithing has been totally ignored.

In conclusion, Paul would not expect his best pupil, Timothy, to follow lower standards than himself. As a Pharisee, lawyer, and teacher of the law, Paul had been taught to refuse payment to instruct others in the honored Mosaic Law. Yet teaching the gospel of Jesus Christ was a much greater honor than that of teaching the law. Since Timothy accompanied Paul from a very young age, it is very likely that Paul became a surrogate father to Timothy and taught him the highly-important trade of tent-making.

Verses 17 and 18 do not teach that a minister should receive double salary for his services. Since Timothy was among "them that were with me" in Acts 20:31-35, he witnessed firsthand how Paul worked night and day for three years at tent-making while not asking the church at Ephesus for money or food. Paul concluded his farewell sermon by telling his co-workers, including Timothy, to follow his example and work in order to help the needy in the church.

It is very difficult to conclude that Paul is now asking the church to pay Timothy a double salary! Claiming that Paul wanted Timothy and church leaders to receive "double-salary" contradicts his convictions about preaching the gospel. In 1 Corinthians 9:12 he refused a "right" to receive compensation "unless we should hinder the gospel of Christ." In 9:15 he stated that, not only had he not accepted support, he did not intend to start accepting it; as a matter of fact, he would "rather die" than have anybody deny him of boasting that he preached for free. Why would Paul expect Timothy to do otherwise, and not follow his own example?

CHAPTER 25

▼

MISCELLANEOUS OBJECTIONS

Objection: The book of Acts demonstrates that all early Christians gave much more than a tithe and set an example for others to follow.

One prominent television speaker and author insists that tithe-giving is demonstrated in the first chapters of Acts. He also says that the difference between "not being under law, but under grace" means "not operating on the basis of the minimum, but on the basis of loving God."

Acts 2:44 And all that believed were together, and had all things common,
Acts 2:45 And sold their possessions and goods, and parted them to all men, as every man had need.

This is an argument from silence that requires no real supporting texts.

There are several basic reasons to reject this reasoning from Acts 2:44-45.

1. This is an example of freewill offerings to the extreme and is not an example of tithing in the early church.
2. The pastor-author referred to above does not live in a communal house and share equally with all the poor.
3. The radical selling of property and communal living seen in the early chapters of Acts was God's opening "kick-off" of the gospel glory and was not habitually repeated after the initial events.
4. These events have absolutely nothing to do with tithing laws because the majority of the Jewish Christians around Jerusalem never stopped paying tithes to the temple and priests.
5. There is no reason to believe that the poor had anything to contribute. The rich followed gospel principles and gave according to their ability.
6. It is very doubtful that many of those who advocate this viewpoint have followed the very same example of above-tithe-giving by selling all their property and by sharing everything in common.
7. The definition of the difference between the law and grace concerning tithing is flippant. Fortunately, this theological doctor does not use similar hermeneutics when discussing other Bible doctrines.
8. When the first great influx of money was gone, the Jerusalem church soon became destitute of funds and even had to ask other churches for famine relief. What would happen today if church members "sold [all] their possessions and goods" and lived until the resources expired?

Objection: Tithing is not mentioned because it was not an issue.

The same prominent author who promotes the first objection also says that all of the early churches of the first century A.D. accepted and practiced tithing. This would naturally include Gentile Christians as well as Jewish Christians. His logic is that, since no New Testament writer accused any individual or any church of *not* tithing, this proves that all *did* tithe. Therefore, since they all tithed (the assumption claims), there was no need to address a problem that did not exist. Thus the silence, or absence of an argument, proves tithing was faithfully observed. In other words, "no texts" *are* their "texts."

This position also assumes that Jewish Christians switched from tithing to the temple priests towards tithing to the church, and that Gentile Christians accepted this one ordinance of the Mosaic Law, while rejecting the rest of its ordinances as non-New Covenant. While misunderstanding parts of the gospel, early Christians, they say, faithfully paid tithes to support church pastors and missionaries.

For the following reasons, this argument from silence must be rejected:

1. Church historians (and probably theologians) of most denominations normally reject this argument.
2. The "silence" is caused by the fact that the New Testament does not contain a single reference or command for any Christian to tithe. This presents a major dilemma for those who support tithing. Beyond quoting Old Covenant texts which are either pagan in origin (such as in Genesis 14) or only refer to national Israel under the Mosaic Law, they have no texts to use from the New Testament after Calvary.
3. If tithing were indeed a genuine New Covenant doctrine, then it must be the only "silent" doctrine *NOT* supported by a single post-Calvary text. This is embarrassing because most conservatives who advocate tithing also insist that all doctrine should come from the post-Calvary New Testament.
4. If the "argument from silence" is the major defense of tithing, it is a poor argument. This approach simply cannot stand alone.

Acts 15:1 And certain men which came down from Judea taught the brothers, and said, Unless you become circumcised after the manner of Moses, you cannot be saved.

Acts 21:20 And when they [the Jerusalem church elders] heard it [Paul's report], they glorified the Lord, and said to him, You see, brother, how many thousands of Jews there are which believe; and they are all zealous of the law. [A.D. 58]

Acts 21:21 And they are informed of you, that you are teaching all the Jews which are among the Gentiles to forsake Moses, saying that they ought not to circumcise their children, neither to walk after the customs.

....

Acts 21:24 Take these men, and purify yourself with them, and pay their expenses, that they may shave their heads, and all may know that those things, whereof they were informed concerning you, are nothing, but that you yourself also are walking orderly, and are keeping the law.

5. Actually, there was no "silence" from Jewish Christians. It is conclusive from Acts 15 and 21, all of Romans, all of Galatians, all of Hebrews, and most church historians that many (if not most) Jewish Christians had simply added Christianity to Judaism. Those in Israel had continued regular worship at the temple and supported the temple financially, including tithing. It is very obvious that many Jewish Christians wanted all Gentile Christians to become circumcised, observe all of the law, and pay temple tithes (Acts 15:1; Gal. 2:4).

6. The Jewish Christians who did tithe gave their tithes, not to the church, but to the temple because they still considered themselves to be Jews first, and under obligation to keep the entire Mosaic Law. Compare Acts 15; 21:21-24; 28:17.

Acts 21:25 Concerning the Gentiles which believe, *we have written and concluded that they observe no such thing*, except that they keep themselves from things offered to idols, and from blood, and from strangled, and from fornication.

7. There was also no "silence" about the Gentile Christians. The Jewish church in Jerusalem specifically excluded them from the necessity of keeping any part of the Mosaic Law, including tithing. Compare Acts 15:19-30; 21:19-25.

8. Israel had been rebuked by God for its failure to pay tithes under the law. God would certainly have rebuked the church for the same sin if the church were in violation. Yet, while Paul, Peter, John, James and Jude correct the church for a very wide variety of sins, including not giving offerings for the poor, they never correct it for not tithing. This is inconceivable if tithing were a legitimate doctrine. It is especially inconceivable that the church at Corinth would be guilty of so many other sins, yet continue to pay tithes.

9. Likewise, a prominent issue with Paul was the failure of Corinth to give "offerings" to help the poor saints in Judea. It is unlikely that they would be faithful in tithing, yet unfaithful in offerings to the poor.

10. In reality, then and now, failure to support God's program is usually the *very first* sign of unfaithfulness—not the last one! Why would failure to support the church possibly be the very last sin and the very least committed that would require a rebuke? Thus, the basic assumption is illogical.

11. According to 1 Corinthians 9:15-19, Paul would have refused tithes, or any offer of full-time support, in order to fully preach the gospel unhindered. And neither was his action disobedience to Christ's command. In Acts 20:26-35, at the end of Paul's many years of missionary service, he still refused a salary and worked for a living. Furthermore, he urged other preachers to follow his example.

12. The "not an issue" claim ignores the strong "issue" of Mosaic Law ordinances, found prominently in Acts, Romans, Galatians, Ephesians, Colossians, and Hebrews. The Mosaic Law *was* an issue! Since tithing was so easy to ascertain, it was particularly enforced in the Mishnah. Legalistic Jewish Christians tried to force the Mosaic

Law on the church. Scripture records that Sabbath-keeping, circumcision, feast-keeping, and food laws were among the law practices they tried to force on the church. If tithing were not viewed as something solely due to the Aaronic priest, then every Jewish-Christian who had been a Pharisee would have certainly tried to impose some kind of tithing on the church. The very fact that the Judaizers did not try to impose it on the church along with these other laws is a strong argument against tithing in the early church.

13.An "argument from silence" much better fits the contention that tithing is not taught for the New Covenant believer. Other than Hebrews 7, which says that tithing was abolished, the word does not once appear in the inspired writings after Calvary.

14.The "silence" argument ignores the fact that Paul and early Jewish church leaders came from a tradition which forbade them from giving up a trade and expecting to be supported by others. It would take centuries for this tradition to be erased by the escalation of the clergy over the laity and the removal of the priesthood-of-believers' doctrine.

By using the Living Bible as a guide, Galatians 3:1-5 could very easily read thus:

Gal. 3:1 O foolish preachers, who has placed an evil spell on you, that you should not obey the whole truth about tithing and other abolished, blotted out, and disannulled ordinances of the Mosaic Law? The meaning of the crucifixion was clearly set forth before you. What do you think was nailed to the cross with him at his crucifixion? What do you think happened to law ordinances when the veil ripped?

Gal. 3:2 I want you to answer one serious question for me. Were you filled with the Spirit because of your obedience to the Mosaic Law, or because of your faith? Should not this logic apply to ALL laws not repeated under the principles of faith?

Gal. 3:3 Your logic is foolish. (You have gone completely crazy: The Living Bible). You *began* your Christian experience by receiving the Spirit through faith. You needed the Spirit because the law never gave you spiritual life in any sense! How can you possibly turn back to the law and try to attain spiritual maturity by works of law? How can the church teach salvation by grace through faith, and then teach financial success by re-applying the unprofitable Mosaic Law of tithing?

Gal. 3:4 If such is your logic, then you have wasted your time! You are discarding every principle you have learned about the gospel. The law is not of faith.

Gal. 3:5 God will work miracles, financially and otherwise, only "when you believe in Christ and fully trust in Him."

Objection: Since New Covenant standards are higher than Old Covenant standards, the tithe is the "minimum" starting place.

For the following reasons, this objection is also rejected:

1. This is another argument from silence which tries to avoid the major dilemma that there are no specific post-Calvary/post-law texts which command tithing to the New Covenant Christian.

2. While the principle of interpretation is sound, the *assumption* is wrong. In order words, while it is true that New Covenant principles are higher than Old Covenant principles, this does not lead to the conclusion that all Christians should begin their giving at the ten percentage level.

3. *The erroneous assumption is that ALL Israelites under the Mosaic Law were required to tithe and started at ten percent.* In fact, only landowners and herdsmen of the land were required to tithe and start at ten percent. Actually, tithing was a targeted ordinance which placed burdens on land owners while not affecting hundreds of tradesman and craftsman occupations who only gave heave offerings. This is exactly why many Jews stopped farming and went into banking and commerce during the Middle Ages.

4. The error of this assumption reveals why New Covenant giving principles are actually *higher than* Old Covenant tithing. Once the tithe
had been paid on the land by the landowner, all those who lived on
that land and were sustained by that land were *required* to give *nothing* at all. The hired servants were already covered by the tithe of the
owner.

This inherent problem with tithing is pointed out in several quotations
in the discussion of 1 Corinthians 16:2. While an Old Covenant wealthy
person could STOP giving at ten percent and meet the requirements of
the Mosaic Law, this same wealthy person is violating the *higher* New
Covenant principles when he stops at ten percent!

**2 Cor. 8:12 For if there is first a willing mind, it is accepted according to
that which a man has, and not according to that which he has not.**
**2 Cor. 8:13 For I do not mean that other men should be eased, and you
burdened.**
**2 Cor. 8:14 But by an equality, that now at this time your abundance
may be a supply for their want, that their abundance also may be a supply for your want, that there may be equality,**
**2 Cor. 8:15 As it is written, He that had gathered much had nothing
over; and he that had gathered little had no lack.**

The New Covenant *higher principle of equality* expects ALL believers to
give freewill offerings spontaneously because they have a new nature and
want to give above that which they normally would. While all give spontaneously from a willing heart, the "above ten percent" of the wealthy
should more than offset the "below ten percent" of the poor.

This principle of "equality giving" is a higher standard of grace giving.
It does not operate on the principle of law. Neither does it shame or
"curse" the poor for not being able to pay a minimum of ten percent.
"Equality giving" does not encourage the poor to stay away from worship
in order to avoid being made a spectacle for not giving much. On the con-

trary, New Covenant giving allows the poor to have some degree of self-respect in knowing that they gave all possible without depriving their families of essential food and shelter.

2 Cor. 8:2 How that in a great trial of affliction, the abundance of their joy, and their deep poverty abounded to the riches of their liberality.
2 Cor. 8:3 For to their power, I bear record, yes, and beyond their power they were willing of themselves.

5. The New Covenant replaces Mosaic Law tithing with many general principles which range from zero percent to one hundred percent. Although they may actually give less than ten percent, even the poor are commended for giving above and beyond their ability. "Ability," not "compulsion," is the operating principle of New Covenant motivation! To this we can add "love" and "the desire to see souls saved"—neither of which were required motivations for law-tithing.

6. While the New Covenant is full of "freewill giving" principles, it contains no exact giving percentages because we are no longer under the law but under grace.

Objection: Tithing was not a form of taxation

Eklund writes, "The tithe was not a form of taxation. The Old Covenant Jews under the authority of kings paid taxes in addition to the tithe (see 1 Sam. 17:25; 2 Kings 23:35; Ezra 4:13, 20; Neh. 5:4). Prior to the monarchy there was no need for taxation. Israel operated as a theocracy and there was no government to fund."[109]

The argument that tithes were not a form of taxation because "Israel operated as a theocracy and there was no government to fund" is contrary

---

109   Eklund, 66.

to both common sense and most theological authorities. An earlier chapter in this book on "taxes" discusses this objection. In summary,

1. The very definition of "theocracy" is "a form of government in which God is the supreme civil ruler." It is a direct government by God. A "theocracy" IS a "government." As a government, even a theocracy needs funds for the sustenance of its authority figures who administer law and justice. In the theocracy portrayed in the Pentateuch, the Levites performed government-type duties and were sustained by tithes and offerings.

2. Many biblical authorities define the tithe as a tax, or tithing as a form of taxation, including the *Encyclopedia Judaica* and the Southern Baptist *Holman Bible Dictionary and Concordance*.[110]

3. The "not a tax" argument ignores the church-state nature of Old Covenant tithing. Although, from King Saul to King Hezekiah, hundreds of years, tithing is not mentioned in the Bible, yet, it is evident that King David and King Solomon assumed the responsibility to gather tithes and redistribute them to the Levites as government officials and religious leaders. However, the prophets registered no complain that this violated the Mosaic Law's underlying purpose of tithing.

Conclusion

This book has thus far completed an exhaustive study of every tithing text in the Bible. Every Christian can, and should, take a few minutes to check the doctrine out personally. Read the texts in several versions if necessary. Become like the Bereans and do not take anything on the basis of what somebody else says. The Bereans "searched the scriptures daily,

---

110   *Holman Bible Dictionary and Concordance (Giant Print)* (Nashville: Holman, 1999), s.v. "tithe." Note: This is a Southern Baptist publication. It differs from the full-sized *Holman Bible Dictionary* which does *not* define the tithe as a form of taxation.

whether those things were so" because they were "more noble...in that they received the word with all readiness of mind" (Acts 17:11).

Obtain an exhaustive Bible concordance and look up the words "tithe" and "tenth." As you check each reference in context, you will discover that the words do not occur in the New Testament after Calvary, except in Hebrews, chapter 7.

The new church had the tremendous task of taking the gospel to the entire world. Yet from the day of Pentecost to the last words of Revelation, not a word occurs which in the least implies that any kind of tithing is expected from the Christian living under grace.

Many theological reference books end their discussion on 'tithe' with statements similar to *The Oxford Companion to the Bible*, "The New Testament nowhere explicitly requires tithing to maintain a ministry or a place of assembly."[111] The *New Catholic Encyclopedia* says, "No law of tithing is found in the New Testament, although the principle of church support is laid down in Matt. 10:10 (see also Luke 10:7) and echoed in 1 Corinthians 9:13-14."[112] One can be sure that both Protestants and Roman Catholics would certainly promote and expect tithes from a biblical basis if it were a legitimate benefit for them.

111   Bruce M. Metzger and Michael D. Coogan, *Oxford Companion to the Bible* (New York: Oxford UP, 1993), s.v. "tithe."

112   *New Catholic Encyclopedia*, s.v. "tithe."

GRACE GIVING:
THE NEWER AND BETTER
REPLACED TITHING

CHAPTER 26

▼

CHAFER AND WALVOORD
ON NEW COVENANT GIVING

Lewis Sperry Chafer, the founder of Dallas Theological Seminary, author of an eight volume *Systematic Theology*, and a leading spokesman for conservative Christianity, wrote an excellent article discussing New Covenant giving in his book, *Major Bible Themes*. That article is reprinted here in its entirety. Sperry is required reading in many conservative schools of theology.

Conservative theologians often remind us that all doctrine should be settled from the epistles of the New Testament and NOT from the Gospels. This advice reminds us that the two events of Calvary and Pentecost, not the birth of Christ, ended the Old Covenant and began the New Covenant. Christ lived and died under the Old Covenant.

From *Major Bible Themes* Lewis Sperry Chafer, Revised by John Walvoord
"The giving of money which a Christian has earned becomes an important aspect of any believer's service for God. Self and money are alike the

roots of much evil, and in the dispensing of money, as in its acquisition and possession, *the Christian is expected to stand upon a grace relationship to God* (2 Cor. 8:1, 7). This relationship presupposes that he has first given himself to God in unqualified dedication (2 Cor. 8:5); and a true dedication of self to God includes all that one is and has (1 Cor. 6:20; 7:23; 1 Pet. 1:18-19)—his life, his time, his strength, his ability, his ideals, and his property.

In matters pertaining to the giving of money, the grace principle involves the believer's recognition of God's sovereign authority over all that the Christian is and has, and *contrasts with the Old Testament legal system of tithing* which was in force as a part of the law until the law was done away with (John 1:16-17; Rom. 6:14; 7:1-6; 2 Cor. 3:1-18; Gal. 3:19-25; 5:18; Eph. 2:15; Col. 2:14). *Though certain principles of the law were carried forward and restated under grace, tithing, like Sabbath observance, is never imposed on the believer in this dispensation.* Since the Lord's Day superseded the legal Sabbath and is adapted to the principles of grace as the Sabbath could not be, so *tithing has been superseded by a new system of giving* which is adapted to the teachings of grace, as tithing could not be.

Christian giving under grace, as illustrated in the experience of the saints in Corinth, is summarized in 2 Corinthians 8:1-9:15. In this passage we discover:

A. Christ was their pattern. The Lord's giving of Himself (2 Cor. 8:9) is the pattern of all giving under grace. He did not give a tenth; He gave ALL.

B. Their giving was even out of great poverty. A striking combination of phrases is employed to describe what the Corinthians experienced in their giving (2 Cor. 8:2): "in a great trial of affliction," "the abundance of their joy," "their deep poverty abounded," "the riches of their liberality." Likewise, concerning liberality in spite of great poverty, it should be remembered that "the widow's mite" (Luke 21:1-4), which drew the commendation of the Lord Jesus, was not a part, but "all that she had."

C. *Their giving was not by commandment [1 Cor. 8:8], nor of necessity [2 Cor. 9:7]. Under the law, a tenth was commanded and its payment was a necessity; under grace, God is not seeking the gift, but an expression of devotion from the giver. Under grace no law is imposed and no proportion to be given is stipulated,* and, while it is true that God works in the yielded heart both to will and to do His good pleasure (Phil. 2:13), He finds pleasure only in that gift which is given cheerfully, or more literally, "hilariously" (2 Cor. 9:7).

If a law existed stipulating the amount to be given, there are those, doubtless, who would seek to fulfill it, even against their own wishes. Thus their gift would be made "grudgingly" and "of necessity (2 Cor. 9:7). If it be said that to support the work of the gospel we must have money whether given hilariously or not, it may also be said that it is not the amount which is given, but rather the divine blessing upon the gift that accomplishes the desired end.

Christ fed five thousand from five loaves and two fishes. There is abundant evidence to prove that wherever the children of God have fulfilled their privilege in giving under grace, their liberality has resulted in "all sufficiency in all things" which has made them "abound to every good work," for God is able to make even the grace of giving to "abound" to every believer (2 Cor. 9:8).

D. The early Christians, first of all, gave themselves. Acceptable giving is preceded by a complete giving of oneself (2 Cor. 8:5). This suggests the important truth that giving under grace, like giving under the law, is limited to a certain class of people. *Tithing was never imposed by God on any other than the nation Israel (Lev. 27:34; Num. 18:23-24; Mal. 3:7-10).* So, Christian giving is limited to believers and is most acceptable when given by believers who have yielded their lives to God.

E. Christians in the early church also gave systematically. Like tithing, there is suggested systematic regularity in giving under grace. "Upon the first day of the week let every one of you lay by him in store, as

God has prospered him" (1 Cor. 16:2). This injunction is addressed
to "every man" (every Christian man), and thus *excuses none*; and
giving is to be from that which is already "in store."

F. God sustains the giver. God will sustain grace-giving with limitless
temporal resources (2 Cor. 9:8-10; Luke 6:38). *In this connection it
may be seen that those who give as much as a tenth are usually prospered
in temporal things, but since the believer can have no relation to the law
(Gal. 5:1), it is evident that this prosperity is the fulfillment of the promise under grace, rather than the fulfillment of promises under the law. No
blessings are thus dependent on the exact tithing.*

The blessings are bestowed because a heart has expressed itself through
a gift. It is manifest that no gift will be made to God from the heart which
He will not graciously acknowledge. There is no opportunity here for
designing people to become rich. The giving must be from the heart, and
God's response will be bestowing spiritual riches, or in temporal blessings
as He shall choose.

G. True riches are from God. The Corinthian Christians were made
rich with heavenly riches. There is such a thing as being rich in this
world's goods and yet not rich toward God (Luke 12:21). All such
are invited to buy of Him that gold which is tried in the fire (Rev.
3:18). Through the absolute poverty of Christ in His death, all may
be made rich (2 Cor. 8:9). It is possible to be rich in faith (Jas. 2:5)
and rich in good works (1 Tim. 6:18); but in Christ Jesus the
believer receives "the riches of his grace" (Eph. 1:7), and "the riches
of his glory" (Eph. 3:16) (italics mine).[113]

---

113   Lewis Sperry Chafer, *Major Bible Themes, Revised,* John Walvoord (Grand
        Rapids: Academie Books, 1974 ed.), 253-55.

CHAPTER 27

▼

2 CORINTHIANS 8 AND 9 GRACE PRINCIPLES OF GIVING OUT-PERFORM LAW PRINCIPLES OF GIVING

Every man according as he purposes in his heart, so let him give; not grudgingly, or of necessity: for God loves a cheerful giver (2 Cor. 9:7).

Financial need was obviously very great for the young New Covenant church. The less time that missionaries had to spend in their trade to earn a living meant more time they could spend spreading the gospel. Those assemblies were actively participating in the most important task ever given to mankind—the spreading of the gospel of Jesus Christ. Although the missionaries did need financial aid, it must be remembered that such was primarily because they chose to be poor and deserved the aid.

Acts 14:23 And when they had *ordained elders in every church....*

Titus 1:5 For this cause I left you in Crete, that you should set in order the things that are wanting, and *ordain elders in every city,* **as I had appointed you.**

There was not just one "elder" or "overseer" but many in each city and in each house assembly where the word was studied and preached (Acts 11:30; 14:23; 15:4, 6, 23; 16:4; 20:17; Tit. 1:5; Jas. 5:14; 1 Pet. 5:1, 5). It would have been impossible to pay full-time support for the many elders of house churches. At least for the first 2-3 centuries they worked at their own trades as did Paul (Acts 18:1-3).

Second Corinthians, chapters 8 and 9, detail how the Apostle Paul used gospel principles to obtain assistance for the poor saints in Jerusalem. However, there is no indication that the support was being collected for missionary salaries or for support of church officers.

1. Giving is Totally "Of Grace" in the Church

No other chapter in the Bible uses the word "grace" more often than 2 Corinthians, chapter 8! Thayer defines "grace" as "that which affords joy, pleasure, delight, sweetness, charm, and loveliness.[114] What a rich word for God to apply to giving. Therefore, those who give to God's work actually receive of the grace of God. God gives us grace in order to give, and then God gives us more grace when we give.

 A. The GRACE that God has given" (8:1)

 B. "GRACE of sharing" (Greek); "favor" (NAS); "privilege" (NIV); "gift" (KJV) (8:4)

 C. "Gracious work" (NAS), "the act of GRACE" (NIV) (8:6)

 D. "Gracious work" (NAS), "this GRACE of giving" (NIV) (8:7)

---

114 Thayer, *"charis."*

E. "The GRACE of our Lord Jesus Christ" (8:9)

F. "But GRACE be to God" (Greek); "thanks" (8:16)

G. "This GRACE" (Greek) (KJV); "offering" (NIV); "this gracious work" (NAS) (8:19)

H. "God is able to make all GRACE abound to you" (9:8)

I. "The surpassing GRACE God has given you" (9:14)

All of the above texts describe the Christian's relationship to grace and giving. It is a grace from God and is based on Christ's example. In contrast to the law which commanded giving, New Covenant giving is grace from beginning to end. It is an act that shares. It rebounds to the giver because one cannot out-give God.

2. Give Yourself to God First

First, you must accept Jesus Christ as your personal Lord and Savior. "They…first gave their own selves to the Lord" (8:5). Until one joins the family of God through conversion, he is still under condemnation and grace cannot govern his life (John 16:9).

3. Give Yourself to Knowing God's Will

A Christian must seek for, and yield to, the will of God. "First to the Lord, and, then, to us by the will of God" (8:5). Concerning the matter of giving, we must seek to know God's will in our lives in this area as in every other area of our lives. In the context, "gave themselves to us" means that they agreed with Paul's request for famine relief for the saints in Judea.

4. Give in Response to Christ's Giving

"For you know the grace of our Lord Jesus Christ, that, though he was rich, yet for your sakes he became poor, that you through his poverty might be rich" (8:9). "Thanks be to God for his unspeakable gift" (9:15). Christians who are yielding to God's will, hastening to know the Word of God, and who are filled with the Holy Spirit are being changed day by day to follow Christ's example. This example includes every part of their lives, including giving.

5. Give out of a Sincere Desire

"To prove the sincerity of your love" (v. 8). Paul reminded them that in the past they were the first "to be forward [have the desire: NAS]" to give (v. 10). "If there is first a willing mind" (v. 12), again emphasizes the desire. This principle is repeated in chapter 9, verse 7, "as he purposes in his heart." A believer in God's will should naturally have that sincere desire to give.

Under the law, a sincere desire was the motive for freewill offerings, but it did not matter concerning tithes. God commanded a tithe and expected it, whether or not it was given out of a sincere desire. The priests still had no inheritance and still deserved their portion under the terms of the Old Covenant.

6. Give, Not Because of a Commandment

"I speak not by commandment" (8:8); "I am not commanding you" (NIV). "And herein I give my advice" (8:10). "Let every man give...not grudgingly or of necessity," "not grudgingly, or under compulsion" (NAS) (9:7); "as God has prospered him." It is clear from these references that there is no hint of any compulsion, demand, or commandment to give under the grace principle.

Scofield wrote at 2 Corinthians 8 and 9, "In contrast with the law, which imposed giving as a divine requirement, Christian giving is voluntary, and a test of sincerity and love."[115] Chafer agreed, "The grace principle contrasts with the Old Testament legal system of tithing.... Tithing has been superseded by a new system of giving which is adapted to the teachings of grace.... Under grace, God is not seeking the gift, but an

---

115   *Scofield*, s.v. "2 Cor. 8 and 9."

expression of devotion from the giver. Under grace no law is imposed and no proportion to be given is stipulated."[116]

Under the New Covenant the Christian obeys God because he has a new nature, is a new creation, and the Holy Spirit is his teacher. "When he said 'a New Covenant,' he has made the first obsolete; but whatever is becoming obsolete and growing old is ready to disappear" (Heb. 8:13). The "commandment" to give has now been replaced by a "sincere desire" of a new creation. The Christian gives spontaneously because the desire to give is part of the new creation.

7. Give as Much as You Are Able, or Even Beyond Your Ability

"For to their power [ability], I bear record, yes, and beyond their power [ability] they were willing of themselves" (8:3). "Now therefore perform [finish] the doing of it...so there may be a performance also out of that which you have [an actual doing from your ability]" (8:11). "...it is accepted according to that a man has, and not according to that he has not" (8:12). "Let every one of you lay by him in store, as God has prospered him" (1 Cor. 16:2).

Rhodes Thompson remarks in his book, *Stewards Shaped by Grace*, "Another discovery is now revealed: God's grace shown in those churches [in India] was complemented by people's voluntary response [quotes 8:3]. Precisely! No legalistic response to the amazing grace of God is appropriate. That is why Paul wrote [quotes 9:7]. God's grace obviously encourages, but does not force, the decision to be made. However, when faith responds to grace, God's power at work within that life...or within the churches...is able to do far more abundantly than all that people can ask or think (Eph. 3:20). What we cannot do or cannot even imagine being done, God's grace working through our faith does."[117]

---

116   Chafer, 253-54.
117   Thompson, 113.

8. Give in Order That There Might Be an Equality

2 Cor. 8:13 For I do not mean that other men be eased, and you burdened,
2 Cor. 8:14 But by an equality, that now at this time your abundance may be a supply for their want, that their abundance also may be a supply for your want, that there may be equality.

1 Tim. 6:17 Command them that are rich in this world, that they should not be high-minded, nor trust in uncertain riches, but in the living God, who gives us richly all things to enjoy;
1 Tim. 6:18 That they do good, that they become rich in good works, ready to distribute, willing to communicate.

Some can afford to give much more than the Old Covenant ten percent, while others are simply not able to give much at all. Circumstances are different from household to household. God understands. Let us not forget the saying "little is much if God is in it." God can do more with the widow's mite or the grain of mustard seed given sincerely than with millions given to purchase his favor.

In connection with giving as much as one is able, is the grace principle of "equality." This does not mean that everybody is to give the same percentage. It means that those who are prosperous should give a lot more—until they actually notice a crimp in their checkbook—"Give until it hurts!" When those who are prosperous give more, and those who are poor give less (but still as much as they can), the results are an "equality" according to what each was able to give.

New Covenant grace-giving principles are fair; they are not set at the same legalistic level for everybody. While some families have good incomes and few bills, others have low incomes and many bills. A family giving ten percent of $200,000 would have $180,000 remaining; while the same size family giving ten percent of $20,000 would have only

$18,000 to survive on; under tithing this is an unfair legalistic burden. If two families both earned $40,000 and only one had free housing, paid expenses, and insurance, should both give the same amount? What would be a burden for one to give would not be felt by another. Also, if two families had the same income and one had oppressive medical bills, God does not expect them both to give the same under principles of grace giving. Yet the tithing law made no exceptions to land owners and did not require non-landowners and craftsmen to tithe at all!. These examples illustrate why grace principles are superior to tithing.

There is no commandment after Calvary concerning how much" to give. God has no desire to cause some to be "hard pressed" or "burdened" (KJV) because of any guilt about how much they must give (8:13). The greater burden of giving falls on those who are able to pay more (1 Tim. 6:17-18.)

9. Give Because of a Burden for Lost Souls

Although not mentioned specifically in these two chapters, this was, and should be, the reason for all spiritual giving. When Paul said "woe is me if I preach not the gospel (1 Cor. 9:16)," he was referring to his calling and burden for souls. Every Christian needs a vision of lost and dying relatives, friends, and the world on its way to hell without Christ. Yet, the Old Covenant tithing principle from law had no evangelistic motive for the lost world and non-Hebrews around it.

10. Give Joyfully

2 Cor. 8:2 How that in a great trial of affliction the abundance of their joy and their deep poverty abounded to the riches of their liberality [rich generosity: NIV].

The secret of the Macedonian churches' abundant generosity in giving included: (1) a great trial of affliction, (2) abundant joy, and (3) deep poverty. "In Christ" they had abundant joy which could not be erased through any amount of persecution or poverty. It was this great joy in the gospel which provoked them to give over and above that which was expected by mortal man. "God loves a cheerful giver" (9:7). Happy and joyful Christians are also "giving" Christians. When the gospel is preached, the forgiveness of sins is realized, and the assurance of salvation is known, God's peace and joy transform lives and giving practices.

11. Giving Is the Result of Spiritual Growth

Not only did they give "to their power," that is, all they could spare, but they gave "beyond their power," that is, they did without some necessities for a while (8:3). "Praying [begging] us with much entreaty that we would receive the gift, and take upon us the fellowship of the ministering to the saints" (8:4). This is true New Covenant giving at its best!

What more could a pastor ask for from his church when money is needed? The church was actually "begging" (NAS) for Paul to let them give *beyond* their means! "Therefore, as you abound in every thing, in faith, and utterance, and knowledge, and in all diligence, and in your love to us, see that you abound in this grace [of giving] also" (8:7). *Giving is the normal result of spiritual growth. The Christian who is fed the right spiritual food grows spiritually and gives naturally.*

12. Giving Produces More Spiritual Growth

"And God is able to make all grace abound toward you; that you, always having all sufficiency in all things, may abound to every good work" (9:8). God will also "both supply bread for your food, and multiply your seed sown, and increase the fruits of your righteousness; being enriched in every thing to [for the purpose of] all [even more] bountifulness [to others], which produces through us thanksgiving to God" (9:10-11).

When we give to God's work, he promises to supply our "sufficiency." This means that he will make us "contented" in what we "need," as compared to what we "want." The purpose of this sufficiency is that we may then, in turn, "abound in every good deed," that is, keep right on performing God's work with that sufficiency.

Phil. 4:15 Now you Philippians know also, that in the beginning of the gospel, when I departed from Macedonia, no church communicated with me as concerning giving and receiving, but you only.

Phil. 4:19 But my God shall supply all your need according to his riches in glory by Christ Jesus.

The wonderful promise of Philippians 4:19 is not an *unconditional* promise to be claimed by all believers. We cannot ignore the context of verses 14-18. Paul made that particular promise *only* to those in Philippi *because* they had supplied his needs. Christians who refuse to contribute to the needs of God's people have no claim to the promised blessings in verse 19!

Giving is a circle: God gives first, we give second, then God gives more, so we can give more. God's spiritual blessings stop flowing into us when we stop becoming a spiritual blessing to others. Since we cannot out-give God, the circle should keep on expanding to include more and more people! Our needs (not our wants) will be met on earth and givers will accumulate spiritual blessings both here on earth and in heaven. God will continue to enrich the believer throughout eternity with him in heaven.

13. Giving Results from Preaching the Gospel

"...they glorify God for your professed subjection to the gospel of Christ (NAS): for your obedience to your confession, and for your liberal distribution to them, and to all men" (9:13). The circle returns to its beginning at the grace of God and the gospel. The text does NOT say "obedience that accompanies your preaching and the practicing of tithing." A church that obeys the grace principles of giving will be blessed. When Christ is preached (which is God's great gift to us), we give ourselves, and then keep on giving as we become burdened for lost souls. Again, preaching Christ grows his church! Preaching tithing is preaching an "unprofitable" Old Covenant principle which has been abolished (Heb. 7:5, 12, 18). Whereas churches that preach tithing regularly without preaching Christ will not grow, churches that preach Christ regularly without teaching tithing will grow. It is that simple!

CHAPTER 28

▼

ACTS 20: 16-35
A SERMON
AND EXAMPLE TO PREACHERS

Paul expected others to follow his example of not receiving tithes or any other full-time sustenance as payment for the gospel ministry. If this is a correct conclusion from Acts, chapter 20, then Paul's statement in 1 Corinthians, chapter 9, verses 16-19 cannot be interpreted as the exception to the general rule. Paul preferred that his principle of "liberty" would become the superior principle which is more important than the principle of "rights."

While I have personally received full-time support in the past, I am now forced to admit that receipt of such, at least in Paul's mind and era, was following the *lesser* principle of my "rights," rather than following the *greater* principle of exercising my "liberty" to preach the gospel un-pressured by those who contribute the most to my sustenance.

This is an uncomfortable subject, to say the least. Every serious Bible student will eventually encounter teachings in God's Word of which he or she will at first find hard to accept. The answer to my question, "Should preachers accept full-time salaries?" was startling to one who has received full-salaried support from the gospel. The answer shook me, and should disturb the very foundation of the modern church system. It was one thing to question whether tithing was the New Covenant principle used to support the gospel ministry. However, my studies led me eventually to 1 Corinthians 9 and the "rights" that gospel ministers had to receive financial support. Next, the thorough cross-referencing and commentary searches led me to Acts 13:1-3; 18:1-4; 20:16-35; 2 Cor. 11:7-9; 2 Cor. 12:13-15; Phil. 4:15-19; 1 Thess. 2:9-10; and 2 Thess. 3:6-15. Although I had read these texts many times over forty years as a Christian, I had never "put them together" to see the entire picture. My conclusions follow.

The Historical Setting of Acts 20

20:16 For Paul had determined to sail by Ephesus, because he would not spend the time in Asia; for he hastened, if it were possible for him, to be at Jerusalem the day of Pentecost.

The historical setting of Acts 20 is important. The event occurred at approximately A.D. 58, which is about twenty-eight years after Calvary and after the church had been established at Pentecost in Acts, chapter 1. After ministering for over ten years, Paul had just completed his third and final missionary journey. At least three of those years had been continuous or from a base at Ephesus (20:31). When Acts 20 is combined with 1 Corinthians 9, a powerful message about gospel priorities and the ethics of gospel workers emerges.

The Sermon Was Specifically for Preachers (20:17-18, 28)

20:17 And from Miletus he sent to Ephesus, and called the elders of the church.

Paul wanted to reach Jerusalem before Pentecost and did not have time to await another ship. He had sent word ahead for the elders of the area around Ephesus to come and meet him at Miletus on the coast west of Ephesus. These texts contain a sermon especially for the leaders of the churches, the elders! The "elders" are also called "overseers"; they are the shepherds of the "flock," the church of God (20:28), the pastors of the various churches in and around Ephesus. Everything Paul had to say about false teachers taking advantage of the flock and about work ethics related specifically to them.

Paul's Example (20:18, 20, 26-27, 35)

20:18 And when they came to him, he said to them, You know, from the first day that I came into Asia, after what manner I have been with you at all seasons....

20:20 And how I kept back nothing that was profitable to you, but have shown you, and have taught you publicly, and from house to house.

Even before presenting the problems which burdened him, Paul offered his own example as the solution. They had observed his manner and lifestyle for three years throughout all seasons (v. 18); they had observed him declare the whole gospel in public (vv. 20, 27); they knew how he had treated everybody fairly (vv. 26, 31); and they knew that he had set an example for them in everything he did (vv. 20, 35). To the best of his ability, Paul was following the example of Christ. Therefore, he then asked his understudies to follow his example.

Paul's Farewell Sermon

20:22 And now, behold, I go bound in the spirit to Jerusalem, not knowing the things that shall befall me there,
20:23 Except that the Holy Ghost is witnessing in every city, saying that bonds and afflictions await me.
20:25 And now, behold, I know that you all, among whom I have gone preaching the kingdom of God, shall see my face no more.

Paul fully believed that this would be his final farewell to the leaders of the many house churches which he had started. He felt convinced by the Holy Spirit that this was his last missionary trip. Being a farewell sermon, he would surely tell them the most important things on his mind to safeguard the church in the future without him. They must first realize that the gospel of the grace of God is a most solemn thing; it is not to be treated lightly. Paul had resigned himself to possible martyrdom, if necessary, in order to preserve the integrity of the gospel and to fulfill his calling (v. 24).

Warning Against False Teachers (20:28-31, 33)

20:28 Take heed therefore to yourselves, and to all the flock....
20:29 For I know this, that after my departing grievous wolves shall enter in among you, not sparing the flock.
20:30 Also of your own selves shall men arise, speaking perverse things, to draw away disciples after them.
20:31 Therefore watch, and remember, that by the space of three years I ceased not to warn every one night and day with tears.

Paul's first concern was that false teachers with false doctrines would arise from outside and from inside the church after he had gone. From past experience he knew that others would follow him and preach a "different" gospel (Gal. 1:6-7). "Take heed," he said, "savage wolves" from outside Ephesus and "men speaking perverse things" within the church would not spare the flock and would draw away disciples to themselves (vv. 28-30).

God's Inheritance Will Suffice

20:32 And now, brothers, I commend you to God, and to the word of his grace, which is able to build you up, and to give you an inheritance among all them which are sanctified.

What a great pity it is! The last four verses of Paul's farewell sermon concern money going in the wrong direction! Surely Paul would have preferred to end his career at Ephesus on a better note. Perhaps he feared that the ravenous wolves he just mentioned were going to pervert the gospel he preached by coming in and fleecing the flock. There must be some connection between those Paul warned about and the direction of the flow of money.

Just think about it! This is an extremely important last farewell sermon to some of his nearest and dearest fellow workers in the gospel. He will never see them again, and, of all things, he warned them about false teachers. Hinting that the elders were concerned about their financial future, Paul told them that God "is able to build you up and give you an inheritance," and then he gave his own example of his attitude towards wealth. It seems as if Paul had peered into the future and had seen filthy rich church leaders and their poor parishioners in the Middle Ages when the worldly church was at the peak of its wealth and political influence. The solution he presented for staying in the center of God's will was to allow God's Word to build them up and to remember our "inheritance," that is, what we have in Christ.

Paul Chose His Right to Liberty Rather Than Financial Support

20:33 I have coveted no man's silver, or gold, or apparel.
20:34 You yourselves know that these hands have ministered to my necessities, and to them that were with me.

1 Cor. 9:18 What is my reward [Greek: *misthos*] then? Truly that, when I preach the gospel, I may make the gospel of Christ without charge, that I do not abuse my power in the gospel.

Paul exercised his higher "right" to refuse adequate sustenance which would have allowed him more time to evangelize. In doing so he refused his inferior "right" to substantial financial assistance which a few other gospel workers had evidently chosen to accept. Evidently Paul was so industrious and efficient making tents that his co-workers in the gospel did not have to ask for sustenance from the churches either. Oddly enough, Paul's co-workers may have been more free to evangelize because their leader worked long hours night and day. Paul provided their "necessities." Although it is true that choosing the principle of liberty involves more sacrifices on our part, it is also true that it yields greater rewards in soul-winning.

At this verse, a very frank and amazing admission is made by George E. Ladd in the *Wycliffe Bible Commentary:* "Paul reminded the Ephesians of his custom of making tents not only to support himself but to provide for the needs of others with him. He quoted a saying of the Lord which is not recorded in any of the Gospels, about the blessedness of giving.... *The main objective of giving in the early church was to provide for the needs of the poor brothers rather than to support the preaching of the gospel, as is the case today"* (italics mine).[118]

---

118   *Wycliffe Comm.*, s.v. "Acts 20:34."

Who Should Give What to Whom?

20:35 I have shown you all things, how that so laboring you ought to support the weak, and to remember the words of the Lord Jesus, how he said, It is more blessed to give than to receive.

Paul was concerned that too much money was flowing the wrong direction in the church! Using his own life as an example for others to follow, he said "so laboring, you ought to support the weak." The Greek word for "labor" means hard work and toil. Thus, the Apostle Paul, in his very last recorded words to a large group of church elders at the *very end* of his missionary career, told them to follow his example, work hard, and help the poor. Robertson says that "support," or "help," is in the middle voice and means to do it personally.[119]

Exactly the opposite of any doctrine of tithing is taught here! Instead of asking everybody to tithe in order to support himself, Paul was asking church *elders* to work harder in order to support the poor church members! Paul's very last words of what he thought might be his very last sermon to the Ephesian elders is a quotation of Jesus which is not recorded elsewhere. In some unwritten tradition Jesus had said "It is more blessed to give than to receive" (see John 21:25). How many times have we heard these words used at offering time! Yet, how much of the offering goes back into the direction of the poor, as Jesus and Paul so earnestly preferred?

It is impossible to conclude from this chapter that Paul wanted tithes, offerings, or any other item provided to him on a regular sustenance basis. It is also clear that Paul preferred that other elders and gospel workers follow his example. Paul preferred the "high road" principle of gospel "liberty" over the "low road" principle of gospel "privilege." Either direction, "gospel" was, and is, the key word. Both principles follow gospel examples.

---

119   *Robertson's*, s.v. "Acts 20:35."

Paul's Work Ethic

Acts 18:3 And because he was of the same craft, he stayed with them, and worked, for by their occupation [Greek: technee] they were tent-makers.

Paul insisted on working for a living. The Apostle was a Pharisee of the tribe of Benjamin (Acts 23:6; 26:5; Phil. 3:5). He was a teacher of the law of Moses trained under Gamaliel (Acts 22:3) and was therefore, a rabbi himself; however, he earned his living by making tents.

The *Wycliffe Bible Commentary says*, "It was customary for Jewish rabbis not to receive pay for their teaching, and therefore, Paul, who had been raised as a rabbi, had learned the trade of tent-making. The apostle did not at once launch into the evangelization of Corinth, but joined Aquilla and Priscilla in practicing his trade during the week. The Sabbaths he devoted to preaching in the synagogues (Acts 18:1-4)."[120]

The *New Bible Commentary* says "even rabbis were expected to earn their living by manual labor and not to make the teaching of the law a means of gain; thus Paul maintained himself by leather."[121]

Acts 18:5 And when Silas and Timotheus came from Macedonia, Paul was pressed in the spirit [better, "the Word'] and testified to the Jews that Jesus was Christ.

Few Christians realize that Paul did not preach for a living! Acts 18:1-4 occurred during the second missionary journey; Paul was still working a secular job for a living! He worked at his trade six days a week and preached at least one day. Although Acts 18:5 is translated in most versions to give the impression that Paul stopped working for a while and

---

120   *Wycliffe Comm.*, s.v. "Acts 18:1-4."
121   *New Bible Comm.*, s.v. "Acts 18:1-4."

preached full-time, these are only guesses about what the word "pressed" means in the context. I believe that the King James' translation is best here. The Greek word is "*suneicheto*" (Strong's 4912) which can also mean "compel," or "pre-occupy." Having been "depressed" from the outcome at Athens, Paul was elated by both the good news from Silas and Timothy and by their assistance to him. He certainly became "taken" with a new drive to witness for Christ. However, there is no compelling reason either in the context of Paul's convictions, or in the varied definition of "pressed" to demand that the text proves that Paul ever worked full-time as a gospel worker. (See "*sun-eicheto*," Strong's 4912).

It is clear that Paul never intended to stop performing manual labor and become a full-time salaried minister! His strict education, respect for tradition, and work-ethic compelled him to work very hard during the week from morning to evening. To the Thessalonians Paul said, "For neither at any time used we flattering words, as you know, nor a cloak of covetousness; God is witness" (1 Thess. 2:5). He would not place himself in a position where he could be accused of preaching for financial gain. "Nor of men sought we glory, neither of you, nor yet of others, when we might have been burdensome, as the apostles of Christ" (1 Thess. 2:6). Although Paul had a right to ask for financial assistance, he did not exercise that right, and he urged others to follow his example (Acts 20:35)!

Instead, Paul exercised his liberty in the gospel and freely chose to work. "For you remember, brothers, our labor and travail: for laboring night and day, because we would not be chargeable to any of you, we preached to you the gospel of God. You are witnesses, and God also, how devoutly and justly and un-blamably we behaved ourselves among you that believe" (1 Thess. 2:9-10). In performing hard physical labor, Paul said he was "devout, upright, and blameless" among believers.

The New Bible Commentary says, "This policy [working night and day] not only reflected a desire to be financially independent of those among whom they ministered, but it also marked them off from the ordinary religious traffickers of the day, and showed the converts a good example."[122] What an amazing statement!

2 Thess. 3:7 For yourselves know how you ought to follow us; for we did not behave ourselves disorderly among you;
2 Thess. 3:8 Neither did we eat any man's bread for free; but worked with labor and travail night and day, that we might not be chargeable [a burden or expense] to any of you;
2 Thess. 3:9 Not because we have not power [right to do so], but to make ourselves an example unto you to follow us.
2 Thess. 3:10 For even when we were with you, this we commanded you, that if any would not work, neither should he eat.
2 Thess. 3:11 For we hear that there are some which walk among you disorderly, working not at all, but are busybodies.
2 Thess. 3:12 Now them that are such we command and exhort by our Lord Jesus Christ, that with quietness they work, and eat their own bread.
2 Thess. 3:13 But you, brethren, do not be weary in well doing.
2 Thess. 3:14 And if any man does not obey our word by this epistle, note that man, and have no company with him, that he may be ashamed.

Since Paul had previously told how he worked night and day (1 Thess. 2:9-10), it is reasonable to conclude then that the repeat statement in his second letter applies especially, though not exclusively, to gospel workers who had stopped performing manual labor for a living. Paul counseled the church to "withdraw yourselves from every brother that walks disorderly, and not after the tradition which he received of us" (2 Thess. 3:6). This was because they should follow his example (2 Thess. 3:7). None of Paul's group ate anything for free; they worked hard night and day to prevent

---

122   Ibid., s.v. "1 Thess. 2:8-10."

owing anybody any favors (2 Thess. 3:8). They did this, not because they had no legitimate rights to assistance, but to be an example of Christian liberty for others to follow (2 Thess. 3:9). In fact, Paul commanded that none should eat if they are lazy and not working (2 Thess. 3:10). He personally considered those who refused to work to be disorderly busybodies who should be avoided (2 Thess. 3:11-13). Of course, tithing is completely foreign to these discussions.

Paul denounced capable persons who depended on others for support. In Galatians 6:2-6 the general work ethic is again discussed. While we should help bear each other's heavy loads (Greek: *baree*), we have an individual responsibility to bear our own portion (Greek: *phortion*). According to Paul, so did gospel workers!

Paul Boasted about Not Burdening Churches for Money

Paul often boasted that he did not ask for money and was not a burden to the churches. Therefore he had much more freedom to preach the gospel with full conviction.

2 Cor. 11:7 Have I committed an offense in abasing myself that you might be exalted, because I have preached to you the gospel of God freely?

2 Cor. 11:8 I robbed other churches, taking wages [daily rations] of them, to do you service.

2 Cor. 11:9 And when I was present with you, and in need, I was chargeable [an expense] to no man; for that which was lacking to me the brothers which came from Macedonia supplied; and in all things I have kept myself from being burdensome to you, and so I will keep myself.

2 Cor. 11:10 As the truth of Christ is in me, no man shall stop me of this boasting in the regions of Achaia.

2 Cor. 11:11 Why? Because I love you not? God knows.

2 Cor. 11:12 But what I want to do, that I will do, that I may cut off occasion from them which desire occasion; that wherein they glory, they may be found even as we.

2 Cor. 11:12 (TLB) I will do it to cut off the ground from under the feet of those who boast that they are doing God's work in just the same way we are.

2 Cor. 11:13 For such men are false apostles, deceitful workers, disguising themselves as apostles of Christ.

2 Cor. 12:13 For in which way were you inferior to other churches, except it be that I myself was not burdensome to you? Forgive me this wrong.

2 Cor. 12:14 Behold, the third time I am ready to come to you, and I will not be burdensome to you; for I do not seek yours, but you; for the children ought not to lay up for the parents, but the parents for the children [i.e. parents should provide for their children].

In its comments on 2 Corinthians 11:8, The *New Bible Commentary* says, "Paul is really indicating that he did not receive wages *at all* for preaching the gospel. If what was given him for his support by other churches was to be regarded as 'earnings,' then he had in effect 'robbed' them since the service given was not to them but to the Corinthians."[123] Also, the Greek word for "wages" means "daily rations" and is that which Roman soldiers were provided. Rather than receive sustenance from the Corinthians, as a spiritual parent, Paul felt that it was his obligation to care for their needs, rather than their obligation to take care of his needs (2 Cor. 12:14; Acts 20:35).

---

123   Ibid., s.v. "2 Cor. 11:8."

Paul Worked to Help the Needy

Jas. 1:27 Pure religion and undefiled before God and the Father is this, to visit the fatherless and widows in their affliction, and to keep himself unspotted from the world.

Paul only received temporary partial assistance from Philippi in Macedonia, not because he was due any tithe, or offering, but because he was in need. In contrast, he told churches in Corinth, Thessalonica, and Ephesus that he refused to be a burden on them. The statements in 1 and 2 Corinthians relating to giving are in the context of giving for the needy, both church members and otherwise. True Christian religion is not found in a system of tithing to support a hierarchy of church officers, but in helping the needy. At least to Paul, every penny given for salaries is one penny not given to the poor. The gospel worker should, according to Paul's ideal, earn his own living and give to the poor.

In its first century context, "giving to the poor" is much more accurately "giving to God," than is "giving to the church." When Zacchaeus said, "the half of my goods I give to the poor," Jesus replied, "This day is salvation come to this house" (Luke 19:8-9). Jesus also told the rich ruler, "Sell all that you have, and distribute to the poor, and you shall have treasure in heaven: and come, follow me" (Luke 18:22). Notice that Jesus did not tell them to give it to the priests at the temple!

Early church history reveals that giving flowed from those who had more toward those who had less. However, today the huge cathedrals, fancy homes, cars, and clothes of the clergy mock Jesus words. Peter was poor and shared what he had to those poorer than himself (Acts 3:6). One proof of the great power of the resurrection was that the early church was fully capable of taking care of its own needy.

As a needy person, Paul received assistance from Philippi because other churches did not contribute. The "main" church in Jerusalem plainly did not instruct Paul to solicit tithes and offerings for their support. Instead they only asked that Paul collect for the poor (Gal. 2:9-10).

Conclusion

Just because one has a "right" to act in a certain way does not make that "right" a necessity. Christ had a "right" to defend himself against false accusers, but often refused to use it. We have a "right" to take the nearest parking spot and force the elderly to walk farther, but that does not mean that we should do so. Paul said that others should follow his example and disregard the "right" for the sake of the liberty of preaching the gospel in all its power. Again, it is a shame that a conservative Bible commentary must admit that, *"The main objective of giving in the early church was to provide for the needs of the poor brothers rather than to support the preaching of the gospel as is the case today"* (italics mine).[124]

Paul's "churches" (rather, "assemblies of believers") met in homes, not fancy buildings. Instead of going "from house to house" to worship, as Paul did in Acts 20:20, the vast majority of money given by believers today goes to pay for buildings and salaries, rather than to the poor. To most believers the word, "church," brings up thoughts of an edifice rather than an assembly of believers. (On houses, see Acts 2:46; 5:42; 20:20; Rom. 16:5; 2 Tim. 3:6; Tit. 1:11).

What this New Covenant conclusion does to tithing is evident. The truth is a radical change from tradition and life under the principles of Mosaic Law. Paul's last letters were written from 30-35 years after Calvary. *Yet not a word is said about tithing.* While specifically discussing the "matter of giving and receiving," he called the gifts "a fragrant offering and an acceptable sacrifice" and, again, no mention is made of tithes (Phil. 3:15-18). On the other hand, Paul seemed concerned about greed,

---

124   *Wycliffe Comm.*, s.v. "Acts 20:34."

covetousness, and the love of money when writing to Timothy. Since such problem definitely existed, Paul addressed the problem of elders and deacons in regard to money matters.

SECULAR HISTORY, ETHICS, AND SUMMARY

CHAPTER 29

▼

A CHURCH HISTORY
OF TITHING SINCE CALVARY

The purpose of this chapter is to trace the early church's gradual teaching of tithing which followed the first apostolic century. For at least the first 200 years after Calvary, early church leaders preferred to be poor and predominantly ascetic, rather than be sustained by any elaborate system of tithes and offerings. It will be clearly seen that, not only did the inspired writers of the New Testament not teach tithing for the church, neither did those who immediately followed them as leaders of the Gentile Christian churches.

From the middle of the second century, the tithe only had the authority of a "suggestion" of a few bishops and presbyters until it became church law almost five hundred years after Calvary. The advocacy of tithing emerged in direct proportion to the gradual disintegration of the doctrine of the priesthood of believers and the emergence of the power of the bishops.

New Testament doctrines concerning the church and giving experienced a drastic change from the end of the first apostolic century to the beginning of the third century. The *first stage* of decline was the removal of spiritual gifts from the laity. The *second stage* was the distinction of the bishop as a level higher than the other (formerly equal) elders in the church. The *third stage* of decline occurred when the bishop was given a high priestly status with spiritual power over the laity. In the *fourth stage*, the bishops, elders, and (sometimes) the deacons were encouraged to stop performing secular work and devote themselves full-time to the church. Tithing became the *fifth stage* of this doctrinal decline.

Instead of the priesthood of every believer replacing the Old Testament priesthood, the church had gradually reorganized itself to resemble the Old Testament hierarchy. The bishop had become the equivalent to the Old Testament high priest, the presbyters to the Old Testament priests, and the deacons to Old Testament Levites. Full sustenance and tithing followed by using the Old Testament pattern of priesthood, sacrifices, and forgiveness controlled by priests. Thus tithing was introduced into the church only after a long period of at least 200-300 years of steady doctrinal decline and only to follow the pattern of Old Testament worship. Even then, tithing was not mandatory or compulsory for many more centuries.

Non-Christian Jews

A noted authority on Judaism, Alfred Edersheim, gives several important points which prove that tithing did not exist in the early centuries of the church. He reminds us of the Jewish customs which were surely followed by at least the Jewish-Christian apostles and disciples. First, tithing was not universal, even in Israel, because it did **not** apply to crafts and trades, "And it is remarkable, that the law seems to regard Israel as intended to be only an agricultural people—no contribution being provided for from trade or merchandise."[125] Second, proper tithes could only

125   Edersheim, *Temple*, CD-ROM, chap. 19.

come from the holy lands of Israel (p. 15-17). Third, most Jews considered it a sin to make a profit from teaching the law, "Then, as for the occupation of ordinary life, it was indeed quite true that every Jew was bound to learn some trade or business. But this was not to divert him from study; quite the contrary. *It was regarded as a profanation—or at least declared such—to make use of one's learning for secular purposes, whether of gain or of honor.* The great Hillel had it (Ab. I. 13); 'He who serves himself by the crown [the Torah] shall fade away'" (p. 118) . Fourth, rabbis, such as Paul, were not expected to earn a living from teaching the law, "For, in point of fact, with few exceptions, all the leading Rabbinical authorities were working at some trade, till at last it became quite an affectation to engage in hard bodily labor..." (p. 173). And, fifth, honest labor was considered a cherished virtue, "And this same love of honest labor, the same spirit of manly independence, the same *horror of trafficking with the law*, and using it either as a 'crown or as a spade,' was certainly characteristic of the best Rabbis." (p. 172) (italics mine).[126] Edersheim leaves no room in his conclusions for any idea that rabbis might have taught God's truth to provide for their own financial sustenance. This very strong tradition among Jews certainly would have been extended into the Jewish Christian church by former Jewish rabbis such as Paul. (See Acts 6:7 i.e. "many priests.")

Later, after the Jews had been banished from the land of Israel, Jewish law was modified concerning tithing. To the question, "How much must a man contribute to charity?", the answer given in the *Code of Jewish Law* involved "tithes," which were essentially alms. The first year required a tithe of his capital; afterwards he was to tithe net profits. He could chose, instead, to give a fifth of his capital each year, but never more than a fifth. *"The tithe money (set aside for charity) must not be used for the purpose of any other religious act, like buying candles for the synagogue; but it must be given to the poor."* However, there were exceptions to this rule. Tithes could be

---

126   Edersheim, *Sketches*, 15-17, 118, 173, 172

used to pay for circumcision, dowry for poor couples wishing to get married, and setting those couples up in a secure trade (p. 1-112).

The Jewish sage was expected to either know a craft or learn a craft in order to avoid idleness. In the event that worker did not know or have a craft, the community was to provide a craft or training and help that person as much as possible to earn a living through a trade (p. 1-114).

Also, the poorest were still not required to tithe, or give to charity, "But he who has barely sufficient for his own needs, is not obligated to give charity, for his own sustenance takes precedence over another's" (p. 1-111) (italics mine).[127]

Jewish Christians (Especially Around Palestine)

Almost every historian of early church history agrees that, until A.D. 70 the Jewish Christians in Palestine faithfully attended the temple in obedience to Jewish law and, as faithful Jews, supported the Jewish temple with tithes and offerings in addition to their church support. The Jewish Christians merely added their unique brand of Judaism into the already diverse Judaism of their day. Although the Sadducees did not accept them, the Pharisees did not oppose them and applauded their high moral conduct within Judaism. Jewish Christians narrowly escaped when the temple was destroyed in A.D. 70 by fleeing to Pella. The final banishment of Jews under Emperor Hadrian in A.D. 132-135 ended all hope of Jewish Christian leadership from Jerusalem. (However, the Gentile Christians had an influential church there in the new Roman city.)

From the destruction of Jerusalem until the end of the fourth century the "Nazarenes" were identified with a small group of Jewish Christians who held themselves bound by the Law of Moses, but did not refuse fellowship with Gentile Christians. While later splitting into Pharisaic Ebionites, Essene Ebionites, and Elkaisites, they also considered Paul an apostate, and eventually found themselves outside the church proper.

---

127 *Code*, 1-112, 1-114, 1-111.

These Jewish Christians never ceased teaching that strict obedience to the Mosaic Law was necessary for salvation. Thus, for Jewish Christians, tithing *never* left the spiritual environment of the Mosaic Law.[128] [129]

The Second and Third Century Apostolic Age Universal Church

It is quite simple to demonstrate from Scripture that none of the first century post-Calvary Apostolic fathers, that is, Paul, Peter, John, James, Jude and Luke, taught tithing. Several chapters in this book demonstrate that no teaching of tithing exists in Scripture after Calvary.

The second and third generation church leaders (c. 100-200) were almost totally devoted to living an ascetic, or semi-ascetic, lifestyle, preaching the gospel, defending the gospel, and helping the poor and needy. Constructing fine houses of worship and accumulating financial independence were completely foreign to their mind set. They took literally Jesus' words in Matthew 19:21, "If you want to be perfect, go, sell that which you have, and give to the poor, and you shall have treasure in heaven; and come, follow me," and Paul's words to elders in Acts 20:35, "I have shown you all things, how that so laboring you ought to support the weak, and to remember the words of the Lord Jesus, how he said, 'It is more blessed to give than to receive.'"

The first generation church fathers wrote very often about the Lord's Supper being the occasion for offerings for the needy. Almsgiving was considered better than both fasting and prayer. *Tithing, however, was not included!* The verifiable *presence* of freewill-giving in their writings, along with the verifiable *absence* of tithing in their writings presents a real dilemma for those who support tithing and insist that it was a valid doctrine of the church from the very beginning. Tithe-advocates do not quote the early fathers in order to validate their doctrinal position.

---

128   Qualben, 73-74.
129   Schaff, 428-434.

Alfred Edersheim, in his book, *Sketches of Jewish Social Life*, devoted an entire chapter to the Jewish work ethic. "Thus…to come to the subject of this chapter…we now understand how so many of the disciples and followers of the Lord gained their living by some craft; how in the same spirit the Master Himself condescended to the trade of his adoptive father; and how the greatest of his apostles throughout earned his bread through the labor of his hands, probably following, like the Lord Jesus, the trade of his father. For it was a *principle*, frequently expressed, if possible 'not to forsake the trade of the father….'" (italics mine).[130]

Lars P. Qualben explains this in detail in, *A History of the Christian Church*. "The local church had elders and deacons who supervised and directed the work of the congregation, administered its charity, took care of the sick, and saw to it that services were regularly held. But the early church organization was not centered in office and in law, but in the special gifts of the Spirit. The teaching, the preaching, and the administration of the sacraments were conducted by the 'gifted men' in the congregation. An elder might also teach, preach, and administer the sacraments, but he did not do so because he was an elder, but because he was known to have the 'gift.' *None of these 'gifted men' held church office in a legal or judicial sense.* The preaching, the teaching, and the administration of the sacraments were not legally confined to any specific office. The gospel could be preached and the sacraments could be administered in the presence of any assembly of believers, gathered in the name of the Lord."

"Toward the end of the first century a change took place. A general lack of confidence in the special gifts of the Spirit, a desire for more specific order, and a pressing demand for proper safeguard against heresy resulted in a gradual transfer of the preaching, the teaching, and the administration of the sacraments from the 'gifted men' to the local elders…."

"During the second and third centuries another important change took place. Instead of government by a group of elders, the local churches were

---

130   Edersheim, *Sketches*, 169.

headed by single officials for whom the name 'bishop' was exclusively reserved…. The election of the bishop became a *legal* ordinance and the bishop alone had a right to preach, to teach, and to administer the sacraments…" (italics mine).[131]

Philip Schaff comments on church growth before the great persecutions which followed, "Until about the close of the second century the Christians held their worship mostly in private homes, or in desert places, at the graves of martyrs, and in the crypts of the catacombs. This arose from their poverty, their oppressed and outlawed condition, their love of silence and solitude, and their aversion to all heathen art (p. 198)." "The first traces of special houses of worship occur in Tertullian, who speaks of going to church, and in his contemporary, Clement of Alexandria, who mentions the double meaning of the word '*ekkleesia.*' About the year 230, Alexander Severus granted the Christians the right to a place in Rome…. After the middle of the third century the building of churches began in great earnest…." (pp. 199-200).

As the early church grew, it became more complex and developed a hierarchy. "Thus we find, so early as *the third century*, the foundations of a complete hierarchy; though a hierarchy of only moral power, and holding no sort of outward control over the conscience…. *With the exaltation of the clergy [in the third century] appeared the tendency to separate them from secular business, and even from social relations…. They drew their support from the church treasury, which was supplied by voluntary contributions and weekly collections on the Lord's Day. After the third century they were forbidden to engage in any secular business, or even to accept any trusteeship*" (as per Cyprian) (p. 128) (italics mine).[132]

While there were many pre-Nicean (pre A.D. 325) early church fathers whose writings still exist, until Cyprian, they did not write about any form of suggested enforced tithing at all. These include Clement of Rome,

---

131 Qualben, 94.
132 Schaff, 128, 198, 199-200.

Mathetes, Polycarp, Ignatius, Barnabas, Papias, Justin, the Pastor of Hermas, Tatian, Theophilus of Antioch, Athenagoras, Clement of Alexandria, Tertullian, Minucius Felix, Commodianus, Origen, Hippolytus, Caius, and Novatium.

Clement of Rome (c. 95) began writing about the same time the Apostle John died. His writings do not use the word, "tithe." He is not specific when he wrote, "He [God] has enjoined offerings [to be presented] and service to be performed [to Him], and that not thoughtlessly or irregularly, but at the appointed times and hours" (*First Epistle to the Corinthians*, chapter 40). Most likely, at this time, Jewish Christians in the Roman church would have objected to any hint that tithes be taken away from Levitical priests.

Justin Martyr (c. 150) wrote, "And *the wealthy among us help the needy*...when our prayer is ended, bread and wine and water are brought, and the president in like manner offers prayers and thanksgiving, *according to his ability*, and the people assent, saying Amen; and there is a distribution to each, and a participation of that over which thanks have been given, and to those who are absent a portion is sent by the deacons. And *they who are well to do, and willing, give what each thinks fit*; and what is collected is deposited with the president, who succors the orphans and widows and those who, through sickness or any other cause, are in want, and those who are in bonds and the strangers sojourning among us" (*First Apology*, chap. 67) (italics mine). In accordance with the first century Scripture, "presidents," or church leaders, are only capable administrators, and not necessarily pastors or teachers of the Word.

Justin's writings only use the word, "tithe," four times: twice from Matthew 23:23 to point out that the Jews did not like Christ, and twice from Genesis 14:20 while proving that Melchizedek did not require circumcision (*Dialogue with Trypho*, chap. 17, 19, 33, 112).

The *Didache*, or *Teaching of the Twelve* (150?), was discovered in the late 19th century at the Jewish Monastery of the Most Holy Sepulcher at Constantinople. It appears to be a Jewish-Christian document from approximately the middle of the second century, and it gives some interesting ideas about how prophets and church leaders were supported.

Paragraph XI:…"Now, as concerning the apostles and prophets according to the teaching of the gospel, so do; and let every apostle that comes to you be received as the Lord; and he shall stay but one day, and, if need be, the next day also; but if he stays three days he is a false prophet. When the apostle goes forth, let him take nothing but bread, until he reaches his lodging: *if he asks for money, he is a false prophet.*… But whosoever shall say in spirit, 'Give me money, or other things,' you shall not listen to him; but it he bids you to give for others that are in need, let no man judge him."

Paragraph XII probably refers to ordinary travelers. "Let every one that 'comes in the name of the Lord' be received" and proven…. "If he wishes to abide with you, being a craftsman, let him work and eat. If he has no craft, use your common sense to provide that he lives with you as a Christian, without idleness. If he is unwilling to do so, he is a 'Christ monger.' Beware of such."

Paragraph XIII: "But every true prophet that desires to abide with you is 'worthy of his food,' In like manner a true teacher is also, like the laborer, 'worthy of his food.' Therefore you shall take and give to the prophets every *firstfruits* of the produce of the wine-press and the threshingfloor, of oxen and sheep. For the prophets are your high priests. *If you have no prophet, give them to the poor.*"

Paragraph XV: "Elect therefore of yourselves bishops and deacons worthy of the Lord, men that are gentle but not covetous, true men and approved; for they also minister to you the ministry of the prophets and leaders" (italics mine).[133]

It is interesting that the document says "firstfruits," not "tithes." Perhaps this is why this document is placed in the middle of the second century—after some elevation of bishops, but before the authority urged

---

133   *Didache*, 64-65.

on them by Cyprian. Noticeably, though, the firstfruits match the description of only food items from Numbers 18. Also, it seems that even these would not be totally supported by the church if it were small, but would be required to retain a trade. It is interesting to note that paragraph XIII says, if there is no prophet in the church, then give the firstfruits to the poor, rather than to a bishop or elder. There must be no doctrine of tithing here!

Irenaeus (150-200), clearly did not teach tithing. "And for this reason did the Lord, instead of that [commandment], 'You shall not commit adultery,' forbid even concupiscence; and instead of that which runs thus, 'You shall not kill,' He prohibited anger; and *instead of the law enjoining the giving of tithes, to share all our possessions with the poor;* and not to love our neighbors only, but even our enemies; and not merely to be liberal givers and bestowers, but even that we should present a gratuitous gift to those who take away our goods" (*Against Heresies*, book 4, chap. 13, para. 3).

"For with Him there is nothing purposeless, nor without signification, nor without design. And for this reason they (the Jews) had indeed the *tithes* of their goods consecrated to Him, *but those who have received liberty set aside all their possessions for the Lord's purposes,* bestowing joyfully and freely not the less valuable portions of their property, since they have the hope of better things [hereafter]; as that poor widow acted who cast all her living into the treasury of God" (*Against Heresies*, book 4, chap. 18) (italics mine). Irenaeus clearly taught that the church was a dispenser of necessities for the poor. His life and writings reveal that he believed that its leaders should live as meagerly as possible.

Tertullian (150-220) was a prolific writer from Carthage in northern Africa whose writings do not teach tithing. He was also a Montanist who lived an extremely ascetic lifestyle. For the Montanists, extreme poverty was a virtue which allowed no room for full sustenance through tithing. Although he agreed that all incoming oblations should be given to the poor, Tertullian would not have taught that church leaders should be supported through tithes. His only recorded uses of the word, "tithe," appear when he quotes Matthew 23:23 to compare Marcion's hypocrisy with that of the Pharisees (*Marcion*, book 4, chap. 27) and Genesis 14:20 when he argued, like Justin Martyr, that Melchizedek was not circumcised (book 5, chap. 9).

Tertullian also wrote, "Our presidents are elders of proved worth, men who have attained this honor not for a price, but by character. *Every man brings some modest coin once a month or whenever he wishes, and only if he is willing and able; it is a freewill offering.* You might call them the trust-funds of piety; they are spent...on the support and burial of the poor..." (*Apology*, xxxix, 1-18) (italics mine). From these it is clear that, at least near the end of the second century, no tithing existed solely to support full-time clergy.

Cyprian (200-258) followed Tertullian in Carthage and was probably the first influential leader to suggest that tithes should support a full-time clergy. It must be remembered that, by Cyprian's time, at least the first departures from the apostolic age doctrine had occurred. Spiritual gifts had mostly been taken from the laity and placed within various levels of the clergy. The office of bishop had been distinguished above that of elder and presbyter, and each bishop had spiritual power over the laity through the crude sacramental system. And the church now compared the bishop to the Old Testament high priest, the presbyters to the Old Testament priests, and the deacons to Old Testament Levites. Cyprian merely took the next logical step (in this scenario of the role of bishops) and insisted that the clergy should cease all secular work and depend on tithes for full-time support. The Old Testament pattern of priesthood, sacrifices, and forgiveness was now controlled by so-called Christian high priests, Christian priests, and Christian Levites. Such is the context of Cyprian's tithing appeals!

However, Cyprian's tithing still does not qualify as "proof" that the early church taught tithing. Although not as ascetic as the Montanists and his favorite teacher, Tertullian, Cyprian was an ascetic who gave up his considerable fortune at his baptism. While he strongly advocated that bishops, presbyters, *and deacons* should receive tithes and devote full-time service to the church, he did not suggest they live above the poverty level (*Epistle* 65, para. 1). At one occasion, in his Epistle 4, he said that the "whole of the small sum which was collected" was given to the clergy *and they distributed it to those in need.* Any person who has read Cyprian knows of his generation's many uses of Christ's injunction, "If you want to be perfect, go and sell that you have, and give to the poor, and you shall have treasure in heaven, and come and follow me." Cyprian's understanding of tithing was that church leaders should only take the bare minimum and distribute the remainder to the poor.

The Constitutions of the Holy Apostles (book 2, section 4), is a fictional account probably dating from the third or fourth century. It was not accepted by the Church until many centuries later. Its use of tithing reflects an evolution of the doctrine to about the same level as that of Cyprian.

"*On the Management of the Resources Collected for the Support of the Clergy and the Relief of the Poor:*"

"Let the bishop esteem such food and raiment sufficient as suits necessity and decency. Let him not make use of the Lord's goods as another's, but moderately; 'for the laborer is worthy of his reward.' Let him not be luxurious in diet, or fond of idle furniture, but contented with so much alone as is necessary for his sustenance."

"*On Firstfruits and Tithes, and After What Manner the Bishop is Himself to Partake of Them, or Distribute Them to Others*"

XXV. Let him use those *tenths and first-fruits,* which are given according to the command of God, as a man of God; as also let him dispense in a right manner the free-will offerings which are brought in on account of the poor, to the orphans, the widows, the afflicted, and strangers in distress, as having that God for the examiner of his accounts who has committed the disposition to him. Distribute to all those in want with righteousness, and yourselves use the things which belong to the Lord, but do not abuse them, eating of them, but *not eating them all up by yourselves:*

communicate with those who are in want, and thereby show yourselves unblamable before God. For if you shall consume them by yourselves, you will be reproached by God...."

"For those who attend upon the Church ought to be maintained by the Church, *as being priests, Levites, presidents, and ministers of God; as it is written in the book of Numbers concerning the priests....*"

"Those which *were then* first-fruits, and *tithes*, and offerings, and gifts, *now* are oblations, which are presented by holy bishops to the Lord God, through Jesus Christ, who has died for them. For these are your high priests, as the presbyters are your priests, and your present deacons instead of your Levites; as are also your readers, your singers, your porters, your deaconesses, your widows, your virgins, and your orphans: but He who is above all these is the High Priest."

XXVI. "*The bishop*, he is the minister of the word, the keeper of knowledge, the *mediator* between God and you in the several parts of your divine worship. He is the teacher of piety; and, *next after God, he is your father*, who has begotten you again to the adoption of sons by water and the Spirit. He is your ruler and governor; *he is your king* and potentate; he is, next after God, *your earthly God*, who has a right to be honored by you."

XXVII. "You ought therefore, brothers, to bring your sacrifices and your oblations to the bishop, as to your high priest, either by yourselves or by the deacons; and do you bring not those only, but also your first-fruits, and your *tithes*, and your free-will offerings to him. For he knows who they are that are in affliction, and gives to every one as is convenient, that so one may not receive alms twice or more often the same day, or the same week, while another has nothing at all" (italics mine).

Author's comments on the *Constitutions of the Apostles*. While attempting to use the language of the Old Testament Law, several differences are apparent. First, now the high priest, not the Levites, receives the tithes directly. Second, the bishop is to maintain a bare sustenance level from what he takes from the tithes and offerings. Third, the bishop is directly responsible for redistributing both tithes and offerings back to the needy. Fourth, the new priestly caste system does not refer to Abraham's tithe to Melchizedek in Genesis 14 for pre-Law justification, nor to "It is holy to the Lord" in Leviticus 27:30 for an eternal principle. Clearly, the justification for re-introducing tithing into the early church, even if only a voluntary offering, was the result of the abandonment of the doctrine of the priesthood of the believer and the elevation of the position of priest and high priest. Therefore, it is easy to understand why modern tithe-advocates do not appeal to the Church Fathers for validation of tithing as a legitimate doctrine.

A Summary of Historical Reasons to Reject Tithing

For the following reasons which have been supported by many reputable authorities in this chapter and elsewhere in this book, tithing cannot be supported as a valid doctrine found in early post-biblical history.

1. It is certain that Jewish-Christians in Palestine continued to send tithes to the temple in obedience to the law (Acts 15 and 21) at least until A.D. 70. Post-biblical history proves that most of these never abandoned the Mosaic Law, refused full fellowship with Gentile Christians, rejected Paul, later split into factions, and disappeared around the end of the fourth century.

2. Jewish Christians, like Paul, who had been trained in the strict traditions of the Mosaic Law would have never accepted full-time support for teaching the Old Testament Sacred Writings concerning Christ.

3. Jewish Christians viewed tithing as purely law, which they directly ordered Gentile Christians *not* to obey (Acts 15 and 21).

4. Jewish Christians were taught to earn their living through a trade and not depend on charity. Both Jewish and Christian sages were supported by the communities through support of their trade.

5. The secular crafts and trades of many rabbis and later church leaders are recorded in history. Many church historians comment on the fact that the early church leaders sustained themselves by a trade (rather

than by tithing). This is documented by numerous footnotes in this book, especially the chapter on 1 Corinthians 9, Acts 20, and this chapter.

6. The church was considered "illegal" since its inception and it was considered an "outlaw" since approximately A.D. 80. The Romans required all citizens to register their livelihood and proof of sustenance. In many places, a full-time gospel worker would have been arrested as an insurrectionist without any evident means of support such as a trade.

7. Since Christians were sporadically killed by mobs and the government for much of the first three centuries, it seems improbable that the earliest leaders would reveal themselves (by not having an obvious trade) that they were full-time church leaders supported by tithes.

8. When the New Testament was written, very few, if any, of the churches were organized into a monarchical bishop system which would require or sustain a full-time minister. The churches were too primitive, too small, too poor, and often had to hide from the authorities to meet. Church buildings did not exist because they would not have been tolerated until about A.D. 200 and did not flourish until after A.D. 260 before being destroyed again in 303.[134]

9. The earliest churches did not distinguish between "clergy" and "laity" for several centuries. Gifted lay members preached and carried out other functions which were later restricted to full-time ordained clergy. For example, a gifted "administrator" may have been in charge while another gifted person "preached" and another gifted person "taught" the Word. This fact would preclude giving tithes when numerous laity exercised their spiritual gifts.

---

134   Schaff, 63.

10. It is very likely that even slaves held leadership roles as elders and bishops in the early church. The noted scholar, F. F. Bruce, says that "Pius, bishop of the Roman church towards the middle of the second century, *if not a slave himself, was at any rate the brother of a slave*; and Callistus, bishop of the same church in the early part of the third century, was an ex-slave" (italics mine).[135] Slaves would certainly not accept tithes for their sustenance!

11. Perhaps the best post-biblical argument against tithing in the Ante-Nicean church is the church's overall attitude towards Christian virtues, ethics, poverty, and asceticism. To state it plainly, *"Poverty was considered a virtue, especially among the clergy!"* While still retaining fresh memories of the first apostles and disciples, the miracles of the first century, and, while still expecting a soon return of Jesus Christ, the pre-Constantine (pre-A.D. 325) church, was a *charity* organization which received offerings only to serve the poor, widows, and orphans of society. See Philip Schaff's detailed comments in the chapter on 1 Corinthians 9.

The Church from the Fourth Century until the Eighth Century

The church in the first centuries had a very different use for money than the typical church today. Williston Walker reports that, in the year A.D. 251, the church of Rome under Bishop Cornelius had a membership of approximately 30,000 members and supported over 1,500 dependents. This amounts to one dependent per 20 members![136]

Although Cyprian tried to enforce his idea that church workers should not pursue secular trades, Walker comments, "By the middle of the third century the higher clergy were expected to give their whole time to the work of the ministry, *yet even bishops sometimes shared in secular business,*

---

135   F. F. Bruce, *The Spreading Flame* (Waynesboro: Pater Noster Press, 1958), 192.
136   Walker, 83.

not always of a commendable character. The lower clergy could still engage in trade" (italics mine).[137]

It may, or may not, be noteworthy that Schaff does not mention church "buildings" until the lapse of persecution between 260-303. It is unclear to what extent church edifices existed prior to this time. As long as Christians were blamed for almost every disaster such as famines, earthquakes, floods, and barbarian invasions, the pagan populace very often punished the church as its scapegoat and would have quickly destroyed highly visible and accessible structures associated with the church.

It is odd that the *Encyclopedia Americana* says, "It [tithing] was *not* practiced in the early Christian church, but gradually became common by the 6th century."[138] The statement probably means that tithing was not practiced "by enforcement of Church or secular law" until the 6th century.

The *Catholic Encyclopedia* (1912 edition only) says, "In the beginning [provision] was supplied by the spontaneous support of the faithful. In the course of time, however, as the Church expanded and various institutions arose, it became necessary to make laws which would insure the proper and permanent support of the clergy. The payment of tithes was adopted from the Old Law, and early writers speak of it as a divine ordinance and an obligation of the conscience. The earliest positive legislation on the subject seems to be contained in the letter of the bishops assembled at Tours in 567 and the Canons of the Council of Macon in 585."[139]

While it may appear that both the *Encyclopedia Americana* and the *Catholic Encyclopedia* ignore all of the tithing references made by Cyprian and the *Constitutions of the Apostles* as invalid, actually, they must be agreeing with the premise of this book that the early church did not teach tithing! When tithing was first re-introduced into the church,

---

137   Ibid., 84.

138   *Americana*, s.v. "tithe."

139   *The Catholic Encyclopedia*, Vol. XIV, 1912, s.v. "tithe."

it was voluntary and was built on an erroneous comparison of the New Covenant bishop as a high priest to the Old Testament priesthood.

Centuries later, the church acquired wealth in the form of land. At first wealthy landowners donated land to the church for parishes, but retained the privileges of nominating the bishops and keeping the profits and tithes from the land in their own secular hands. Therefore, tithing soon became a source of abuse. Eventually, however, the church gained enough secular authority to regain appointment of its own priests and bishops again, along with keeping the tithes in the church. The church soon owned from one half to one fourth of the land in many European countries and enacted tithes from those who rented its lands.

Historians usually agree that, not until A.D. 567, five hundred and thirty seven (537) years after Calvary, did the Church's *first* substantial attempt to enforce tithing under its own authority appear in history! The Council of Tours in 567 and the Council of Macon in 585 enacted regional church decrees for tithing, but did not receive authority from the king to enforce collection through civil decrees. It is significant that tithing did not emerge historically until the church became powerful in the secular realm. Eventually, the Roman Church even refused to administer last rites if it was not given wealth or land in wills.

Between 774 to 777 the Frankish king, Charlemagne, destroyed the Lombard kingdom which separated his empire from northern Italy. After his defeat of the Lombards, Charlemagne's unopposed rule included northern Italy and Rome. By quoting the Mosaic Law as its authority at a Church synod, the pope finally convinced Charlemagne to allow enforced tithing in support of the fast-growing parish system of churches. In appreciation of his church support, on Christmas Day, A.D. 800, the pope crowned Charlemagne as Holy Roman Emperor, thus making official the renewed "Holy" Roman Empire.

Pope Innocent III (1198-1216), in order to strengthen and purify the church, ordered that tithes for the support of the church be given precedence over all other taxes, excluded all lay interference in ecclesiastical affairs, and prohibited any one man from drawing the income from more than one church office. Theologian Thomas Aquinas defended tithing by stating, "During the time of the New Law the authority of the Church has established the payment of tithes" (*Summa Theologica,* Vol. 3, The Second Part of the Second Part) .

In 10th century England tithing was made obligatory under ecclesiastical penalties by Edgar. In 1067 and 1078, at the Church Councils of Gerona, and in 1215 at the Fourth Lateran Council, tithing was increasing applied to all lands under Christian rule. All citizens, including Jews, were required to tithe to the Roman Catholic Church. A typical peasant was giving the first tithe of his land to ruler or landlord (which was often the church) and a second tenth to the church outright. In 1179 the Third Lateran Council decreed that only the pope could release persons from the obligation to tithe, and he exempted the Crusaders.

Exacting tithes from Jews became especially severe in England and Germanic countries. Beginning around the 14th century, Jews were not even allowed to own land in many nations. This forced the Jews off the land and many went into banking and commerce (occupations which were not required to tithe. In 1372 even the clergy in Germany revolted at having to pay tithes to the pope.

Not long after the Bible had been translated into the vernacular, Otto Brumfels, in 1524, proclaimed that the New Testament does not teach tithing. Later that century, Pope Gregory VII, in an effort to control abuses, outlawed lay ownership of tithes which had once more become a problem.

In 1714 the English and Anglican minority were in control and exacted tithes from Roman Catholics and Presbyterians for the support of the Church of Ireland. Soon revolt became ripe in France. Some of the earliest stages of the French Revolution were actions which struck at the privileges and status of the Roman Catholic Church. In 1789, tithes were abolished in France by the secular authority.

Other revolts against tithing followed. Between 1836-1850 tithing was mostly abolished in England. It was later commuted to a rental to be paid in cash. In 1868, as a result of agitation which began at least as far back as the 1830s and which was pushed by Dissenters, the compulsory payment of local parish tithes for the maintenance of the church was abolished and was made purely voluntary. However, the final tithe rent charges were not abolished until 1936 in England.

In Canada, as late as 1868, the Fourth Council of Quebec declared that tithing was mandatory. For a while tithes were even made mandatory in the French lands of the New World until the territory was sold in the Louisiana Purchase. In 1871 tithes were abolished in Ireland. In 1887 they ended in Italy. In West Germany residents must formally renounce church membership in order to avoid mandatory church taxation. Elsewhere, the Eastern Orthodox Church has never accepted tithing and its members have never practiced it. The Roman Catholic Church still proscribes tithes in countries where they are sanctioned by law, and some Protestant bodies still consider tithes obligatory.

Today most religious bodies have abandoned the practice of compulsory tithing, particularly in the United States, where no system of tithing was ever generally employed after the American Revolution. Tithing was never a legal requirement in the United States. Nevertheless, members of certain churches, including the Latter Day Saints and Seventh-Day Adventists are required to tithe and some Christians in other churches do so voluntarily. Southern Baptists define tithing as an "expectation." For further study, most books on church history briefly discuss the history of tithing since Bible times. As Europe slowly rejected church-state taxation and the divine right of kings, it also rejected enforced tithing to state-supported churches.

Relevant to this book, the biblical model of tithing best fits a church-state economy similar to Israel's theocracy. History reveals that tithing became a "Christian" doctrine only after the Roman Catholic Church joined hands with secular and political forces. However, just as tithing was an unprofitable ordinance which never produced spiritual growth in national Israel under the Old Covenant, even so tithing never led to spiritual growth when used by Christians and was eventually forced into retirement a second time by state churches.

Both Roman Catholics and Protestants have been guilty of oppression and persecution regarding state mandated tithing laws. And, like Old Covenant tithing in national Israel, nothing good has ever resulted from such attempts to enforce tithing on another.

Note: The historical source material from this chapter has come from the following: *Encyclopedia Americana; Encyclopedia Britannica; The Catholic Encyclopedia* (1912 and New); Baker, *A Summary of Christian History;* Durant, *The Reformation;* Latourette, *A History of the Christian Church;* Qualben, *A History of the Christian Church;* Schaff, *History of the Christian Church*, Vol. 2; and Walker, *A History of the Christian Church*. See Bibliography.

CHAPTER 30

▼

ETHICAL CONSIDERATIONS
OF TITHING UNDER GRACE

Experience 1: A visiting stewardship director delivered a message on giving to my congregation. He arrived in an expensive new automobile and was wearing a very expensive suit. In his sermon he boasted about how he had convinced a poor church widow on welfare to donate money which she had been saving for many years to buy false teeth.

Experience 2: Several widows who lived in welfare housing have personally told me that they tithed their welfare checks and social security checks and depended even more on charity to meet their other needs.

Experience 3: A mother with little income, a disabled out-of-work husband, and deeply in debt from medical bills worked several jobs in order to survive and pay her tithe. She had been told that she would be cursed by God if she failed to tithe.

Experience 4: A 15 year old girl, the oldest of 6 children, told a Christian financial adviser that her father had been laid off work and that the only income the family had was her baby-siting money from which she tithed. As a strong advocate of tithing, he did not suggest that she stop paying tithe and meet the pressing needs of the family first. Neither did he obtain her address and seek help for her from the church.

Experience 5: The God-called evangelist to whom this book is dedicated has won many hundreds, if not thousands, of precious souls for the glory of God. Like myself, he has grown up both physically and spiritually under the nurture of churches that are dispensational and agree with the basic premises of this book concerning the law and tithing. How very sad it is to discover that this great man of God is not considered qualified to teach a Sunday School class merely because he believes that tithing is not a New Covenant doctrine! What a terrible waste of God's gifts and calling which he has placed in the church for its edification. The church of God across this nation and world is suffering because of this sin of not using its talent.

Experience 6: I personally have been refused leadership roles in church after church because of my convictions about tithing. Several years ago I changed my membership and immediately became active teaching adult Sunday School. After teaching in this church for about two years, I noticed that much less experienced and less qualified persons than myself were being asked to preach and take leadership roles. Upon questioning the pastor, I was told that it was because I did not teach my Sunday School class that tithing was a mandatory New Covenant doctrine. Yet I had personally never heard this pastor mention the word "tithe" from his pulpit in two years!

Other Experiences: Unfortunately, these, and similar stories, can be found by the thousands across the country. I have witnessed too many who tithe simply out of the fear of being cursed if they fail to do so. At testimony time, I have heard many say that they tithed because they feared the wrath of God. All their lives they have heard Malachi 3:8-10 hurled at them as a threat. I have also personally interviewed many strong Christians who have left tithe-preaching churches and faithfully support other churches that put more emphasis on evangelism. They had become tired of hearing sermons about money once a month. Sadly, though, I have also interviewed many who have simply stopped attending church altogether because they have felt embarrassed by not being able to tithe, or put enough into the offering plate.

Gal. 3:13 Christ has redeemed us from the curse of the law, being made a curse for us....

Something is wrong with these true stories! No Christian is under any curse of the Old Covenant Law! It is un-ethical to preach out-of-context proof texts about tithing sermons only from Malachi and Genesis 14. Is there not some obligation to teach, as Paul Harvey would say, "the rest of the story"? Should the poor fear that God will punish them if they do not give as the preacher says? Even in the Old Covenant, after the tithe was paid, God commanded the tithe-paying landowner to let the poor enter his property and pick up the loose grain for themselves (Lev. 19:9-11; Deut. 24;19-21). "Do not steal," in Leviticus 19:11, means "do not take food out of the widows' hand." The farmer got his 90%; God got his 10%, and the poor widow and stranger got the gleanings; they were not asked to tithe. The church that expects the *poor* to tithe above their freewill offerings is stealing from them!

1 Tim. 5:8 But if any provide not for his own, and especially for those of his own house, he has denied the faith, and is worse than an infidel.

What does the poor do about his/her obligation to their own family? No church should pressure the poor to contribute when it means they must then turn to the welfare system for food and help with housing and utility bills. It is also dishonest to tell church members that 1 Corinthians 16:2 is about giving tithes on Sunday to pay the preacher and building expenses. True historical and exegetical context is completely ignored!

I have been a member of several very large successful churches that did NOT preach tithing. They succeeded by preaching sound New Covenant giving principles. When the heart is right with God, the Holy Spirit will supply the needs of the church. Churches grow by preaching the gospel, because that is where the power is! When a church has financial problems, the answer is not to preach a lot of sermons on tithing and giving, but to emphasize soul-winning. On the plus side, there are churches that have volunteer "tentmaker" preachers who distribute donations to the poor in the congregation. There are many preachers like this who have ministered for years, as Paul did, for free (Acts 20:26-35).

Serious Thoughts about Tithing

1. If tithing were indeed a valid New Covenant doctrine, one can be sure that most other churches would grasp it and teach it. Financial need is great everywhere. Yet when one looks at most of the Christian Churches, Churches of Christ, Episcopalians, Evangelicals, Lutherans, Methodists, Presbyterians, Roman Catholics and even the official statement of Southern Baptists, one finds a lot of talk about tithing, but no "definitive commandment" for church members to give ten percent of their gross income to the church! See the footnote discussion for a detailed statement concerning Southern Baptists.[140]

2. If tithing were a sound New Covenant doctrine, then why do many leading conservative institutions such as Moody Bible Institute and

---

140   "Stewardship," *The Baptist Faith and Message* (Nashville: Lifeway Christian Resources, rev., June 1998), 18. Article XIII, concludes: "According to the Scriptures, Christians should contribute of their means cheerfully, regularly, systematically, proportionately, and liberally for the advancement of the Redeemer's cause on earth." Although Genesis 14:20, Leviticus 27:30-32, and Malachi 3:8-12 are among the many texts listed, the word, "tithe," oddly, does not appear in the *text* of the article.

Dallas Theological Seminary not teach it? Where is the literature from top theologians at university levels of other denominations which defend it? Why do the many comprehensive volumes of Christian theology omit this doctrine? Why do seminary level textbooks on hermeneutics and exegesis not teach tithing? Why do those who write about tithing usually come from the lower echelons of denominations? Where are the Bible scholars and their literature which teach tithing using sound biblical principles instead of prooftext methodology? Why do the church historians usually disagree with the theologians on this issue?

3. The only specific "titing" groups mentioned in the *Encyclopedia Americana* and *Encyclopedia Britannica* are the Latter Day Saints (Mormons) and Seventh Day Adventists—both considered cults by most conservative Christians. However, to this select twosome should be added many Assemblies of God, Baptists, Churches of God, Pentecostals, and Holiness churches. How many of their church members tithe and then turn to tax-supported welfare for survival?

4. Why do some of the most fundamental and conservative churches, the very ones who insist on understanding doctrine through the

---

Page 4 of this pamphlet says that its statements constitute a "consensus of opinion," but "are not intended to add anything to the simple condition of salvation revealed in the New Testament." "Baptists should hold themselves free to revise their statements of faith as may seem to them wise," and that "any group of Baptists have the inherent right to draw up for themselves and publish to the world a confession of faith." Page 5 adds, "confessions are only guides to interpretation, having no authority over the conscience." The statements are "not to be used to hamper freedom of thought or investigation in other realms of life." "*Such statements have never been regarded as complete, infallible statements of faith, nor as official creeds carrying mandatory authority*" (italics mine). Although this is the official stance, there has historically been considerable pressure placed on all Southern Baptists to accept the published statement of faith, or else, drop out of the convention. This "authority" debate is still raging in 2000.

New Covenant alone, cling to tithing without sound New Covenant reasons? Yet, while most of these do not teach twenty or twenty-three percent tithing, they usually must give pastoral workers much more than the "tenth of the tenth" (Num. 18:26-27; Neh. 10:38); they do not return large portions of the total tithe to the poor (Deut. 12:17-18), and they are allowed to own and inherit land (Num. 18:21)— all contrary to tithing principles!.

5. It is difficult to give up something one has believed for many years. Lewis Sperry Chafer admits that "tithe-payers" are blessed…but only because of God's blessings under grace. He says they are NOT blessed "because of" obedience to a commandment of the law. Does not God have a blessing in store for those who accept, teach, and preach the truth of his Word? Even though tithing was practiced, the sacred cows of Ephraim still brought the scorn and disapproval of God. Is not a fear or lack of dialogue about tithing treating it as another taboo "sacred cow"?

2 Cor. 3:6 Who also has made us able ministers of the new testament; not of the letter, but of the spirit; for the letter kills, but the spirit gives life.

Also, although the official statement of faith quoted above is widely distributed for all to read, the *Stewardship Position Paper*, adopted in June 1997, is the current leadership's interpretation and application of the general stewardship statement. It is the *Position Paper*, and not the *Faith and Message* statement, *which must* be followed for all stewardship-related teaching and publications such as Sunday School literature. The *Position Paper*, which is not permitted to be quoted in part, and is not widely distributed, is the denominations' criteria for stewardship and *must not* by replaced by any other criteria. The *Position Paper* also makes it clear that tithing is an act of obedience which is expected from every church member.

6. Does not "by grace through faith alone" also apply to principles of giving? Most Bible-centered churches believe this regarding other doctrines. Why do they not believe it concerning giving? *Teaching the letter of the Old Covenant will kill a church*! It is the Spirit that gives life to the church. The Spirit's ministry is "more glorious" (v. 8), and "how much more glorious" (v. 9). "For even that which was made glorious had no glory in this respect, by reason of the glory that excels" (v. 10). According to God's Word, there is "*no glory*" in teaching the law. A church in love with Jesus Christ and yearning to witness will grow by the Spirit's enabling power.

7. Those who preach Christian tithing accuse those who disagree with them of "rationalizing," or "trying to justify," what they insist are "sound Bible principles." While many of these same preachers use the principle of interpretation that Christian doctrine should be clearly stated after Calvary from Acts to Revelation, they offer no legitimate texts from the Epistles and no exegetical rationale for their own position. If indeed a Christian is required to give one tenth of his gross income to the church, then where is that "principle" stated to the church? Surely God would not leave out such an important principle!

8. When tithing is preached from the Old Covenant books of Malachi, Deuteronomy, or Leviticus, the preacher is not on New Covenant ground. All three major theological approaches admit this. If using the approach of covenant theology, tithing is discarded when the eternal moral commandments are separated from the

---

While it seems that the *Baptist Faith and Message* and the *Stewardship Position Paper* far from complement each other regarding tithing, many other denominations are forced to follow this same pattern of *outwardly* stating one position, while *operationally* following differing guidelines. This is probably so because denominational leadership shifts back and forth between liberal and conservative interpretations of Scripture and leadership approaches.

temporary ceremonial religious ordinances. If using dispensational theology, tithing is discarded along with the entire law because it is not repeated to the church after Calvary. The third leading theological approach dismisses tithing as purely cultic, and not a moral issue.

"But their minds were blinded: for until this day the same veil remains un-taken away in the reading of the old testament; which veil is done away in Christ. But even to this day, when Moses is read, the veil is upon their heart" (2 Cor. 3:14-15). Preaching tithing from the law ignores Christ's new and better principles of grace and places a veil over those superior principles.

9. If tithing were for the church, then why do New Testament writers NOT quote Genesis 14, Numbers 18, Leviticus 27 and Malachi 3 in appeals for Christians to tithe? The New Testament's only use of "tithe" after Calvary is the account of Abraham's tithe to Melchizedek in Hebrews 7, and it teaches that God abolished tithing and all other ordinances relating to the Levitical priesthood (Heb. 7:5, 12, 18).

Questions for Christian Pastors

1. Is the salary of your pastoral staff one-tenth of ten percent as required by Numbers 18:26. If not, how do you justify this?
2. Is the salary of your non-pastoral staff ninety percent of the first/total tithe according to Numbers 18:21? If not, how do you justify this?

As mentioned above, I personally have been refused active leadership rolls in several churches merely because of my position on tithing. This is also true of the evangelist whom God used to inspire my call to the ministry. While tithing is not once specifically mentioned in the official *Baptist Faith and Message*, the *Position Paper* on tithing is the official "expectation" to be followed in all published literature for Sunday School and church use.

3. What percentage of your budget is allocated to care for the poor, widows, orphans, and those who depend on welfare in your church? Does your "tithe" income pay these costs as it did in the Old Covenant, or do you collect tithes and leave most of their care for government agencies?

4. Do you ask the poor to tithe and then give them back less than they gave? If so, are you not robbing the poor like those in Malachi 3:5-8? Does your action cause them to do without basic necessities?

5. Have you consciously, or subconsciously, succumbed to using legalistic principles to finance God's church? Is this action an admission that law principles are better than faith principles, and that God is not capable of blessing in better ways?

6. Do you refuse to believe that God's people give more from free-will principles of love than when compelled or threatened by law?

7. How can any true blood-bought born-again child of God possibly be under a curse for breaking an ordinance designed to displace the priesthood of every believer? How can any believer spiritually "sit with Christ in heaven" and be under a curse? Do you need to reconsider the curse of Malachi 3:9?

8. While Malachi 3:7 says, "from the days of your fathers you have gone away from my ordinances," does not the New Covenant say in Hebrews 8:9, "not according to the covenant I made with their fathers"? Was not tithing an ordinance which lost its glory and was done away (2 Cor. 3:10-13)? Are you still blinded to the plain truth of this doctrine?

9. Are you missing out on God's blessings that come through grace giving principles such as beholding Christ (2 Cor. 3:16-18)? Mixing grace and Mosaic Law actually weakens the church's integrity (Gal. 3:3-5; 5:23). Such mixture of law and grace is against Paul's detailed instructions in Galatians and Romans. There are many very successful soul-winning churches which do not teach tithing—AND—they do not suffer financially. Why should a church fear that it will

not survive if it does not teach tithing? Successful grace-giving churches prove that God blesses when churches follow his sound New Covenant principles. Love out-gives and out-produces law every time (2 Cor. 8:2-5).

CHAPTER 31

▼

SUMMARY OF REASONS TO REPLACE TITHING

Exegetical preaching takes a Bible verse and explains it in the context of surrounding verses, chapters, the book, the testament in which it is found, and the entire Bible. Exegetical preaching takes into consideration the historical setting and application of the text. It is "critical," meaning "exact" and "accurate," in that it forces the expositor to research. Unlike topical proof-text preaching, exegetical preaching does not risk as much misinterpretation or false doctrine. The excuses of "it's always been that way," "that's what my professor told me," and "it's the principle that counts" do not impress exegetical preachers.

The subject of "tithing" presents a bonanza for topical proof-text preachers and a nightmare for exegetical preachers. Yet it is amazing how many good exegetical preachers switch to topical proof-text preaching when it comes to tithing. Whereas topical preachers can make the Bible say almost anything they desire by taking verses out of context, true exegetical preachers let the Bible tell them what to speak as God intended for his people.

1. *Genesis 14 and Abraham.* Context teaches that Abraham gave a tenth of the spoils of war, but not his own possessions, to a pagan priest-king who worshiped the Canaanite gods, El and Baal. He did so in obedience to well-known pagan war custom, and not as a result of a command from Yahweh. While almost all commentaries admit to pagan reasons for the ninety percent in Genesis 14:21, they fail to extend the same logic to verse 20 concerning the ten percent. Since neither Old nor New Testament writers used Abraham's tithe as an example to others, neither should Christians use it as an example. The "typical" Melchizedek of Hebrews 7, and not the "historical" one of Genesis 14 should be our pattern.

2. *Genesis 28 and Jacob.* Since we know Jacob's early character, context teaches that Jacob was bargaining with God. Jacob's promise was a bad example of "you give me first, and I'll give to you next." To whom he gave the tithe and how he gave is not revealed. The temple in Haran was to the moon goddess.

3. *Numbers 18 and the purpose of tithing.* This most important foundational "chair" passage for tithing is often ignored. The Levitical priests received tithes for two very specific reasons. First, they replaced the priesthood of believers and performed service for God for all Israel, and, second, the tithe was their inheritance because they were not allowed to own property or receive any inheritance. Christian preachers divide the tithing ordinance when they expect to receive the tithe, and still own land. Numbers 18:20-21 should be the most important tithing texts in the Bible—not Genesis 14:20 or Malachi 3:8.

4. *Numbers 18 and the percentage to the priest.* The priests only received one tenth of the tithe, or one percent of the total (18:26; Neh. 10:38).

Since most preachers could not accept a salary of only one tenth of one percent, they do not follow basic law principles for its use.

5. *Leviticus 27 and the contents of the tithe.* As the last listed of the many priestly ordinances in Leviticus, these verses, along with every other "tithe" verse in the Mosaic Law, limit tithes to landowners and herdsmen. Strange, but true, biblical tithes are always *only* crops and herds. Tithes were only commanded to the nation Israel under the Mosaic Law. The poor and those whose professions did not result from land use are never included among tithers. Therefore, since the Bible does not define the tithe as one tenth of all gross "income," neither should New Covenant Christians re-define the word for their own purposes.

6. *Leviticus 27: It is holy unto the LORD.* The correct interpretation of this phrase does not interpret tithing as an eternal principle of God which must be observed by Christians. The phrase is an extremely common designation for almost all ordinances and items associated with the Old Covenant Mosaic Law. The two preceding verses describe men under a death decree as being "*most* holy to the Lord."

7. *Deuteronomy 12, 14, and 26.* Biblical tithes could only come from the *land of Israel* and should *stay in Israel*. At least the second tithe must be brought *to Jerusalem*. Tithes should help feed the poor and widows. Under certain conditions, tithes could even be converted into strong drink.

Those who try to combine the three tithes into one tithe of ten percent are obligated under Old Covenant guidelines to give much of it to the poor, or eat most of it at festivals. Those who admit to two or three different tithes are obligated to teach tithing of either twenty or twenty three percent. However, while most tithe churches *receive* the tithe under the pretense of Old Covenant principles, they do not *dispense* it under those same principles.

8. *First Samuel 8:14-17; 2 Chronicles 31 and Nehemiah 10, 12, and 13.* Tithing was fundamentally a political tax of a state-church theocracy.

Kings received a first tithe of the best of the land and clean animals. Public servants were responsible for collecting, protecting and re-distributing the tithes. The Levites who received the tithes clearly became the political core of King David's divine-right theocracy. Also those who received tithes were separated into orders and each Levite only served in the temple a few weeks a year.

What preacher today would suggest that tithes be collected, protected, and distributed by a political authority? Does this Old Covenant example not give credence to state churches like those found in Europe? Yet this is exactly the example given to us by the Old Testament writers and God's prophets never objected! It is dishonest to preach from Malachi 3 and Genesis 14 and then ignore all other legitimate examples which might contrast with one's modern new definition of tithing.

9. *Malachi 3 is purely Old Covenant.* Malachi is addressed only to Israel under the Mosaic Law and its curses. The book is most specifically addressed to dishonest priests who did not share their tithes with the poor. The governor (from Nehemiah 10-13) was in charge of collecting tithes, and the storehouse was provided by and protected by him. Galatians 3:10-13 removes the curses. If Malachi 3 were such a good text to preach tithing for the church, then why is it not quoted by any inspired New Testament writer?

10. *Ezekiel 40-48.* "Significantly, the tithe is not introduced as a part of the restored temple and priesthood in Ezekiel's vision (Ezek. 40-48)."[141] This confusion might be reconciled by the fact that the Levites will possess land.

11. *Matthew 23:23; Luke 11:41-42 and Jesus.* Exegetically speaking, Jesus was rebuking teachers of the Mosaic Law about their abuse of it. Pharisees had exempted themselves from Jewish taxation and could afford to tithe more; they also only traded within their peers to avoid extra tithing. While living under the the authority as

---

141   *Wycliffe Dict.,* s.v. "tithe."

interpreters of the law, Jesus encouraged obedience to their abusive interpretations. By supporting the tithes of spices, Jesus was even supporting their extravagantly altered definition of tithes in respect to those who sit in the seat of Moses (Matt. 23:2-3).

These are pre-Calvary texts which belong to the Old Covenant. They have no relevance to the post-Calvary New Covenant Christian. At Calvary the veil in the temple split, thus ending the priesthood, ritual, and tithing that supported it.

12. *Luke 18:10.* Works of the law, including tithing, will not justify. The man who did not tithe went home justified.

13. *Hebrews 7:1-19 (especially 5, 12, 18).* This lone biblical mention of tithing after Calvary does not support tithing. Just the opposite is true! Context demands a conclusion that the Mosaic Law of ordinances which was annulled per verses 12, 18, and 19 must include tithing from verse 5.

14. *The priesthood of believers removes the need for tithing.* When part of God's original purpose for Israel (Exod. 19:5-6) was restated under New Covenant principles (1 Pet. 2:5, 9-10), all believers became priests. This negated tithing to a Levitical priesthood. *Every function performed by the Old Covenant priest who received tithes is NOW performed by every believer-priest!* The individual believer, and not the pastor-teacher, replaced Old Covenant priests!

15. *Old Covenant ordinances were abolished.* Tithing was an ordinance, or statute, of the Old Covenant (Num. 18:23-24; Mal. 3:7). All Old Covenant ordinances were clearly abolished at Calvary (Eph. 2:15; Col. 2:14; Heb. 7:18; 9:26).

16. *Christians are not under the Mosaic Law.* (John 1:7; Rom. 6:14; 7:4, 6; 8:2-3; 2 Cor. 3:6-11; Gal. 3:19, 23-25; 5:18; Eph. 2:15; Col. 2:14; Heb. 8:13).

17. *New Covenant gospel workers are to live under gospel principles of grace, not law* (1 Cor. 9:14; Gal. 3:12; Rom. 14:23).

18. *Although full-time gospel workers are acceptable, the higher gospel road is self-support* (1 Cor. 9:18-19; Acts 20:32-35).

19. *Some of the best known conservative authorities do not teach tithing.* (For example: Dallas Theological Seminary, Moody Bible Institute, Lewis Sperry Chafer, Theodore Epp, John MacArthur, Charles Ryrie, C. I. Scofield, and Merril F. Unger.

20. *The O. T. poor gave freewill offerings, not tithes.* Even the *Code of Jewish Law* states, "He who has barely sufficient for his own needs, is not obligated to give charity, for his own sustenance takes precedence over another's."[142] Those who were not landowners or herdsmen, were not required to tithe (Lev. 27:30-34 cf. Lev. 1:14; 2:24; 12:1-8; 14:21-22; 25:35-36; 27:8; Deut. 15:7-81; 24:12-15; Mal 3:5-6.).

21. *Jesus did not tithe!* There was no reason for Jesus to pay tithes! First, he was not a landowner or herdsman (Lev. 27:30-34), and, second, he was poor; therefore he was not required to tithe, but gave offerings. His parents paid the offering for the poor (Luke 2:24; cf. Lev. 5:7-11). His disciples gleaned freely because they were poor (Matt. 12:1) and were not rebuked for not tithing.

22. *Tithing is not commanded after Calvary.* It is illogical to say that the Holy Spirit "forgot" to include this doctrine. While every other New Covenant doctrine is plainly stated after Calvary, tithing is not.

23. *Tithing did not support New Covenant preachers.* It is also illogical to believe that the early church taught tithing when there is no indication that its leaders ever received a full-time salary! One should study the following texts and come to his/her own conclusion. (Acts 13:1-3; 18:1-3; 20:17-35; 2 Cor. 11:7-9; 2 Cor. 12:13-15; Gal. 6:2-10; Phil. 4:15-19; 1 Thess. 2:90; 2 Thess. 3:6-15).

---

142   *Code,* 1-111.

24. *O.T. tithing contrasts with basic N.T. principles of giving as stated in 1 Corinthians 16:2 and 2 Corinthians, chapters 8 and 9.*

25. *The early church fathers did not teach tithing.* Included are Clement of Rome (93-97), Ignatius (110-117), Polycarp (110-117), Hermas (100-140), Barnabas (131), Justin Martyr (100-166), Irenaeus (130-200), Hippolytus (170-236), Clement of Alexander (150-200), and Tertullian (150-220). The pro-tithe advocates do not quote these in support of their position on tithing. Tithing did not appear in history as an expectation of the church until a church synod demanded it in A.D. 567. It was first legally enforced in A.D. 777.

26. *The existence of successful churches that do not teach tithing proves that tithing is not an essential doctrine for church growth.* Almost every community has large successful churches that never preach mandatory tithing. They are burdened for souls and prosper without adding law to principles of grace. They believe God's New Covenant promises and operate successfully on the New Covenant principles of grace giving.

27. *It is illogical to assume that tithing is not mentioned because it was not an issue.* First, why would worldly Christians break every other "moral" law and yet continue to tithe? Second, the issue of "law" was a very debated issue in Acts 15, 21, Romans, Galatians, Ephesians, Colossians, and Hebrews. Third, the Jerusalem church specifically released Gentile Christians from any obligation to observe the Mosaic Law.

28. *Modern Jewish synagogues do not teach tithing* They operate on a dues-system of support. No collections are made and no money is even handled on the Sabbath because exchanging money on the Sabbath is considered a sin. Ask any knowledgeable Jew! They understand that tithes were only food for taxation.

29. *The Greek Orthodox Church has never taught tithing.* Yet these are the direct descendants of many of the earliest churches.

30. *Love-giving out-gives law-giving every time.* Since preaching the "weak and beggarly elements of the law," such as tithing, could not sustain the Levitical priesthood (Heb. 7:5, 11-12, 18-19), then, how could those same principles prosper a church spiritually? A church that loves God, loves each other, and loves sinners grows spontaneously through the blessings of the Holy Spirit. A church that gives out of compulsion and fear of being cursed may temporarily succeed, but eventually it too will falter.

Those who teach compulsive tithing fail to understand the basic differences between the moral and cultic laws, Old and New Covenants and/or law and grace. Christ's priesthood, equipped by "the power of an endless [indestructible] life," assures the success of his church (Heb. 7:16).

CHAPTER 32

▼

SPREADING THE GOSPEL REMAINS OUR CALLING

Rom. 1:16 For I am not ashamed of the gospel of Christ; for it is the power of God unto salvation to every one that believes—to the Jew first, and also to the Greek.

Rom. 1:17 For therein is the righteousness of God revealed from faith to faith; as it is written, The just shall live by faith.

1 Cor. 1:18 For the preaching [the word] of the cross is to them that perish foolishness; but to us which are saved it is the power of God.

2 Cor. 3:18 But we all, with open face beholding as in a glass the glory of the Lord, are being changed into the same image from glory to glory, even as by the Spirit of the Lord.

When Peter exclaimed, "You are the Christ, the Son of the living God (Matt. 16:16), Jesus replied, "Upon this rock I will build my church; and the gates of hell shall not prevail against it" (Matt. 16:18). All Protestant preachers understand that the church is built on the great rock, Peter's inspired statement about the person of Jesus Christ—nothing more, nothing less!

The gospel IS "Jesus Christ"—his pre-existence, virgin birth, life, death, resurrection, ascension and intercession—nothing more, nothing less! (Compare also Rom. 1:1-5; 1 Cor 1:17-18; 1 Cor. 15:1-4). *Anything*, including principles of giving, which is *added* to the gospel from the *New* Covenant is merely "fruit" of the gospel and food for spiritual growth. "Against such there is no law" (Gal. 5:23) means that there is "no law" to counteract, or negate, the fruits of the Spirit. Anything, including tithing, which is added to the gospel from the Old Covenant without New Covenant re-authorization is neither of the gospel, nor of its fruit.

"I marvel that you are so soon removed from him that called you into the grace of Christ to another gospel, which is not another; but there are some that trouble you, and would pervert the gospel of Christ" (Gal. 1:6-7). From Galatians, chapters 2-4, it is clear that these "distortions" were additions from the old law back into the gospel preached by Paul.

A dead or dying church cannot be permanently revived by preaching law, whether it is the law of tithing, or even the Ten Commandments. The revival message MUST be the Christ of Calvary! In comparison to the power of the Spirit and the gospel, the law has completely lost all of its glory and power (2 Cor. 3:10). Permanent revival and increased giving will only come when the pastor and his church hear and respond to the gospel and all that it says about the love of Christ. "The gospel is the power of God" and the gospel reveals God's righteousness from faith to faith, not from faith to law. Paul was sustained totally by faith, trusting in God's ability to provide for him.

As in the parable of the sower, the power of God's Word falling on fertile souls brings forth a bountiful harvest. Thousands were converted at

Pentecost and in the weeks following through the preaching of Christ and him crucified for our sins. Everywhere the apostles went, the gospel was preached, souls were saved—and the church grew.

When the Philippians saw Paul's need, they sent aid to him again and again (Phil. 4:16). When Christ is preached, believers will see the "needs" of a lost world without Christ. They will also see and strive to meet the needs of gospel workers and fellow-believers. Inspired by the Holy Spirit, Paul said to the Philippians, "But my God shall supply all your need according to his riches in glory by Christ Jesus" (Phil. 4:19). This is a conditional, but sure promise, *only* to those who see the need of God's people and respond by giving out of love created by the gospel.

According to the New Covenant, eternal spiritual riches, not physical riches, flow from a knowledge and love of God in Christ. When Scripture is compared to Scripture, the "hundredfold increase" is not money. Moses left his money and chose the "reproach of Christ greater riches than the treasures of Egypt" (Heb. 11:26). God abounds in those riches for all who call upon him (Rom. 10:12). Paul told the true believer, "Now you are full, now you are rich" (1 Cor. 4:8). The riches of God's grace fall, not as money, but in the assurance of "redemption through his blood, the forgiveness of sins, according to the riches of his grace" (Eph. 1:7). Mercy, kindness, love and power flow from God's wealth to the believer throughout eternity (Eph. 2:4, 7; 3:16). This was the message of riches preached by Christ (Rom. 3:8; Col. 1:27).

Colossians 2:2 describes the church and believer that are being "being knit together in love, and to all riches of the full assurance of understanding, to the acknowledgment of the mystery of God, and of the Father, and of Christ." A free democratic society will out-give (and out-produce) a forced labor society. The Apostle Paul received neither tithes nor any full-time support. He used his gospel freedom to refuse wages, yet he was perhaps history's most successful church-builder and evangelist. Likewise, the Christian church, with its freedom in Christ, will out-give and out-serve Old Covenant Israel.

God saves, blesses, and fills the believer with his Holy Spirit solely because of the believer's faith in Jesus Christ. Having done so, he continues to use principles of grace, not law, to supply the needs of his church (2 Cor. 8:1-15; 9:6-8; 1 Cor. 16:1-2; Gal. 3:1-5).

When Christ is preached, every doctrine must be in the light of its relationship to him. A Christian does not obey God in order to please him. Instead a Christian obeys God *because* he has been saved, his nature is changed, he is studying to know God's will, and is yielded to the Holy Spirit. Believers who are being transformed into Christ's likeness by learning sound doctrine want to give as Christ gave. With a burden for lost souls, they respond by giving from a sincere desire and from their best ability. They give their lives, their time, and their money.

BIBLIOGRAPHY

Alexander, Pat, ed. *Lion Encyclopedia of the Bible*. Orig. *Eerdman's Family Encyclopedia of the Bible*, 1978. 3rd ed. Batavia: Lion Publishing, 1987.

Baker, Robert A. *A Summary of Christian History*. Nashville: Broadman, 1959.

Barclay, William. *Daily Study Bible Series: The Letter to the Hebrews*. Philadelphia: Westminster, 1976.

Barnes, Albert. *Barnes' Notes*. CD-ROM, Seattle: Biblesoft, 1999.

Bettenson, Henry, ed. *Documents of the Christian Church*. 2nd ed. New York: Oxford UP, 1963.

Bruce, F. F. *The Spreading Flame*, Grand Rapids: Eerdman, Waynesboro: Pater Noster Press, 1958.

Chafer, Lewis Sperry. *Major Bible Themes*. Dallas Theological Seminary, 1926. Revised, John F. Walvoord. Grand Rapids: Zondervan, 1974.

Clarke, Adam. *Adam Clarke's Commentary*. CD-ROM, Seattle: Biblesoft, 1996.

Dana, H. E. *The New Testament World*. 3rd ed., rev. Nashville: Broadman, 1937.

Davis, John D. ed., *Westminster Dictionary of the Bible*. Philadelphia: Westminster Press, 1964.

Davidson, F., ed. *New Bible Commentary*. London: Inter-Varsity, 1953.

Durant, Will. *The Story of Civilization: Part VI, The Reformation, A History of European Civilization from Wyclif to Calvin: 1300-1564.* New York: Simon and Schuster, 1957.

Edersheim, Alfred

—. *Sketches of Jewish Social Life: Updated Edition.* Peabody: Hendrickson, 1994.

—. *The Temple, Its Ministry and Services,* CD-ROM, Packard Technologies, chapter 19.

Eggenberger, David I., ed. *New Catholic Encyclopedia.* New York: McGraw-Hill, 1967.

Eklund, Bobby, and Terry Austin. *Partners with God: Bible Truths About Giving.* Nashville: Convention Press, 1994.

Eliad, Mircea, ed. *Encyclopedia of Religion.* New York: MacMillan, 1987.

Elwell, Walter A., ed. *Baker's Evangelical Dictionary of the Bible.* Grand Rapids: Baker, 1996.

Epp, Theodore H. *Moses, Vol. III, Great Leader and Lawgiver.* Lincoln: Back to the Bible, 1976.

Evans, Louis H., Jr. *The Communicator's Commentary: Hebrews.* Waco: Word, 1985.

Fausset, Andrew Robert. *Fausset's Bible Dictionary.* CD-ROM, Seattle: Biblesoft, 1999.

Fee, Gordon, and Douglas Stuart. *How to Read the Bible For All Its Worth.* Grand Rapids: Zondervan, 1980.

Ganzfried, Solomon. *Code of Jewish Law.* Translated by Hyman E. Goldin. Spencetown, New York: Hebrew Publishing, 1961.

Harrison, Everett F., Geoffrey W. Bromiley, and Carl F. Henry, editors, *Wycliffe Dictionary of Theology.* Orig. *Baker's Dictionary,* 1960. Peabody: Hendrickson, 1999.

Henry, Matthew. *Matthew Henry's Commentary on the Whole Bible.* CD-ROM, Seattle: Biblesoft, 1999.

Holman Bible Dictionary and Concordance (Giant Print), Nashville: Holman, 1999.

Jamieson, Robert, A. R. Fausset and David Brown., *Jamieson, Fausset, and Brown Commentary.* CD-ROM, Seattle: Biblesoft, 1999.

Jones, Clifford A., Sr. *From Proclamation to Practice, A Unique African-American Approach to Stewardship.* Valley Forge: Judson Press, 1993.

Kaiser, William C., Jr., and Moises Silva. *An Introduction to Biblical Hermeneutics: The Search for Meaning.* Grand Rapids: Zondervan, 1994.

Keil, C. F., and F. Delitzsch. *Keil and Delitzsch Commentary on the Old Testament.* CD-ROM, Seattle: Biblesoft, 1999.

Klein, William W., Craig L. Bloomberg, and Robert L. Hubbard, Jr. *Introduction to Biblical Interpretation.* Dallas: Word Publishers, 1993.

Lang, J. Stephen. *1001 Things You Always Wanted to Know About the Bible.* Nashville: Thomas Nelson, 1999.

Latourette, Kenneth Scott. *History of Christianity, Vol. 1.* New York: Harper and Row, 1975.

MacArthur, John F. *God's Plan for Giving.* Chicago: Moody Press, 1985.

Metzger, Bruce M. and Michael D. Coogan. *Oxford Companion to the Bible.* New York: Oxford UP, 1993.

New Bible Dictionary. London: Inter-Varsity, 1962.

Orr, James, ed. *International Standard Bible Encyclopedia.* CD-ROM, version 3.0B. Seattle: Biblesoft, 1999.

PC Study Bible's Greek-Hebrew Dictionary and Englishman's Concordance. CD-ROM, Seattle: Biblesoft, 1999.

Pfeiffer, Charles F. and Everett F. Harrison, editors. *Wycliffe Bible Commentary.* Chicago: Moody Press, 1962. Nashville: Southeastern, 1968.

Qualben, Lars P. *A History of the Christian Church.* New York: Thomas Nelson, 1942.

Rhodes. Ron. *Complete Book of Bible Answers.* Eugene: Harvest House, 1997.

Robertson, Archibald Thomas. *Robertson's Word Pictures in the New Testament (Volumes 1-4).* CD-ROM, Seattle: Biblesoft, 1999. Copyright: Broadman Press 1985.

Roth, Cecil, ed. *Encyclopedia Judaica.* New York: MacMillan, 1972.

Ryrie, Charles C. *Ryrie Study Bible: Expanded Edition.* Chicago: Moody Press, 1995.

Schaff, Philip. *History of the Christian Church, Volume II, Ante-Nicean Christianity, A.D. 100-325.* Copyrighted by Charles Scribner's Sons, 1910. Reprinted by Wm. B. Eerdmans Publishing: Grand Rapids, 1995.

Scofield, C. I. *New Scofield Reference Bible.* Revised by E. Schuyler English, chairman, 1967. New York: Oxford UP, 1967.

Smith, Jerome. *Treasury of Scripture Knowledge.* CD-ROM, Seattle: Biblesoft, 1999.

Strong, Augustus Hopkins. *Biblesoft's New Exhaustive Strong's Numbers and Concordance with Expanded Greek- Hebrew Dictionary.* CD-ROM, Seattle: Biblesoft, 1999.

Thayer, Joseph Henry. *Thayer's Greek-English Lexicon of the New Testament.* CD-ROM. Seattle: Biblesoft, 1999. Grand Rapids: Zondervan, 1962.

Thompson, Rhodes. *Stewards Shaped by Grace.* St. Louis: Chalice Press, 1990.

Unger, Merrill F., ed. *New Unger's Bible Dictionary.* Chicago: Moody. Revised and upgraded, 1985. CD-ROM, Seattle: Biblesoft, 1999.

Walker, Williston. *A History of the Christian Church.* 3rd ed. New York: Charles Scribner's Sons, 1970.

Youngblood, Roland F. *Nelson's Illustrated Bible Dictionary.* CD-ROM, Seattle: Biblesoft, 1999. Copyright: Thomas Nelson, 1986.

Zodhiates, Spiros, *Zodhiates' Hebrew-Greek Key Study Bible,* Chattanooga: AMG Publishers, 1984 ed.

About the Author

After receiving a B.A. in Theology, Russell Earl Kelly served churches in Georgia, Tennessee, South Carolina, and North Dakota before leaving the full-time ministry in the early 1980s. Although legally blind since 1988, he has never stopped a rigid schedule of Bible study and preaching. He has always been a very serious Bible student and thoroughly enjoys discovering and researching the beliefs of those who are of different denominations.

In August 2000 Russell fulfilled a life-long desire by receiving a Ph.D. in Religion at Covington Theological Seminary in Rossville, Georgia. This book is the revised product of his dissertation for graduation requirements. Now Russell is again seeking to re-enter much more active service for Christ in preaching the Word. Janice, his wife, fully supports him in his desire to return to full time ministry soon. He has two children, one stepdaughter, and currently has three grandchildren.

Printed in the United States
4258

9 780595 159789